COALBROOKD
THE DARBY

This book is dedicated to my wife Barbara Thomas and our
daughter Caryl, without whose support and indulgence
it would not have been completed.

*The cover is based on a design concept by David de Haan, deputy director of
the Ironbridge Gorge Museum. The pencil sketch of Coalbrookdale, dated 1789,
by Joseph Farington, R.A. (1747-1821) has been pastel coloured by Bryan
Blackwell (see also page 92). The emblem in the roundel on the back cover is
derived from a design formerly used by the Coalbrookdale Company as a trade
mark, and is now the seal of the Ironbridge Gorge Museum Trust.*

The Family Tree of the Darbys of Coalbrookdale

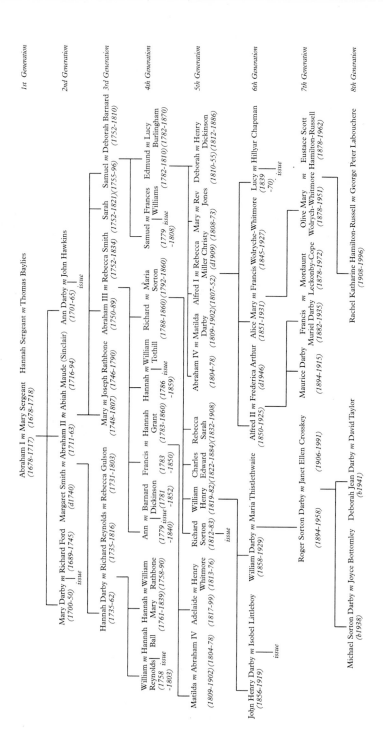

Coalbrookdale and the Darby Family

The story of the world's first industrial dynasty

by
Emyr Thomas, CBE, LL.B, DL

SESSIONS BOOK TRUST
in association with the
IRONBRIDGE GORGE MUSEUM TRUST

© Emyr Thomas and the
Ironbridge Gorge Museum Trust 1999

ISBN 1 85072 217 X

Printed in 10 on 11 point Plantin Typeface
from Author's Disk
by Sessions of York
The Ebor Press
York, England

Contents

Illustrations
(including maps)

Unless otherwise stated, all illustrations are from the collections of the Ironbridge Gorge Museum Trust.

Acknowledgments and Thanks

IN 1950, a book entitled "*Quakers in Science and Industry*", by Arthur Raistrick, Ph.D., M.Sc. was published. It contained an account of the Coalbrookdale Company and of the Darby family. Three years later in 1953, Dr Raistrick published another definitive book entitled "*Dynasty of Ironfounders*". This was based on extensive and scholarly research and it was immediately recognised as the seminal and authoritative work on the Darbys and Coalbrookdale. Later in 1973, Dr Barrie Trinder published his monumental and equally authoritative book on "*The Industrial Revolution in Shropshire*" which inevitably incorporated an immense amount of information about the Company and the family. These books have formed the bedrock of our information about Coalbrookdale and the family whose name will forever be associated with it.

Since then, a considerable amount of information has become available for study, notably through the cataloguing of family documents made available to the Shropshire Record Office and the Library of the Ironbridge Gorge Museum Trust by Rachel Labouchere, LL.D., a descendant of Abraham Darby I. Prior to her death in 1996, Lady Labouchere had herself made an enormous contribution to the history of the Darby family through the publication of her books on Abiah Darby and Deborah Darby. Before her death she had almost completed a third book based on the journals of Adelaide Darby.

It is, of course, impossible to write a book about the Coalbrookdale Company without mentioning the Darby Family. It is equally impossible to write about the Darby Family without detailing their involvement with the Company over two hundred years. The effect of cataloguing the family documents in recent times, however, has been to make available more information about the family than was previously known. Rachel Labouchere in her last years was anxious that this information should be incorporated into an account of the history of the family through to modern times, with a consequent emphasis on the family, rather than the Company. This present account is an attempt to undertake that rather daunting task.

In this venture, I have been immensely assisted by David de Haan, Deputy Director, Ironbridge Gorge Museum Trust and also by John

Powell, Librarian, and Diana Tapley, Archivist. To them I express my deepest thanks. My special thanks also go to Linda Birch, David de Haan's Secretary, who has diligently transformed my illegible handwriting into a text suitable for the publishers.

I would also like to express my appreciation of the helpful way in which the staff of the Shropshire Records and Research Centre at Castle Gates, Shrewsbury, guided me through the records which are safely in their care. Likewise, a special mention needs to be made of the outstanding work undertaken by the Victoria County History under its editor George Baugh M.A. The publication of Volume XI (Telford) in September 1985 provided a wonderful basis for tracing the ebbs and flows of industrial development across the whole of the Coalbrookdale Coalfield throughout the entire period. It provided an authoritative structure for the story which the book seeks to tell.

When I left Shropshire in 1995 to return to Hampshire some of the research which I had left uncompleted in the Shropshire Record Office was continued on my behalf by Ken Jones. I am truly grateful for that valuable help. Ken and Dorinda Jones have been with the Ironbridge Gorge Museum Trust since its earliest days and represent the very best of the volunteer spirit on which the Museum has been so successfully built.

I would also like to make a special mention of the help and encouragement I have received from my daughter Caryl Thomas in transcribing the voluminous parchments in the Public Record Office which make up the Chancery Proceedings which rocked the Company to its foundations between 1756 and 1762. Without her enthusiastic assistance I could not have completed what proved to be an important piece of research.

Finally, a special word of thanks to Philip Trevor-Jones, D.L., M.A.(Cantab), and Michael Lowe, J.P., F.C.A., respectively President and Chairman of the Ironbridge Gorge Museum Trust. They are fellow trustees of the Museum Trust and are long-time friends. They have shown their special friendship to me by sponsoring the publication of this book. I am deeply indebted to them and would like to express to them my sincere thanks. I am also most grateful to Bill Sessions of the Sessions Book Trust (co-publishers of this book with the Ironbridge Gorge Museum Trust) for the enthusiasm and helpful encouragement which he has demonstrated throughout the long process of preparing the book for publication.

EMYR THOMAS
March, 1999

"The works at Coalbrookdale are of very great publick utility, being one of the most capital, if not the greatest, ironfoundries for cast iron in the Kingdom."

Chancery Proceedings 1759.

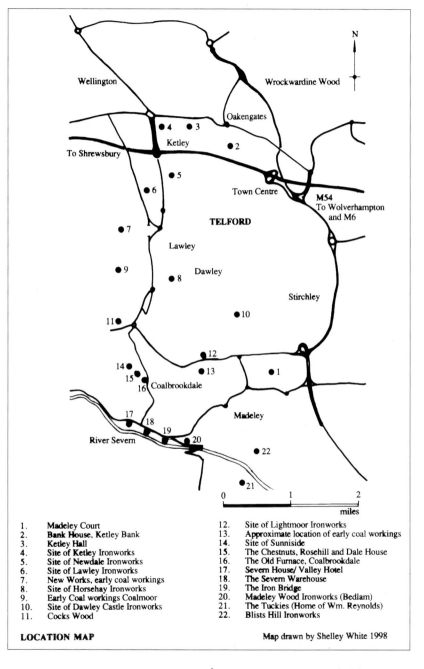

N

Wellington

Wrockwardine Wood

Oakengates

● 4   ● 3

Ketley

To Shrewsbury

● 2

● 5

● 6

Town Centre

M54
To Wolverhampton
and M6

TELFORD

● 7

Lawley

● 9

● 8

Dawley

Stirchley

11●

● 10

● 12

14 ●

● 13

15

16   Coalbrookdale

● 1

17

18

19

River Severn

20

Madeley

● 22

● 21

0   1   2

miles

1.	Madeley Court	12.	Site of Lightmoor Ironworks
2.	Bank House, Ketley Bank	13.	Approximate location of early coal workings
3.	Ketley Hall	14.	Site of Sunniside
4.	Site of Ketley Ironworks	15.	The Chestnuts, Rosehill and Dale House
5.	Site of Newdale Ironworks	16.	The Old Furnace, Coalbrookdale
6.	Site of Lawley Ironworks	17.	Severn House/ Valley Hotel
7.	New Works, early coal workings	18.	The Severn Warehouse
8.	Site of Horsehay Ironworks	19.	The Iron Bridge
9.	Early Coal workings Coalmoor	20.	Madeley Wood Ironworks (Bedlam)
10.	Site of Dawley Castle Ironworks	21.	The Tuckies (Home of Wm. Reynolds)
11.	Cocks Wood	22.	Blists Hill Ironworks

LOCATION MAP

Map drawn by Shelley White 1998

Preface

IN 1707 QUEEN ANNE was on the throne of the newly-united kingdom of England and Scotland. John Churchill, the recently-created Duke of Marlborough was on the continent ensuring that the War of the Spanish Succession would be settled in England's favour. Against this background of the nation's constitutional and military progress, nobody would have taken more than a passing interest in a young man, named Abraham Darby, then aged twenty-nine, examining the remnants of an iron furnace in Coalbrookdale in Shropshire which had been wrecked a few years previously by an explosion. Nor would anybody have particularly noticed his companion, named John Thomas, one year younger. These two men had between them devised a method of casting iron pots in sand, and had entered into a bond in January 1707 [1] ensuring the secrecy of the process, for which Abraham Darby had been granted a patent. [2]

Although unnoticed, this incident led within the next twelve months or so to the technological discovery, which, slowly at first and then with increasing speed, initiated the industrialisation of Britain and later of the world. This new industrial progress, combined with Britain's already proven military and commercial prowess, laid the foundations for what was to become within a century, the British Empire and subsequently the Commonwealth of Nations. Britain's predominantly agrarian and rural economy gradually gave way to a new industrial and urban economy. The industrial revolution as it came to be called started in Britain and spread to much of the rest of the Western world. The seminal event in this process occurred in Coalbrookdale in 1709. It is for that reason that the Ironbridge Gorge which includes Coalbrookdale, has been designated by the United Nations as a World Heritage Site.

NOTES

1. Raistrick, p.22; SRO 1987/58/13.
2. IGMT Archives – Patent No. 380, dated 18 April 1707.

CHAPTER I

Abraham Darby I – The Early Years

ON 14 APRIL 1678, Abraham Darby was born at Old Lodge Farm, Wren's Nest, which is a hilly area one mile to the north west of Dudley Castle (now in the West Midlands, but then a detached part of the County of Worcester). He was the son of John Darby (1649-1725) and Ann Baylies.[1] A daughter Esther was born to them two years later in 1680 just before the mother died. John Darby married again, so the two children, Abraham and Esther, were brought up by John Darby and his second wife Joan Luccock.

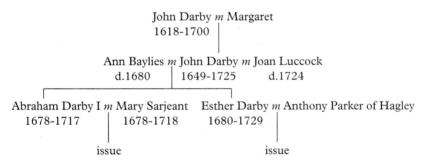

John Darby *m* Margaret
1618-1700

Ann Baylies *m* John Darby *m* Joan Luccock
d.1680   1649-1725   d.1724

Abraham Darby I *m* Mary Sarjeant   Esther Darby *m* Anthony Parker of Hagley
1678-1717   1678-1718   1680-1729

issue   issue

The family were small farmers who also undertook the trades of nailer and locksmith. At that time the iron industry was fairly small scale, sometimes little more than a cottage industry and it was commonplace for families to be engaged in farming and at the same time to own a forge at which various iron trades were carried out. The family were also members of the newly formed Religious Society of Friends. As he grew to manhood, Abraham became subject to the two great influences of his life, his knowledge of the iron industry and his upbringing as a Quaker.

The Quakers belong to the mainstream of ecclesiastical dissent which can be traced at least as far back as the Lollards (the anti-papal followers of John Wycliffe) in the fourteenth century. Through the centuries can be traced other movements such as the Puritans in the time of Elizabeth I, the Anabaptists, Familists, the Jacob Circle and the Baptists (Calvinist and non-Calvinist), increasingly seeking separation from the established Church.

With the start of the Civil War in the 1640s separatism became a substantial movement in which political and religious objectives co-existed. The Levellers, Diggers, Ranters, Fifth Monarchy Men, Seekers and Muggletonians all belong to this period of turmoil and unrest. The Quakers arrived on the scene in the early 1650s, a relatively late stage.

George Fox is regarded as the founder of the Society of Friends, but there were others who were also regarded as leaders at the time. It may well be that it was George Fox who more than any other articulated the views of a movement, which spread rapidly throughout the land. Conversion to the Quakers from the other sects was widespread and in this way the development of the Quaker philosophy derived from many sources including the Army, from whose ranks came many Quakers.

Anti-clericalism had been a strong feature of life since the Reformation and this strand is evident amongst the early Quakers who wanted a movement away from the university-bred, privileged clergy towards a ministry of simple men and women *"who spoke plaine words and reached to the consciences of men of the meanest capacity"*. They pressed for religious tolerance and they campaigned strongly against tithes. They refused to pay tithes and formed the vanguard of popular agitation against them. They went further and interrupted church services; they refused to remove their hats before social superiors or to acknowledge titles. In short, in their origins they were religious radicals of near-revolutionary fervour.

By 1659 reaction had set in and there was deep popular hostility to the trend of events. In particular there was hostility towards the religious sects, notably the Quakers whose numbers had increased to an astonishing degree.

There was a widespread fear of Quakers and throughout the country anti-Quaker incidents took place. Even in Shropshire, men were engaged to *"go and fight against the Quakers"*. It was this feeling against the sects that contributed as much as anything else to the restoration of the Monarchy. And so in May 1660 Charles Stuart came back on the crest of a wave of reaction against "the immense and boundless liberty" of 1659.

The Restoration began badly for the Friends. The Quaker Act of 1662 provided for fining, imprisonment and transportation of Quakers taken at Meetings. The previous year when the peaceable intentions of Friends had been questioned, a declaration was addressed to Charles II "from the Harmless and Innocent People of God called Quakers", which said *"We utterly deny all outward wars and strife and fighting with outward weapons, for any end, or under any pretence whatever, this is our testimony to the whole world...".* This is the source and origin of the Friends' constant policy against war and in favour of peace.

The Quaker Act of 1662 was followed by the Conventicle Act of 1664, which forbade Meetings of dissenters, and the Five Mile Act of 1665 which forbade any minister who had refused to sign the "Act of Uniformity" to dwell within five miles of any city or corporate borough.

These Acts, with other measures, were collectively known as the Clarendon Code, named after Edward Hyde, Lord Clarendon, Chief Minister of the realm under Charles II until 1667. The object of the Clarendon Code was to prevent the revival of the Roundhead party, but the spirit of persecution was much more widespread.

Without doubt the Friends felt themselves to be under siege during the Restoration, and as it has been put, "they retreated into their tents after 1660". There was a transformation of the movement and Quaker self-censorship prevented provocation and curbed religious over-enthusiasm. Under the guidance of George Fox the organisation of the Sect began. By the 1670s the Society of Friends had a nationwide system of local, regional and national business Meetings – the Yearly Meeting, Meetings for Sufferings, Second Day Morning Meetings, Six Weeks Meeting, Quarterly Meeting, Monthly Meetings and various separate Womens' Meetings.

And so it was into this organisation that people like John Darby II (Abraham's father) entered when they became convinced Friends. Abraham himself was brought up in the Quaker culture, a Protestant culture rejecting the ritual and imagery of the old religion in favour of simplicity, lack of ornamentation in language and prose, in furniture, architecture, gardens and dress.

After William and Mary came to the throne in 1688, the Toleration Act 1689 was passed bringing to a close the severe persecution which the Friends had suffered during the previous thirty years. By then they had settled down to an ordered existence within which to pursue their religious beliefs. At the heart of these beliefs is the conviction that each man and woman is enlightened by the divine light of Christ. The emphasis therefore is on the light or spirit within each person.

It was during the period of persecution under the Clarendon Code that Abraham and his sister Esther were born. This may have been the reason which prompted John Darby to place his son Abraham as an apprentice in Birmingham, a free non-corporate town in which there were already many Friends at work. Abraham was, therefore, apprenticed to Jonathan Freeth, a maker of malt mills (small instruments which processed grains of malt for use in brewing). Jonathan Freeth had a reputation as a

3

'weighty' Friend, i.e, one whose contributions to the Meetings of the Friends were influential.[2] Abraham, too, showed great commitment to the Society for he was described as having *"a gift in the Ministry...there were four in the same Shop that worked together all Public, and us'd to sitt together one evening in the week."* [3]

On completion of his apprenticeship, Abraham moved to Bristol, another city where the Friends were strongly represented.[4]

In 1699, the year after his arrival in Bristol, Abraham gave notice to the Meeting on the 31st of the 5th Month of his intention to marry Mary Sergeant, whose father was a bleacher of linen yarn of Fulford Heath in Worcestershire. Their marriage took place in Bristol on the 18th September that year.

Mary had had a terrible experience when quite young, for *"by some accident she fell into the furnace when it was boiling and when taken out thought her dead or near it, they laid her on the hearth before the Fire and she came to herself and told how it was with her at the time that she was in appearance Dead. She thought there came two Angels all in white and took her to a very fine place, finer than she had ever seen in the World, and she desired to stay there it was such a glorious Place, but they told her she must return to the World again and if she lived a sober Religious life till the end of her time she might come there again..."* Before this she was a hearty young woman but after she married, she was troubled with an asthmatic complaint and if her husband was away from home she would sit all night and sleep by the fire.[5]

Abraham set up as a Malt Mill maker and founded the Bristol Brass Company with works at Baptist Mills sited on the River Frome, upstream a mile or so from where the river joins the Avon, and on the north eastern side of the city boundary. Bristol was the second largest city in the kingdom, with a large overseas trade and an inland trade up the rivers, including the River Severn. The works were established as early as 1702 and Abraham's partners were Edward Lloyd, a cider maker, John Andrews a vintner and Arthur Thomas a pewterer.

Abraham, who appears to have been manager of the Brass Works soon established himself as an innovator, for he seems to have been responsible for introducing the use of coal rather than charcoal in brass-making furnaces,[6] thus foreshadowing his later work in Coalbrookdale. Indeed he shortly afterwards started a new enterprise, a foundry for casting iron pots, in Cheese Lane, Bristol.[6] In this he seems to have been alone in the enterprise for a time but later he was joined in partnership by James Peters and Griffin Prankard.

There were two other men whom Abraham came to know very well and who were to have a profound influence on his life.

The first was John Thomas a young Quaker who came from near Welshpool in Montgomeryshire. After growing up as a shepherd, he was sent to work for Charles Lloyd of Dolobran. His maternal grandparents, Grace and Edward Edwards had shared the same prison accommodation, on account of being Quakers, as Charles Lloyd's parents.

John Thomas was sent by Charles Lloyd to find work with his kinsman, Edward Lloyd, who was Abraham's partner in the Bristol Brass Works. He had to have a settled job for "*it being Queen Anne's War he was afraid of being pressed for a Soldier if out of place*".

In a letter to Thomas Goldney, Mary Darby, Abraham's wife, speaks of John Thomas' arrival. Abraham had been seeking for some years to cast iron pots in sand instead of loam or clay. Using techniques developed in Holland he had succeeded in producing brass pots, but Dutch workers he employed had failed to produce iron pots by the same method. Mary, after Abraham's death wrote to Thomas Goldney; "*It was not a question of sand for the moulds ... for nearly a year the brass pots had been cast with success, but the attempt to use the cheaper metal of iron failed because the Dutch brassfounders could not be prevailed upon to allow for the greater heat of the melted iron and to make more air holes accordingly, in consequence their moulds blew to pieces from the compressed and heated air when the hot iron was poured in*".[7]

In the same letter Mary Darby speaks of John's arrival saying that he was "*sent by Charles Lloyd of Dolobran in January 1707 to my husband's partner Edward Lloyd. They sat up at the pot making and the lad made the wise suggestion about an under air hole and between them they cast a pot of iron before morning*".[7] There was fierce competition in new discoveries and processes and the need for secrecy was such that they had to "block the key hole". John Thomas was "*offered double wages to leave his Master Darby, but would not do it.*"

Abraham petitioned for and was granted a patent for his method in 1707[8] and it sets out that this was a new way of "*casting iron-bellied potts and other bellied ware in sand only without loam or clay.*" This shape of pot which had the larger diameter in the middle was to become familiar all over the world. In the same year that the patent was granted, Abraham signed articles of agreement with John Thomas for three years whereby he paid him £7 a year for the first two years and £8 for the third year, and to provide him with good and sufficient meat, drink, washing and lodging. John for his part agreed that although "*he was not brought up employed in this trade, he would not serve any other person on or about casting Iron Potts nor will disclose the method to anyone.*"[9]

Abraham's future daughter-in-law, Abiah Darby (married to Abraham II) wrote of this period "*the Moulding and casting in sand instead of loam was of Great Service, both in expense and expedition. If we compare little things with great as invention of printing was to writing, so was the moulding and casting in sand to that of loam."*[10] Indeed it can be seen with hindsight that the years spent in Bristol were a necessary and unique preparation for the events which were to take place a few years later in Coalbrookdale.

The other person who had a profound influence on Abraham's life at this time was Thomas Goldney II, a Quaker merchant of Bristol.[11] He was the son of Thomas Goldney I and Mary Clements, who had joined the Society of Friends early on. Despite persecution the family prospered and in 1694 the young Thomas Goldney II and his wife leased a house at Clifton to the west of Bristol. This house had been rebuilt since the Civil War as the whole of Clifton had been burnt down on the orders of Prince Rupert, commanding the King's troops, in order to deny access to Parliamentary troops approaching Bristol. In 1705, he purchased Clifton House and the adjoining land, and he had become a prosperous merchant. It was during this period that Abraham Darby needed financial assistance which was readily forthcoming to him from Thomas Goldney as Abraham made arrangements to move his interests from Bristol to Coalbrookdale.

NOTES – CHAPTER I

1. John Darby's father, also named John Darby, had moved to Sedgley, near Wolverhampton, Staffordshire, from Fladbury, Worcestershire earlier in the 17th century. The family had been residents of Fladbury and Feckenham for several generations, and traced their history back to John Darby of Hereford, born c1410. See family tree in IGMT Archives.
2. Raistrick, *Dynasty of Ironfounders*, p.18-19.
3. Hannah Rose's Account, IGMT Archives; Hannah Rose was the daughter of John and Grace Thomas, who accompanied Abraham Darby to Coalbrookdale. She married Thomas Rose in 1764.
4. His certificate of removal from Birmingham Monthly Meeting was dated 14 September 1698.
5. Hannah Rose's Account, IGMT Archives; see note 3.
6. Barrie Trinder, *The Darbys of Coalbrookdale*.
7. Copy made by Matilda Darby of Mary Darby's letters to Thomas Goldney after Abraham Darby I's death. Private family papers.
8. IGMT Archives – Patent No. 380, dated 18 April 1707.
9. SRO 1987/58/13.
10. SRO 1987/46/1.
11. See Goldney – a house and a family, by P K Stembridge.

CHAPTER II

Abraham I in Coalbrookdale

COALBROOKDALE, in Shropshire, little known in the early eighteenth century, was to give its name to the East Shropshire coalfield, which was roughly rectangular in shape and covered about twenty-four square miles in area. Below the surface lay geological strata known as the Upper, Middle and Lower coal measures, and carboniferous and silurian limestones. The coal measures included not only coal but also clay and ironstone. The River Severn, flowing through the southern part of the coalfield had for long been one of the principal commercial highways of the country.

Coalbrookdale lies near the western edge of the Parish of Madeley which in monastic times was under the jurisdiction of Wenlock Priory. After the dissolution of the monasteries the Manor of Madeley (which was substantially co-terminous with the Parish) was purchased by Sir Robert Brooke, a zealous papist, who in 1554 became Speaker of the House of Commons and Chief Justice of the Court of Common Pleas. His grandson, Sir Basil Brooke held the Manor from 1598 to 1646. He was a prominent industrialist who probably established the iron furnace in Coalbrookdale. He was also a leading Roman Catholic and Civil War conspirator and it was because of these latter activities that the Manor was forfeited to parliament in 1652. The lands were recovered soon afterwards but the family remained under constraint. By the 1690s the Manor was seriously encumbered by debt, so that in 1695 an Act of Parliament, the Madeley Manor Act, was passed, under which Trustees were appointed with power to sell off land, but were charged with the *"better managing and carrying on the Coleworks and Ironworks"*. [1] During the next ten years substantial parts of the Manor were sold. Within Coalbrookdale, farmland, part of Cawbrook Farm, (later known as Stanleys Farm) and Furnace Bank Farm, (with Glazebrook's Coppice) and a large holding (Duddell's tenement and adjoining lands) were in private ownership. [2] The floor of the valley including the course of the brook and a system of pools together with the related furnace, forges and mines remained in the ownership of the Manor. This included waste land not at that time appropriated for industrial purposes.

In accordance with the Madeley Manor Act 1695, the furnace and forges, etc, in Coalbrookdale were leased to one Shadrack Fox for twenty-one years from 1696.[3] Fox seems to have been quite a colourful character and something of an adventurer. However, he suffered a serious setback a few years after the start of his lease when the furnace was destroyed by an explosion, caused by the Pool Dam breaking. He then emigrated to Russia, leaving behind his wife and children to suffer great poverty.

He did not survive long in Russia. The following is an account of his life there, described in a dispatch from the British Ambassador in Moscow covering the period 10/12 March 1707, shortly after Fox died:-

"Here also was one Fox, an Englishman brought over by Mr Stiles; he gave himself out to have been many years employed in furnishing the tower with warlike stores. He was freighted with new fashioned mortars, square musketons, grandoes to burn ships (probably Captain Haley's experiment) and other new inventions, some whereof he had not...thought fit to produce in England. He was entertained here with a salary of five hundred pounds a year, but how far his performance would have answered his undertaking is uncertain, for he died suddenly of the collick some days ago; at least time enough to save his reputation and that of his partners."[4]

The date of the explosion which caused Shadrack Fox's departure to Russia is not known, but is thought to have been between 1700 and 1705. At that time Abraham Darby was operating in Bristol, having established the Bristol Brass Works in Baptist Mills and initiated the iron foundry in Cheese Lane. He was also broadening his horizons because in 1706 he was involved with the Quaker community in Broseley, on the opposite banks of the River Severn from Coalbrookdale. In that year he was witness to the purchase of the piece of ground which became the Quaker Burial Ground in Broseley. It also seems likely that he was involved in a brass works in Coalbrookdale at that time and it therefore seems probable that he would have known of the destruction of the Coalbrookdale Furnace. He may have sensed an opportunity to expand his business enterprises for not only was he a great innovator but he was also a man of tremendous energy and drive.

The following year 1707 he had secured his patent for the casting of iron bellied pots in sand, and had entered into his bond with John Thomas regarding the secrecy of the process. The same year he had been admitted a Freeman of Bristol, so that he had secured a position as a trader in the Bristol market.[5] While maintaining his activities in Bristol he started to explore the possibilities of establishing a business in Coalbrookdale. Doubtless he realised the potential of his patent, as the demand for pots and other useful iron utensils was increasing. In this context, Coalbrookdale offered a favourable opportunity. It was one of four

8

A.D. 1707 . . . . Nº 380.

Casting Iron Pots.

DARBY'S PATENT.

ANNE, by the grace of God, &c., to all to whom these presents shall come, greeting.

WHEREAS our trusty and welbeloved ABRAHAM DARBY, of our city of Bristol, Smith, hath by his petition humbly represented vnto vs that by his study and industry and expence he hath found out and brought to
5 perfection "A NEW WAY OF CASTING IRON BELLIED POTTS, AND OTHER IRON BELLIED WARE IN SAND ONLY, WITHOUT LOAM OR CLAY, BY WHICH IRON POTS AND OTHER WARE MAY BE CAST FINE AND WITH MORE EASE AND EXPEDITION, AND MAY BE AFFORDED CHEAPER THAN THEY CAN BE BY THE WAY CŌMONLY VSED, AND IN REGARD TO THEIR CHEAPNESSE MAY BE OF GREAT ADVANTAGE TO THE POORE
10 OF THIS OUR KINGDOME, WHO FOR THE MOST PART VSE SUCH WARE, AND IN ALL PROBABILITY WILL PREVENT THE MERCHANTS OF ENGLAND GOING TO FORREIGN MARKETS FOR SUCH WARE, FROM WHENCE GREAT QUANTITIES ARE IMPORTED, AND LIKEWISE MAY IN TIME SUPPLY FORREIGN MARKETS WITH THAT MANUFACTURE OF OUR OWN DOMINIONS," and hath humbly prayed vs to grant him our Letters
15 Patents for the sole vse and benefit of the said Invention for the terme of fourteen yeares.

KNOW YEE THEREFORE, that wee, being graciously pleased to condescend to that his request, and willing to encourage the inventors of such arts as may be of publick vse and benefit, of our especial grace, certain
20 knowledge, and meer motion, have given and granted, and by these presents, for vs, our heires and successors, do give and grant, vnto the said Abraham Darby, his executors, administrators, and assignes, especiall lycence, full

Patent, dated 1707 for casting iron pots in sand.

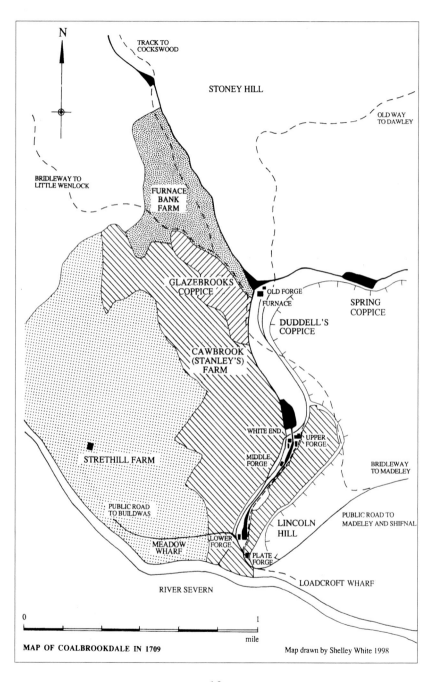

N

TRACK TO
COCKSWOOD

STONEY HILL

OLD WAY
TO DAWLEY

BRIDLEWAY TO
LITTLE WENLOCK

FURNACE
BANK
FARM

GLAZEBROOKS
COPPICE

OLD FORGE
FURNACE

SPRING
COPPICE

DUDDELL'S
COPPICE

CAWBROOK
(STANLEY'S)
FARM

WHITE END

UPPER
FORGE

STRETHILL FARM

MIDDLE
FORGE

BRIDLEWAY
TO MADELEY

PUBLIC ROAD
TO BUILDWAS

PUBLIC ROAD TO
MADELEY AND SHIFNAL

LINCOLN
HILL

MEADOW
WHARF

LOWER
FORGE

PLATE
FORGE

LOADCROFT WHARF

RIVER SEVERN

0   1
                                                  mile

MAP OF COALBROOKDALE IN 1709   Map drawn by Shelley White 1998

10

furnaces located in the Upper Severn region (the others being Leighton, Willey and Kemberton) and was, therefore, part of an established iron working area. It was close to sources of iron ore (known at the time as "Mine") and limestone, and although the connection with coke had not yet been made, there were ample supplies of coal in Madeley and immediately to the north of Coalbrookdale in the neighbouring parish of Little Wenlock. Above all it was immediately accessible to the River Severn with its direct connection to Bristol.

Also, there were four forges in Coalbrookdale, forming part of a wider regional market. With the benefit of hindsight, it is clear that he made a brilliant choice of location, although of course it would have required a major act of faith at the time.

It is evident that Abraham Darby started operating in Coalbrookdale in 1708. Account books show that he spent money on rebuilding the old damaged furnace and bellows during that year.[5] No documentation has survived relating to the tenancy of the furnace at that time but the accounts contain an entry:-

April 20th 1709.   My Landlord Richard Corfield
and Thomas Dorsett.
By Cash paid Tho Dorsett in
full for ½ a years rent
ending on Ladyday last for
ye ffurnis & White End   £20.0.0

The tenancy therefore started in September 1708, and was probably a sub-tenancy. After the departure of Shadrack Fox to Russia, the head-lease appears to have been acquired by Richard Corfield of Harley who possibly held the furnace, etc, before Shadrack Fox and was also involved in the coal and iron business.[6] It was Richard Corfield to whom Abraham paid rent (Thomas Dorsett was perhaps his agent). At some stage whether from 1708 or not, Abraham became sub-tenant for the remainder of Shadrack Fox's lease, ie until 1717 (in a letter dated 12th, 5th month, 1712 to Mr Wm Rollason of Kendal, he refers to himself "*as being fixed at this furnes for 5 years*").[7]

The furnace was in blast by January 1709 and the wages for the first week of blowing was as follows:[8]

			s.	d.
11 month 17th	By cash pd	Jno Tyler, founder	10.	0
(January 1709)		Jno Felton, keeper	8.	0
		Richard Hart, filler	7.	0
		Edward Bear, mine burner	6.	6
		Richard Knowles, stocker		
		of ye bridge	6.	6

11

Between the middle of 1708 and later in 1709, furnace equipment was moved from Bristol to Coalbrookdale, and workmen, including John Thomas also moved there. Abraham and Mary took up residence in White End which was included in the rent paid to Richard Corfield (see above). White End was a black and white timbered house near the Upper Forge which survived until 1939 when it was demolished during road-widening work undertaken by the local authority. Before 1708 it had been the residence of one Lawrence Wellington who had been operating the furnace in 1688 before Shadrack Fox and who subsequently took a sub-lease from Shadrack Fox of the Great and Plate Forges.[9] Lawrence Wellington died in 1708[10] thus making the property available to Abraham and Mary.

Although material and workmen moved from Bristol during this period, Darby continued with his interests in Bristol and in 1709 after a period of operating the Bristol Iron Works as a solitary venture, he entered into partnership with James Peters and Griffin Prankard and also became involved with them in a lease of the water-mill on the River Tern as it nears its confluence with the River Severn at Atcham near Shrewsbury, where a "joint work" was planned for bringing wrought-iron from Coalbrookdale pig-iron, and rolling plates from brass manufactured at Coalbrookdale.[11] One Thomas Harvey, related by marriage to Abraham's sister Esther was appointed manager of the Joint Work. At this period Darby's activities seemed to reach a frenetic level for he had as already mentioned become concerned in a brass works in the Dale before 1708[12] and by 1710 he was developing a copper smelter adjacent to the blast furnace.[12]

His principal activity was, however, the furnace which as stated was producing iron from the beginning of 1709. All furnaces at that time were constrained by the availability of charcoal for firing and it seems inevitable that Abraham would have been reminded of the work of "Dud" Dudley, who, working at Pensnett in the previous century only a few miles from Abraham's birthplace at Wren's Nest, Dudley, had claimed to have succeeded in producing iron using coal, albeit of non-commercial quality. There is no direct evidence of the occasion on which Abraham first used coke as a fuel, although it seems clear that it was in the year 1709. Certainly the account book for that year shows the purchase of "coles" and also two small sums paid for "charking coles". The best family recollection of the event was made later, in 1763, by Abiah Darby,[13] in a letter written after the death of her husband, Abraham Darby II. The following is the relevant extract:-

"I now make free to communicate what I have heard my Husband say, and what arises from my own knowledge; also what I am inform'd from a person now living, whose father came here as a workman at the first beginning of these Pit Coal Works.

Then to begin at the original. It was my Husband's Father, whose name he bore (Abraham Darby who was the first that set foot the Brass Works at or near Bristol) that attempted to mould and cast Iron pots &c., in sand instead of Loam (as they were wont to do, which made it a tedious and more expensive process) in which he succeeded. This first attempt was tryed at an Air Furnace in Bristol. About the year 1709 he came into Shropshire to Coalbrookdale, and with other partners took a lease of the works, which only consisted of an old Blast Furnace and some Forges.

He here cast Iron Goods in sand out of the Blast Furnace that blow'd with wood charcoal; for it was not yet thought of to blow with Pit Coal.

Sometime after he suggested the thought, that it might be practable to smelt the Iron from the ore in the Blast Furnace with Pit Coal: Upon this he first try'd with raw coal as it came out of the Mines, but it did not answer. He not discouraged, had the coal coak'd into Cynder as is done for drying Malt, and it then succeeded to his satisfaction. But he found that only one sort of pit Coal would suit best the purpose of making good Iron – These were beneficial discoveries, for the moulding and casting in sand instead of Loam was of great service, both in respect to expence and expedition. And if we may compare little things with great – as the invention of printing was to writing, so was the moulding and casting in sand to that of Loam. He then erected another Blast furnace, and enlarged the Works. The discovery soon got abroad and became of great utility."

After his initial experiment with coal and coke, it took Abraham a year or two to establish his new process. Writing in 1863, Samuel Smiles, refers to a "Blast Furnace Memorandum Book" which has since disappeared, from which he drew the following conclusions:-[14]

"The fuel used in the furnaces appears, from the Darby Memorandum Book to have been at first entirely charcoal; but the growing scarcity of wood seems to have gradually led to the use of coke, brays or small coke, and peat. An abundance of coals existed in the neighbourhood; by rejecting those of inferior quality and coking the others with great care, a combustible was obtained better fitted even than charcoal itself for the fusion of that particular kind of ore which is found in the coal-measures. Thus we found Darby's most favourite charge for his furnaces to have been five baskets of coke, two of brays, and one of peat; next followed the ore, and then the limestone. The use of charcoal was gradually given up as the art of smelting with coke and brays improved, most probably aided by the increased power of the furnace blast, until at length we find it entirely discontinued".

By 1711 it seems that Abraham was sufficiently confident of his position to bring his father and step-mother from Wren's Nest to live in Coalbrookdale. In that year John and Joan Darby took up residence in White End, when Abraham and Mary moved to live in a part of Madeley

13

Court which they rented from Mathias Astley. Madeley Court was, and still is, the most distinguished property within the Parish. Dating back to the thirteenth century, and extended in each subsequent century, it was originally the summer residence of the Priors of Wenlock. After the dissolution of the Monasteries, the last prior, John Bayley was allowed to live there until his death in 1553. After that the manor was purchased by Sir Robert Brooke and Madeley Court as the Manor House was occupied by the Brooke Family until 1699. Four years later it was purchased together with two neighbouring farms by Mathias Astley, who in turn rented a part of the building to Abraham Darby in 1711.[15]

By then Abraham and Mary had a young family, all girls, the eldest Mary, born in 1700, followed by Ann (b1701), Esther, Sarah and Hannah. The elegant surroundings of Madeley Court must have been a welcome change from the industrial environment of Coalbrookdale and the earlier surroundings in Philip's Place, Bristol, where they previously lived. Soon after they moved to Madeley Court, their first son Abraham II was born on 12 March 1711[16] followed by Edmund (b.2 June 1712)), Sergeant (b.28 July 1713) and John (b.27 July 1716). Although the move to Madeley Court must have been beneficial to family life, the location was not favourable to close supervision of the works which was three miles away by a bridle-way which descended into Coalbrookdale along the line of the present day Church Road. The initial experiments to use coke had been completed but it is clear that the period of experimentation was not over because difficulties were being experienced until 1713 reaching the point where some of Abraham's partners were seeking to withdraw their capital.[17]

This does not seem to have deterred Abraham, because the furnace was prospering and although trade down-river to Bristol diminished in 1710-11, the production of castings seems to have increased substantially thereafter.[17] Abraham did not seem to have difficulty in raising capital during this crucial period. Two Indentures dated 21 September 1711 and 28 February 1712 show that Abraham and his partners were able to raise and pay back £1282 between these dates, from Richard Champion of Bristol, underlining the success of the furnace at that time.[18] In fact Abraham was offering the success of his coke-smelting further afield. In 1712 he raised that possibility with William Rollason of Kendal who had founded the Blackbarrow Company in Furness and was suffering difficulties due to the increasing cost of fuel. Nothing came of the proposition however.[19] Indeed although attempts were made to extend the process to other sites, there is no evidence of these being successful, largely because the pig-iron then produced by coke-smelting, although suitable for the production of castings, was not acceptable to the many forges which converted the pig-iron to wrought-iron, and which preferred for

14

Cast iron pot, dated 1714.

Madeley Court.

15

that purpose the pig-iron produced by charcoal-smelting. Even so, the business of producing castings was prospering and the work at the furnace was expanding.

By this time there were but three years left of Shadrack Fox's lease of 1696. The need to secure the future of the enterprise was therefore becoming pressing. The administration of the Manor was still in the hands of the Trustees appointed under the Madeley Manor Act 1695.

Abraham visited London late in 1714, and as a result a new lease of the works was granted in December 1714 for twenty-one years from 1717.[20] It seems that Abraham's previous partners, James Peters and Griffin Prankard were no longer involved as they were replaced in the new deed by John Chamberlain of Stow-in-the-Wold and Thomas Baylies, Abraham's recently appointed Clerk.

The lease related primarily to the *"Iron Furnace commonly called or known by the name of Colebrookdale furnace"* with its site of half an acre of land, but it also included four forges and a building called the Steel House, with their respective sites amounting to one acre. These forges located down the Dale between the furnace and the River Severn were included in Shadrack Fox's lease. There was a fifth forge not mentioned in the lease known as the Old Forge, then disused, located close to the furnace and on the same site. The forges were variously sub-let and it is difficult to comprehend that they could have been of great significance at that time to Abraham. Normally they would have related to the furnace from which they took the pig-iron for conversion into a form suitable for use by the wrought-iron traders such as nail-makers, etc, but it had already become clear that the pig-iron being then produced from the furnace was not acceptable to the forgemasters of the period.

The lease also included all the pools, watercourses, dams, etc, and most significantly an area of waste ground adjoining the forges *"to be inclosed by setting up a gate on the roadway there"*. The signing of the new lease gave rise to a new burst of energy. In 1715 he built a new furnace on the waste land, thus expanding the production capacity of the partnership. He was able to do this because he was no longer constrained by the capacity of the charcoal industry to provide fuel. He was able for the first time to demonstrate the freedom given by his new coke-smelting process, there being virtually no limit on the availability of the local clod coal which produced an admirable low sulphur coke for the two furnaces.

He clearly had in mind the possibility of expanding the horizons of his enterprise. Despite the failure of his earlier attempt to interest William Rollason of Kendal in his new process, his thoughts encompassed the possibility of using Cambrian ores from the Cader Idris range which were similar to the Cumbrian ores used by Rollason at Furness. Between 1713

16

and 1714 he started to extend his organisation to take expansion on to other sites. The method he used was to appoint clerks to manage different sites under his personal direction. The first to be appointed was John Kelsall, a Quaker who was managing iron forges and furnaces for the Lloyds of Dolobran.[21]

He was first approached in 1713 and then spent three weeks in Coalbrookdale at the beginning of 1715 before inaugurating a new furnace at Dolgyn, two miles east of Dolgellau in mid-Wales. Two other clerks were appointed in 1714. They were both Quakers and belonged to the wider Darby/Sargeant family. The first was Thomas Baylies, a cousin, who was also married to his wife's sister, Hannah Sargeant. He moved to Coalbrookdale from Stourbridge in April 1714. The second clerk, Richard Ford, also moved from Stourbridge to Coalbrookdale in 1714, but his relationship to the family was more distant. His sister Elizabeth was married to Thomas Sargeant, brother-in-law to Abraham.

Another 'relative' who moved to Coalbrookdale at this time was Thomas Luccock, a kinsman of Joan Darby (née Luccock) who was Abraham's stepmother. He was taken into apprenticeship in June 1714 by a deed in which Abraham is described as "of the City of Bristol, Smith, on behalf of himself and his Co-partners with ironworks in Coalbrookdale in the County of Salop".[22] Despite the reference to Bristol, Abraham was by now fully committed to Coalbrookdale, following the signing of the new lease, and the brass works in which he seems to have been first involved in the Dale probably ceased operation in 1714 when its movable equipment was transported down the Severn to Bristol.[23]

Of the two new clerks appointed in 1714, the senior was Thomas Baylies, who as has been noted became a party to the new lease of the works. He also seems by his own account to have been involved in the new venture at Dolgyn in Merionethshire. He and Abraham had known each other all their lives and there is evidence that they were in correspondence back in the Bristol days.[24] Building on this trust, he became involved in the next expansion of the partnership in the Vale Royal Furnace in Oulton, Cheshire. According to a statement later made by Thomas Baylies[25] this project was proposed to Abraham by Charles Cholmondeley of Vale Royal and culminated in articles of partnership signed on 25 April 1716.[26] The partners, in addition to Charles Cholmondeley were Abraham Darby, John Chamberlain and Thomas Baylies, thus following the pattern already established in Coalbrookdale, and probably Dolgyn.

With John Kelsall and Thomas Baylies committed in the two new expansions it fell to Richard Ford to accept responsibility for the development of Coalbrookdale including the new furnace. By this time the number of Quaker families in the Dale was increasing. There were eight families in 1716 including John Thomas, Abraham's oldest colleague who in 1714 had travelled to Bristol to marry Grace Zean whom he had met in his Bristol days and brought her back to the Dale where they lived for the rest of their lives. [27]

In the meantime, with all the activity of expanding the operation, Abraham was finding it inconvenient to be living three miles away at Madeley Court. He, therefore, bought a piece of land close to the works, and started to build a new house for himself and his family in 1715. This was destined to become Dale House.

The site had until 1715 been part of Glazebrook's Coppice, which comprised some 14 acres of what was described as "woody ground". This had been acquired in 1705 by George Dukesell along with the adjoining Furnace Bank Farm. [28] Glazebrook's Coppice was situate to the west of the furnace and stretched up the hill to the west of a bridle-way from Coalbrookdale to Little Wenlock (now Darby Road). The land was purchased for £8 and was probably about an acre in extent.

The deed of conveyance was subsequently lost but the transaction was ratified in a later deed in 1734 [29] between the sons of Abraham Darby and George Dukesell. According to family records "it was built slowly of good old oak and bricks". A walled garden was constructed with a summer house and a walk of yew trees with a flower garden below the walk. The whole project was to take two years to complete.

While the house was being built, Richard Corfield, Abraham's landlord of the works, who held the residue on Shadrack Fox's 1696 lease died and was succeeded by his two sons. This led to an agreement dated 4 June 1716 under which the two sons assigned the residue of their late father's interest in the lease from 26 March 1715 until Michaelmas 1717 for a nominal consideration of 5 shillings. The partners, John Chamberlain, Abraham Darby and Thomas Baylies undertook to purchase all the *"charck coale"* at the Upper and Lower Forges at the rate of £2.6.0 per load. This document regularised the position of the partnership through to the beginning of the new lease. [30]

The period of expansion which had been sustained since 1714 made considerable demands on capital and during this period, Abraham raised money from Thomas Goldney II of Bristol and mortgaged the works as security. Plans for the works at Dolgyn and at Vale Royal were underway and John Chamberlain had taken up residence in the Dale. John Kelsall visited early in 1717 and recorded dining with John Chamberlain and Thomas Goldney. [31] They went on to Dolgyn with Thomas Baylies the following month to set out the foundations of the new furnace. One senses that the project had been losing impetus. Significantly, Abraham was not

18

present at these meetings through illness and his absence was having an effect. His health had in fact been deteriorating for some time, and sadly he died shortly afterwards, aged only 39.

Through all his activities he had maintained his overwhelming commitment to the Friends and he frequently signed the minutes of Monthly and Quarterly Meetings as Clerk. He was attended at the end by his loyal comrade John Thomas. Mary Darby in a letter written later to Thomas Goldney spoke thus of him – "*He stood at my dying Husband's side and heard his mind, and as much as I had cared for him when poor and of low estate, has in these later troubles been to me as a son*".[32]

The last Meeting attended by Abraham was in Dale House. John Thomas' daughter, Hannah Rose, in an account written later[33] wrote:- "*The last Meeting he was at was in the new house which he built in Coalbrookdale. It was not quite finished so not inhabited. The Meeting was held in the room now called the best parlour and he was greatly favoured in prayer. My Father and Mother said they never heard him so fine but he was too ill to sit the Meeting out*". He died not long after at Madeley Court and was brought to the new house to be buried from there at Broseley. "And so he came to rest amongst the people who shared the faith which had sustained him through his all-too-short life. His future daughter-in-law Abiah Darby, wrote his finest epitaph – "*My Husband's Father died early in life, a religious good man and an Eminent minister amongst the people called Quakers*".

His immense secular attainments were also achieved amongst the people called Quakers. It so happened that the iron industry in the West Midlands and the Borders was heavily peopled by Friends and wherever Abraham moved, first to Birmingham, then Bristol and finally Coalbrookdale he was always within reach of Quaker support. His work was predominantly a Quaker achievement.

This occurred within a short period of less than fifteen years. During that time he had by 1707 invented the method of casting iron in sand instead of loam. This in itself would have secured his reputation but after his arrival in Coalbrookdale he was able to show how to secure a bountiful supply of pig-iron through the use of readily-available coke, rather then the severely restricted charcoal, which was the only alternative. This created a virtually new industry, through the supply of cast-iron objects, starting with the famous three legged pot or 'furnace', and developed a new trade for small domestic and industrial utensils at affordable prices, for which there soon came an insatiable demand.

It was, of course, a disappointment that the new pig-iron proved unacceptable to the wrought-iron trade which continued for several decades to prefer the old charcoal-smelted iron. It was to be left to Abraham's son,

The old furnace, Coalbrookdale, during excavation.

The old furnace, preserved.

20

also named Abraham, to solve that problem and to lift the industry into a higher gear. At the time of Abraham's death in 1717, his son was still only six years of age.

NOTES – CHAPTER II

1. Madeley Manor Act, 7 & 8 Wm III C.8 Priv.Act.
2. SRO 1987/19/3.
3. SRO 1987/35/1.
4. Labouchere, *Abiah*, p.23; Information from British Ambassador Wentworth to the Honorary Secretary of State Harley, dated Moscow 10/21 March 1707, now in Public Record Office, Russia.
5. Account Book; SPL Coalbrookdale Company Papers MSS. No.328.
6. SRO 1681/139/1; SRO 1987/35/1.
7. Raistrick p.41; National Library of Wales NLW., MS10823, E.
8. Raistrick p.33; SPL Coalbrookdale Company Papers, MSS No.328.
9. VCH XI p.49; SRO 4406/1 pp94-5.
10. VCH XI p.50; TSAS Ivi85; SPL MS 328 f.(36) January 1709/10.
11. Trinder, *Darbys of Coalbrookdale*, p.12.
12. Trinder, *Darbys of Coalbrookdale*, p.11.
13. SRO 1987/46/1.
14. Smiles S, Industrial Biography: Iron Workers and Tool Makers 1863, p.82. Also Raistrick, *Dynasty of Ironfounders*, p.39.
15. VCH, XI pp 37, 38 and 39; SRO 2280/2/9.
16. Register of Shropshire Monthly Meeting of Friends.
17. Trinder, *Darbys of Coalbrookdale*, p.10.
18. Raistrick p.40; Norris MSS; VIII pp 41-4.
19. Raistrick p.42.
20. SRO 1681/139/1.
21. Raistrick p.44.
22. Labouchere, *Abiah*, p.27.
23. Trinder, *Darbys of Coalbrookdale*, p.13.
24. Labouchere, *Abiah*, p.26.
25. SRO 1987/58/54.
26. Raistrick p.42; Norris MSS VIII p.134.
27. Labouchere, *Abiah*, p.28.
28. SRO 1987/19/1-2.
29. SRO 1681/131/5.
30. SRO 1987/35/1.
31. Raistrick, p.44.
32. Labouchere, *Abiah*, p.28. Private family papers.
33. Hannah Rose's Account IGMT Archives.

CHAPTER III

"Interregnum" – 1717-1720

THE DEATH OF ABRAHAM I in 1717 was a major setback to the enterprise. Although he had secured a new lease to start in September 1717 and although he had appointed clerks to administer the three separate projects in Coalbrookdale, Dolgyn and Vale Royal, his early demise deprived the operation of his exceptional innovative drive and vision. Much would depend on his partners Thomas Baylies and John Chamberlain. In the event, the next year or so developed into a period of discord during which the two partners were replaced by a new partnership.

Information on this period derives mainly from an undated and unsigned memorandum in quasi-legal form which has survived amongst family papers[1] and also to a lesser extent from the recollections of Hannah Rose written later in the century, in which she recorded what she had heard from her parents[2] John Thomas, Abraham's closest colleague, and Grace Thomas his wife.

Abraham died without making a Will, leaving his widow Mary at Madeley Court with seven children, survivors of the eleven children born to them. The situation was not helped by the fact that Thomas Baylies and his wife Hannah entered into possession of Dale House when it was completed and became its first occupiers. Seemingly, he based his claim on a right of survivorship through joint tenancy of partnership property although such evidence as has survived[3] suggests that Abraham had bought the land in his own name. As a result, Mary and her family went back to live in White End.

She took out Letters of Administration under which, according to the Memorandum, *"she became posest of ye Dale Works"*. A creditor of the works was Thomas Goldney II who had lent £1600 on a mortgage of one moiety of the Works. It was, therefore, agreed that the works should be valued at £3200 and that sixteen shares of £200 should be created. Of these six were assigned to Thomas Goldney in respect of £1200 of the debt, and two more representing £400 held against the balance of the mortgage. Mary Darby also sold two shares to Richard Ford for £400, retaining eight shares in her own hands. Four of the eight shares were assigned to John Chamberlain for £800 but he failed to pay the money.

Thomas Baylies also claimed to be a creditor in the sum of £1200 and it was agreed that Mary Darby and John Chamberlain would assign to Thomas Baylies their rights and interest in the Vale Royal Furnace and that Thomas Baylies would assign to Mary Darby and John Chamberlain his rights and interests in the Dale Works and the Lease. He was given a separate bond in respect of the debt of £1200.

Unfortunately Mary Darby became ill at this stage and moved from Coalbrookdale to Bewdley where she died on 30 January 1718, leaving her seven children as orphans, the eldest being Mary who was 17 and the youngest, Sergeant, who was 5. Rather strangely it was Thomas Baylies who took out Letters of Administration on the basis of "survivorship in a joint tenancy" and he thus became possessed of the remaining eight shares. The future of the children then arose and it was their uncle Joshua Sergeant (Mary's brother) who intervened on their behalf and offered to pay £400 plus £100 interest to Thomas Goldney for his two mortgaged shares, a proposition which Thomas Goldney seemingly readily accepted. Thereafter, however, there seems to have developed a power struggle between Thomas Baylies and Thomas Goldney for the control of the Company, which Thomas Goldney won.

The first move seems to have taken place when Thomas Goldney pressed Baylies to execute his bond for £1200. This he did and appropriated to himself the four shares which John Chamberlain had been unable to pay for. He then received £400 from Joshua Sargeant on behalf of the children and went to Bristol to secure the mortgage on two shares which Thomas Goldney had previously agreed to surrender. Goldney, however, would not part with his rights to the two shares, thus leaving Joshua Sergeant without security for his money. Upon being pressed, Thomas Baylies eventually transferred two shares to Joshua Sergeant leaving four shares in his own hands, the remaining two shares being mortgaged to Goldney. Not long after, Baylies became pressed for money and was declared bankrupt. As a result the four shares were sold by the assignees, two to Thomas Goldney II, one to Thomas Goldney III and one to Joshua Sergeant.

As a result of these complicated manoeuvres the Company was then held in sixteen shares, owned as follows:

Thomas Goldney II	10 shares
Richard Ford	2 shares
Joshua Sergeant	3 shares (for the children)
Thomas Goldney III	1 share
	16 shares

In July 1718 an inventory of the works was carried out in meticulous detail, six months after the death of Mary Darby.[4] The stock was valued at £2957.15.0 and the buildings were valued at £1242.5.0, giving a total of £4200.

It can be seen, therefore, that the valuation of the shares at three quarters of that sum (£3200) was a considerable undervaluation. It placed no value on Abraham's discovery (for which he had not taken out a patent) and took no account of the fact that the furnaces represented a thriving business with a full twenty-one year lease in hand. It was in effect a forced sale, particularly ironic when it is recalled that in 1711 only a few years before, Abraham had had no difficulty in repaying a loan of £1282 within five months. The acquisition of eleven out of sixteen shares by the Goldney family can be regarded as a fortunate investment which was to bring great rewards over the next fifty years.

By contrast, Abraham's family were in hazard of being excluded from all benefit and in the process of being deprived of the home which their father had built. All this was the consequence of the early death of both Abraham and Mary before the benefits of their work could be consolidated and safeguarded. It was the first example of a pattern which was to repeat itself in succeeding generations of the family. That the family eventually succeeded in buying back its inheritance is largely due to the action of Joshua Sergeant in purchasing three shares in the Company and also due to the fact that Abraham's eldest daughter, named Mary after her mother, married Richard Ford on 1 August 1718. (At that time Richard Ford owned two shares which was increased to four by the time of his death in 1745).

The exact sequence of events in 1718 and 1719 is not clear. Thomas Goldney spent some time in Coalbrookdale during this period and Richard Ford was appointed manager in 1718. A new account book was started and both furnaces were in blast. This seems to suggest that by then Thomas Baylies had ceased to have anything to do with the works. Exactly when he left Dale House is not clear, Hannah Rose writing about these events later in the century[2] stated: .. "*about this time the late Thomas Goldney came up and went into the Old House* (i.e. White End) *and he and R Ford when they had got T Bailiss out of the New house went and lived there, then my parents* (i.e John and Grace Thomas) *went into the Old one... T Goldney staid about one year.*" This seems to imply that Thomas Baylies was out of Dale House by the end of 1718 and that his connection with the company had come to an end. He felt aggrieved by his treatment and in 1721 published a private account of his treatment entitled "The Case of Th-m-s Ba-l-s in relation to his affairs with Ab-h-m D—by and family before and since their deaths." Certainly he enjoyed Abraham's trust during his lifetime and was not only a clerk but also a partner named in the leases of the Coalbrookdale, Dolgyn and Vale Royal works. He also claimed to be owed £1200 not greatly different from the £1600 owed to

Thomas Goldney. Crucially, however, Goldney's loan was secured by a mortgage of half of the works, whereas Baylies' was not. Above all, his plea of joint tenancy was not accepted.

Within the family the reaction to Baylies seems to have been universally hostile. A document of 1734[3] dealing with a small piece of land at the rear of Dale House refers to *"the affairs of the said Abraham Darby after his decease falling into bad hands."* Hannah Rose in her account states: *"He proved a very bad man, borrowed Money in A Darby's name and my Father was cheated and some of the Workmen by him."*

One is left with the impression that his financial probity was suspect, a fact which would have been unacceptable to the Quaker fraternity. He left Coalbrookdale, presumably in the early 1720s and went to Pennsylvania where in partnership with one Thomas Rutter he erected a blast furnace at Manatawny in the Schuylkill Valley. The furnace was called Colebrookdale and was the first blast furnace in Pennsylvania, and one of the earliest in America. Regrettably he again got into financial difficulties and did not prosper.

In the meantime the upbringing and education of the children of Abraham and Mary needed attention. The eldest child Mary married Richard Ford in 1718. The next eldest child, Anne married John Hawkins and moved to Bersham near Wrexham where she and her husband became involved in the Iron Works. Another daughter Hannah was sent to Bristol to be trained in service but she died in 1727. A daughter Esther had died between 1709 and 1712 and another daughter had died in infancy. A sixth daughter Sarah, was sent to school with Gilbert Thompson at Penketh, Lancashire. She was accompanied there by her three younger brothers Abraham II, Edmund and Sergeant (two other brothers had died young).

The expenses of education and clothing appear in the company accounts until about 1730.[5] Sadly two of the four children who went to school at Penketh died (Sergeant in 1725 and Sarah in 1726) leaving just Abraham II and Edmund in education until 1730 when they entered the Works. Of the eleven children of Abraham and Mary, only four, two daughters and two sons survived to adult years:

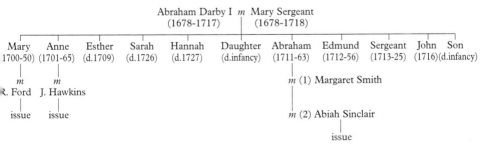

Of all these children, it is only the eldest daughter, Mary and the eldest son, Abraham II, who continued the family. The second daughter Anne, married to John Hawkins had one son who died as a young man. The second son Edmund died in 1756 without issue.

The children's shareholdings were finalised when Joshua Sergeant assigned two shares in 1723 in return for £700[6] being a sum less than his expenses to that date and the remaining share in 1726.

By then a new regime was in existence in Coalbrookdale. Soon after the death of Abraham I in 1717, the partnership which he had established had been replaced by a new partnership in which the dominant interest was held by Thomas Goldney II of Bristol. The vital point, however, was that Abraham's enterprise, embodying his two great inventions of casting iron pots in sand, and of smelting iron with charcoal had survived the crisis and was well placed to consolidate and to advance the tremendous progress which had been made under his leadership.

On the wider national scale, the War of the Spanish Succession had concluded to Britain's advantage with the Treaty of Utrecht of 1713, and perhaps more importantly for the nation's commercial future, with the signing of the Asiento, the collateral Agreement whereby the Spanish trade monopoly in South America was breached.

The Hanoverian succession to the throne of George I had occurred on the death of Queen Anne in 1714, followed the next year by the failure of the Jacobite Rebellion of the Old Pretender, James Stuart. The accession of George I indirectly facilitated the establishment of cabinet government, consolidated by Sir Robert Walpole as the nation's first prime minister (1721-42) whose policies gave the country a valuable period of peace for the next twenty years.

During this period while Britain's commercial capacity was expanding, the country's industrial potential, from its small beginnings in Coalbrookdale, started to move forward, albeit slowly at first.

NOTES – CHAPTER III

1. SRO 1987/58/54.
2. Hannah Rose's Account. IGMT Archives.
3. SRO 1681/131/5.
4. Raistrick, *Dynasty of Iron Founders*, 2nd edition, Appendix 2.
5. Raistrick, *Dynasty of Iron Founders*, 2nd edition, p.48.
6. IGMT Archives.

CHAPTER IV

The Ford/Goldney Years

DESPITE THE DIFFICULTIES encountered by the partnership after the death of Abraham I, the impact on the Works seems to have been minimal. Within a year the new regime of Thomas Goldney II and Richard Ford had taken over full command of the operation. They were the majority shareholders, and they proved to be a remarkable team. Both were good businessmen, well able to consolidate and exploit the innovations introduced by Abraham. Indeed, Richard Ford clearly understood the directions in which the new technology was heading and was able to build upon Abraham's work. Thomas Goldney, for his part, was soon able to return to Bristol, confident in being able to leave the management of the enterprise in the capable hands of Richard Ford. New accounts were started from 1718 and there began a regular business correspondence between the two men. [1]

The position of Richard Ford was clearly reinforced domestically when in addition to becoming Manager of the Works, he married Abraham's eldest child, Mary, on 1 August 1718 at Shrewsbury Meeting. [2] Mary was then eighteen years old and Richard was twenty-nine. It is not known when Thomas Baylies vacated Dale House but it could have been as early as 1718. As soon as this took place, Richard Ford and Mary took up residence in Dale House. Their first child, Mary, was born in 1719. They were to have three daughters and four sons. They lived in Dale House until 1738 when they built the fine house next door, now known as Rosehill. [3]

Richard Ford and Thomas Goldney developed a relationship whereby the markets based on Bristol, including export markets, were looked after by the latter, whilst responsibility for the works and for the markets in the Midlands, Wales and elsewhere vested in Richard Ford. Under these arrangements trade expanded vigorously during the next ten to twenty years.

In 1718, the previously disused Old Forge close to the Old Furnace was brought into operation and the following year trials were undertaken about the suitability of the Coalbrookdale pig iron, which proved sufficiently satisfactory for the Company to take back control of the Middle Forge in Coalbrookdale. In 1722 William Cranage was appointed Forge master. He and his family were to become important residents in the Dale during the next one hundred years.

During this critically important period the Works started to provide cast-iron parts for steam engines and by 1722 cylinders were being cast in iron to replace the brass cylinders previously used. This trade, although small at first was to bring Coalbrookdale to national prominence. In the meantime the pot and kettle trade was considerably expanded and the number of customers soon doubled.

The link with Bristol was of special importance, as Britain's overseas trade was expanding. Nehemiah Champion and his family of Bristol were very good customers and there can be no doubt that much of the Coalbrookdale ware was exported. This applied particularly to the three legged pot or furnace which went all over the world and was very much a Coalbrookdale trade mark. In addition to pots and kettles there was a considerable trade with Bristol in cast-iron pigs in which Thomas and Gabriel Goldney specialised.

A national 'first' was scored when in 1729 the first iron railway wheels were cast, and supplied to Richard Hartshorne, a prominent local coal master, for use on a railway from Little Wenlock to Strethill, immediately to the west of Coalbrookdale. The trade soon extended to other coal masters and thereafter became a feature of the Company's output.[4] Similarly the supply of cast-iron railings was initiated, eventually to become a major part of the product range, as also did the supply of screw-presses for the rapidly-developing hardware trades in Birmingham.[5]

All in all, the enterprise was clearly prospering and was reaching the stage when it was becoming difficult to keep up with demand. The upper and lower furnaces were each producing about five tons of iron per week and Richard Ford was becoming hard pressed. This led to expansion of the operation by the acquisition of two additional furnaces, first at Bersham near Wrexham and then at Willey, near Broseley on the south side of the River Severn.

The Bersham Furnace was built by Charles Lloyd as a charcoal-burning furnace in 1717 and was brought into blast in 1719. Two years later in 1721 it was converted to the use of coke, following the example of Coalbrookdale.[6] In 1727 it was sold to John Hawkins who in 1731 married Anne (b.1701) who was Abraham Darby's second daughter.[7] There was, therefore, a family connection. John Hawkins was involved in financial and legal difficulties and so the furnace was transferred to Coalbrookdale control with John Hawkins continuing as manager. This gave additional capacity of about 5 tons a week and was used to supply the trade around Chester and North Wales.

In the early 1730s, Richard Ford was giving thought to increased trade which would result from the expiry of the patent for Captain Savery's steam engine in 1733.[8] This led to the leasing by Richard Ford and Thomas Goldney of the old furnace at Willey from the Weld estate. After reconstruction the furnace was able to supplement the down-river trade to Bristol in pig iron.

During this period of the 1720s and early 1730s, Richard Ford and Mary his wife were living at Dale House. Seven children were born to them between 1719 and 1734 (Mary, Richard II, Edmund, Hannah, Susannah, Abraham and Darby). Also living with them at Dale House were Mary's surviving brothers and sisters (Anne, Sarah, Hannah, Abraham II, Edmund and Sergeant). Of these, two girls and a boy (Sarah, Hannah and Sergeant) died in the 1720s, leaving Anne (until she married John Hawkins of Bersham in 1731), Abraham II and Edmund resident at Dale House, (when not at school in Penketh). It was a large household, and yet despite this, Mary started to establish the family tradition of hospitality to visitors to the Works, particularly Friends for whom there was always an open door. One of the earliest contacts with North America occurred in 1735 with the visit of Thomas Story who had taken a prominent part in Government in Philadelphia. In his Journal Thomas Story recorded – *"On the 25th in the evening, I had a Meeting at Coalbrookdale, at the house of our Friend, Richard Ford, who looks after some Ironworks in that Place; it was a very open Meeting: and some Persons of Account in these Parts were there, all very sober and attentive."*

Other than occasional references of this sort, there is little description of the domestic way of life in the Ford household. One episode, however, intruded into the rigidly business-like letters of Richard Ford to Thomas Goldney. On 18 April 1735 he wrote – *"My wife for near 3 weeks past have been violently ill of a Fever, which hath brought her very weak, but the Fever is now gone and she begins to get strength"*. It was obviously a serious illness but thankfully she recovered well.

As increasing business and prosperity pressed on Richard Ford he was pleased to welcome into the works Abraham Darby II. In 1732 at the age of twenty-one he had been appointed as assistant to Richard Ford, and having acquitted himself well[9] he was given a salary of £50 a year in 1734.[10] This was additional to his income from the shares in the partnership and he was, therefore, in a position to contemplate marriage. His journeys on behalf of the Company took him through Shifnal and Newport where there were a few Quaker families. Abraham visited their Meetings as his father had done before him and this is probably how he met Margaret

Smith of Shifnal whom he married in 1734. It has to be assumed that the young couple took up residence in Dale House.

The following year, 1735, Edmund Darby came of age and his trustees consented to him "*going into business for himself*", which appeared to have been that of grocer and general merchant and to have been connected with the Works and their Coalbrookdale customers further afield. [11]

And so finally, all four surviving children of Abraham I and Mary were established in life, the two daughters Mary and Anne married to Richard Ford and John Hawkins respectively, Abraham II also married and pursuing a career in the Works, and the youngest son Edmund, established in business on his own account.

At this same time, outside events were beginning to impinge on the Company's affairs. Thomas Goldney II who had been central to the events following the death of Abraham I in 1717, died in 1731 [12] at the age of sixty-eight. He was succeeded in his business by his son Thomas Goldney III, who had visited Coalbrookdale with his father just before Abraham's death. Thomas Goldney was anxious for his son to be involved in the working of the Company but this was not possible at that time because of Abraham's illness. Thomas Goldney III did, however, spend some time in the Works after Richard Ford took over management, beginning as a cashier and then becoming involved in the Dale trade and its finances. [12] This grounding enabled both the Goldneys, father and son, to provide financial and banking services from Bristol. This all-important facility was continued by Thomas Goldney III after his father's death.

The lease of the Works which Abraham I had negotiated in 1715 was due to expire in 1738 and negotiations for its renewal were initiated by Richard Ford and Abraham II. The Lordship of the Manor of Madeley had been vested since 1727 in Catherine Brooke who married John Unett Smitheman of Little Wenlock and in her sister Rose Brooke married to John Giffard, a London merchant and younger brother of the owner of Chillington, Staffs. [13] A new lease was granted by them to Richard Ford and Abraham I on 7 January 1734 for a period of twenty-one years from 1738, [14] and this was followed in 1735 by an agreement between Richard Ford and Abraham II declaring that they held the lease as tenants in common and that Richard Ford would pay three-quarters of the rent and Abraham II the remaining quarter. Strangely neither document made reference to the other partners.

Having re-negotiated the lease, it came as a shock in January 1735 when they were informed by John Hawkins of Bersham that the land and lease of Bersham furnace had been used by him as security for a loan and that the loan was being called in the following month. Richard Ford, Thomas Goldney and Abraham II raised one-third each to pay off the debt. [15] John Hawkins held half a share in Coalbrookdale through his wife Anne and he offered to sell his interest. The half share was offered to Abraham II and Edmund but they declined (or were unable) to purchase it and it was, therefore, bought by Richard Ford, increasing his shareholding to two and a half shares. [16]

This seems to have prompted a discussion with Thomas Goldney III about the respective shareholdings of the families. In a letter dated 20 February 1736, [17] Richard Ford writes to Thomas Goldney III

"I have often treated about a Lease, and through the interest of my Wife and the regard of the Landladys have for her and the children of Abraham Darby deceased there will be a Lease granted to us upon paying a handsome fine, which we left entirely to 'em.

In this future Lease I hope you will not think it hard for us to come in to a Larger Share of the Works than heretofore, for you art not unsensible how easy thy Father come in to 'em and what large profits you have received to say nothing of ye 2 shares with the Proffitts which in Equity did belong to the Children."

Clearly the events of 1717/18 still rankled! As a result a new partnership was negotiated to take effect in 1738 with the new lease. A new account was started in November of that year with a balance of £1050 transferred from the previous account. The sixteen shares in the new company were revalued from £200 each to £1000 each giving the Company a nominal value of £16,000. The result of the negotiations was that the sixteen shares were distributed between the families as follows:

Goldney Family[18]	9 shares
Richard Ford	4 shares
Abraham II and Edmund Darby	3 shares
	16 shares

By this time accommodation for the family had become a problem. Dale House (with or without the adjoining property known as the Tobacco House) must have been proving inadequate. Abraham II and Margaret had a daughter, Hannah, born in 1735 and two sons, Abraham born in 1736 and Edmund two years later. There was clearly need for another house.

The opportunity for freehold residential development occurred on the western side of the Dale, because all the land to the north-east of the Coalbrookdale brook in the adjoining Manor of Dawley was manorial land. In 1705 Furnace Bank Farm had been sold to the Dukesell family, including fourteen acres of Glazebrooks Coppice which stretched along the western side of the brook and of the bridle way from Coalbrookdale to Little Wenlock.[19] It was these fourteen acres which became the location for housing development, as the coppice was progressively cleared. Abraham Darby I purchased just over one acre of the coppice in 1715 to provide for the building of Dale House and a garden at the rear. In 1717 two acres were sold to John Thomas just before Abraham died.[20] These two acres were located immediately to the south of Abraham's land and to the west of the brook; thus providing the opportunity not just for John Thomas' first house, but also for all the housing development which took place to the west of the Upper Furnace over the next one hundred and fifty years, or more.

In 1734 when Abraham II married Margaret Smith, the title deeds for Dale House etc were missing, perhaps because of the dispute with Thomas Baylies. The title was, therefore, reaffirmed by George Dukesell, son of the original vendor.[21] The document states that after the death of Abraham I his affairs had "*fallen into bad hands*" and the deed and conveyance had been lost and not found. The opportunity was taken of regularising the position, including the acquisition of a small irregular piece of land at the rear, about one-eighth acre in extent not included in the original conveyance.

In 1738 a further transaction took place when George Dukesell conveyed to Richard Ford some seven acres of land to the north and west of Dale House. This included the site of the house now known as Rosehill, the first five dwellings of Tea Kettle Row (later extended), a building used as a granary, together with a summer house with garden, orchard and arable land.[22] The essential elements of this development are shown on the engraving "*A View of the Upper Works at Coalbrookdale*" by Vivares dated 1758. It seems likely that by the end of the 1730s the two adjoining houses, Dale House and Rosehill were complete and that Abraham II and Margaret lived in the former and that Richard Ford and Mary lived in the latter. The remainder of Glazebrook's Coppice, the northern part, was acquired by Abraham II in 1738[23] and 1743[24] the first being two acres north of the seven acres acquired by Richard Ford and three and a half acres beyond that. These two pieces of land were to become the site of Sunniside, built by Abraham II in 1750/51.

The start of the new company in 1738 coincided with the end of Walpole's twenty years of peace. Relationships with Spain had deteriorated and in 1739 war was declared by a reluctant Walpole who memorably proclaimed "*Ring your bells now but you will soon be wringing your hands*". In Coalbrookdale, however, the war, followed by the longer War of the Austrian Succession actually increased the new prosperity which was being experienced. This was due to the fact that the Company, somewhat surprisingly, became involved in the gun trade. This was quite contrary to Quaker beliefs. If Richard Ford and Abraham had reservations

A view of the Upper Works at Coalbrookdale (Vivares, 1758).

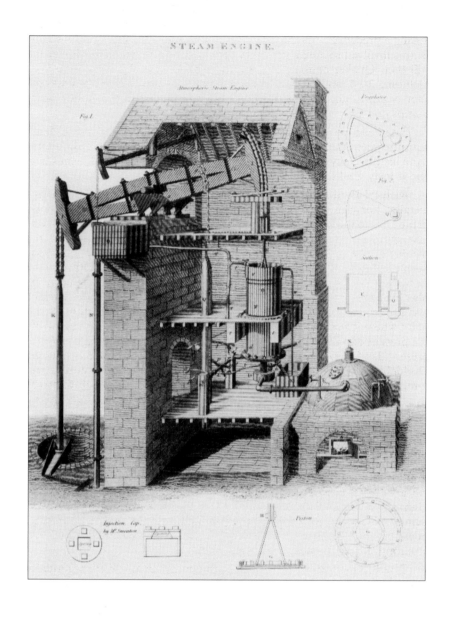

Newcomen engine, similar to the 'Fire Engine', installed in Coalbrookdale in 1742-3.

of conscience, these were effectively over-ruled by Thomas Goldney III who being involved in merchant shipping was under pressure to arm the ships sailing out of Bristol and other British ports. In doing so, he was following a precedent established by his father thirty years previously when he was involved in the privateering trade. Both father and son felt able to still their Quaker consciences. As a result large consignments of guns, including 2-, 4- and 6-pounders and ½-pounder swivel guns and casks of shot began to accompany the pots and kettles, cast-iron cylinders and pumps down river to Bristol.[25]

The need for greater production brought the Company face to face with the perennial problem which had faced furnacemen over the years – the insufficiency of water power to sustain furnaces in blast longer than about forty weeks every year, sometimes much less.

Richard Ford had already addressed this problem in 1735 when he installed horse-driven pumps to return water from one of the lower pools in the Dale to the Upper Furnace Pool. In 1742-3 this system was replaced and improved by a steam pumping engine, known in the terminology of the day as a "*Fire Engine*". This was the first time that a steam engine had been applied to the making of iron and made an important contribution to the development of the industry as it enabled furnaces to be kept in blast even in years of drought.[26] "The Fire Engine", a Newcomen engine was erected on the eastern side of the road through the Dale, close to the point where it was joined by the bridleway from Madeley (the junction of the present day Church Road and Wellington Road in the vicinity of the present day Methodist chapel). As a result the engine was partly built in Duddell's Coppice which was owned by the Manor of Madeley and therefore, outside the lease held by the Coalbrookdale Company. This fact was to cause difficulty when the Company's lease came to be renewed fifteen years later.

On the domestic front, a devastating blow was suffered in 1740 by Abraham Darby, when his two infant sons Abraham and Edmund died, probably of an infectious disease, followed even more unhappily by the death of his wife Margaret later the same year. Abraham was, therefore, left a widower at the age of twenty-nine with his five year old daughter Hannah, living in Dale House.[27] Once again, his sister, Mary Ford, living next door at Rosehill helped to see him through this crisis. It was, however, the ever-increasing activity in the Works which absorbed his attention during the next few years.

There is no doubt that there had been a transformation in the economy of the Dale. When Abraham I first came to the Dale at the beginning of the century it was described as "*barren with little money stirring amongst the inhabitants*".[28] Thirty years later, the Dale had become a dynamic centre of industrial activity. It was not only the partners who prospered but also the work people employed in and around the Works. Notwithstanding the increasing industrial processes within the coal field area, East Shropshire was still a predominantly agricultural area. The work people in the local industries were relatively small in number and were essentially craftsmen and rewarded accordingly. Ownership of property was just starting. Apart from the three acres of land bought by Abraham I and John Thomas in 1715 and 1717, a half acre of land was purchased in 1720 by Andrew Carter (Cartwright) a collier from Wrockwardine Wood, near the junction of the Rope Walk and the bridle way leading to Little Wenlock.[29] This initial purchase was followed in the 1740s by further sales of land to Thomas Cranage and to John Thorpe (who had married into the Dukesell family). These acquisitions saw the development of a small settlement at the southern end of the Rope Walk of some sixteen or so dwellings, almost all associated with the Works.

Homes were also provided for rent when Richard Ford built the first five houses of Tea Kettle Row also for occupation by families associated with the Works. Some of these were Quakers, although their numbers remained relatively small.[30]

To provide for their religious requirements, Richard Ford built a small annexe at the southern end of Tea Kettle Row and this, as extended later, was the first Meeting House in Coalbrookdale until 1808, when a second Meeting House was built just to the east of the Quaker burial ground.

A somewhat surprising element of the early residential development was the quality of landscape which was achieved, in spite of the close proximity of the Works. Even as early as the building of Dale House, Abraham I and subsequently Richard Ford, was laying out a garden with a summer house, a walk of yew trees and a flower garden.[31] The acquisition of seven acres of land by Richard Ford offered a much greater opportunity for landscaping leading to the walled garden, summer house and tower shown on the Vivares engraving of 1758. There can be little doubt that a factor in this was the association with the Goldneys, particularly Thomas Goldney III who had purchased land adjoining Clifton House, Bristol for expansion of the garden he had inherited in 1731. At the time Richard Ford was acquiring seven acres of land in Coalbrookdale, Thomas Goldney was starting to develop what was to become the famous West Country gardens at Clifton, including a grotto, terrace, rotunda and tower. Some of these features, notably a tower[32] and canal[33] were also features at Coalbrookdale. It is a measure of this achievement by Richard Ford that the view of Coalbrookdale by Vivares was included by Josiah Wedgwood as one of the scenes depicted in his famous Frog dinner and dessert service commissioned in 1773 and completed a year later for Catherine the Great of Russia. Within a period of forty years Coalbrookdale had changed beyond belief.

Richard Ford died in 1745 at the age of fifty-six. He had presided over a huge advance in the fortunes of Abraham I's great enterprise. As a businessman he had consolidated and built upon Abraham's epoch-making discoveries. He had moved the business forward in ways that Abraham would have wished, and he had also been responsible for technical innovation such as the first cast-iron wheels and the introduction of steam power to the iron industry. Without him, the business might have faltered and failed, but having sustained it through its most vulnerable period, he had the talent to carry the venture forward to the point at which Abraham I's son was able to take over the reins and make even more progress.

NOTES – CHAPTER IV

1. Ford/Goldney correspondence. IGMT Archives.
2. Rachel Labouchere: *Abiah Darby*, p.32.
3. Lease and Release dated 12/13 April 1738. S.R.O 1681/179/3.
4. Barrie Trinder: *The Darbys of Coalbrookdale*, pp.16 and 17.
5. Raistrick: *Dynasty of Iron Founders*, 2nd edition, p.57.
6. Raistrick: *Dynasty of Iron Founders*, 2nd edition, p.59. John Kelsall's diary 1721.
7. Rachel Labouchere: *Abiah Darby*, p.35.
8. Ford letter book 1732-7. Letter of 16 March 1733.
9. See Ford letter book 23 April 1733. Also Raistrick p.57.
10. Raistrick: *Dynasty of Iron Founders*, 2nd edition, p.63.
11. Rachel Labouchere: *Abiah Darby*, p.35.
12. P.K Stembridge: Goldney, a House and Family, pp. 11 and 13.
13. VCH Vol XI Telford, P.36.
14. S.R.O 1987/35/2.
15. Raistrick: *Dynasty of Iron Founders*, 2nd edition, p.61.
16. Ford letter book 1732-7. Letter of 20 September 1736.
17. Ford letter book 1732-7. Letter of 20 February 1736.
18. The Goldney shares were held as follows:

Thomas Goldney	3
Gabriel Goldney	1
John Ball (husband of Hannah Goldney)	1
Martha Vanderwall (nee Goldney)	1
Mehetable Goldney	1
Anne Goldney	1
Elizabeth Goldney	1
	9

See Raistrick, *Dynasty of Iron Founders*, 2nd edition, pp63 and 64.
19. S.R.O 1987/19/1-2 Lease and Release dated 24/25 May 1705.

20. S.P.L 10330-10330A. Lease and Release dated 5/6 February 1717.
21. S.R.O 1681/131/5 Enfeoffment dated 10 May 1734.
22. S.R.O 1681/179/3 Lease and Release dated 12/13 April 1738. referred to in Abstract of Title dated 1827.
23. S.R.O 1987/14/1-2 Lease and Release dated 23/24 March 1738.
24. S.R.O 1987/14/3-4 Lease and Release dated 16/17 January 1743/4.
25. P K Stembridge: Goldney, a House and Family, p.13.
26. Barrie Trinder: *The Darbys of Coalbrookdale*, pp.17 and 18.
27. Rachel Labouchere: *Abiah Darby*, p.36.
28. Letter written by Abiah Darby 1763. S.R.O 1987/46/1-3.
29. S.R.O 1987/26/1-2. This was to become home to five generations of the Cartwright family. The property was eventually acquired by Francis Darby in 1841 and demolished (S.R.O 1987/26/16-17).
30. The parish register for 1753 only shows nine heads of families registered as Quakers. S.R.O 2280/2/10.
31. S.R.O 1681/131/5.
32. Engraving by Vivares "A View of the Upper Works at Coalbrookdale" 1758.
33. S.R.O 1681/138/1-2 Lease and Release dated January 1789.

CHAPTER V

Abraham II

WHEN RICHARD FORD died in the autumn of 1745, Abraham II was thirty-four years old and fully conversant with the management of the Works which he had first entered in 1728. Some months after Richard's death he married Abiah Sinclair (née Maude) of Sunderland, County Durham. Abiah (1716-94) was the youngest of thirteen children of Samuel and Rachel Maude, important and wealthy residents of that town. Samuel Maude had made his money in the coal mining industry and in property and had become a committed Quaker. His wife Rachel was also a Quaker, daughter of William Warren of Scarborough, a well-known minister in the Society of Friends. [1]

At the age of seventeen, Abiah met and married John Sinclair, somewhat against the wishes of her parents and friends. John Sinclair had a 'gift in the ministry' but he was considered not of the same social standing as the Maudes. The marriage lasted about two years. By the time she was twenty-one, Abiah was widowed, having lost her husband and a child of smallpox. In the following years she spent much time with Quaker friends in and around Kendal in Cumberland. [2] It was at Sedgewick, near Kendal, that she met Abraham II. It seems that the young couple formed an immediate attraction for at their next meeting in Staffordshire in April 1745, Abraham initiated the courtship which led to their marriage at Preston Patrick, near Kendal, in March 1746. [3]

The courtship of Abraham and Abiah took place against the background of the 1745 Jacobite Rebellion by the Young Pretender, Charles Edward Stuart, Bonnie Prince Charlie. Little is recorded locally of these momentous events although they clearly had an impact. Abiah herself was involved in an incident in Kendal when she was called upon to 'taste' food prepared for the Duke of Cumberland to demonstrate its freedom from poison. [4]

Abraham and Abiah set up home at Dale House, with Hannah, Abraham's ten year old daughter by his first marriage, to whom Abiah was to become a kind stepmother. Next door at Rosehill lived Mary Ford, soon to become known as Widow Ford and her family, and together the two houses became the scene of regular and frequent hospitality to Friends and other visitors to the Works.

From the beginning of the marriage, Abiah's life was dominated by her commitment to her Quaker beliefs. Before Abiah's time, Meetings were at first held at Broseley, but later they were held in the laundry, probably at Rosehill and then in the small annexe adjoining the south end of Tea Kettle Row, provided by Richard Ford. Abiah recorded in her diary:

"...since I came here we had a Meeting on first and fourth days at a Meeting House set apart by the late Richard Ford, but which I hear he intended to give Friends, but his son refused to give up, as his father made no will. But he let Friends meet in it, and sister Mary Ford became a constant attender with her daughters and some of her sons." (5)

The Quakers in Coalbrookdale belonged to the Wales Yearly Meeting which Abraham and Abiah attended at Leominster that year and the Yearly Meeting of the Society in London. Their first child, Rachel was born in December 1746 but only lived fifteen weeks, much to Abiah's distress. Some eighteen months later, however, in August 1748, she was safely delivered of another daughter Mary, known as Mally, the first of her children destined to reach adult years.

The birth of Mary seemed to be the prelude to the climactic moment of her life when she committed herself to the arduous life of a minister of the Society of Friends. The moment had been a long time coming. She first felt the calling when she was still a teenager but conflicts within her and an overriding shyness prevented her from declaring herself, though others clearly expected it of her. Finally, however, in Coalbrookdale towards the end of 1748 she spoke the words *"My Friends, I am engaged to invite you all to get inward and taste and feel with my Soul how good the Lord is"*. She confided to her journal *"How I got up, and how I spoke I know not, some invisible hand seemed to lift me up. I was out of the Body filled with surprise and tender astonishment so that for a time I hardly knew where I was. But full of joy, I could hardly believe for joy"*. From that moment onwards her life was transformed as she increasingly became committed to her new responsibilities as a minister.

Abraham, too, was equally committed in his beliefs and he fully supported Abiah in her new-found role. He, however, had responsibilities for the management of the Works, where a period of dynamic change was just beginning. The next fifteen years were to prove perhaps the most critical in the history of the enterprise. It is evident that Abraham II already had ambitions for further development of the Works and of the new technology which it represented. But first it was necessary to assure the mineral resources which were vital for success. The all-important clod coal which

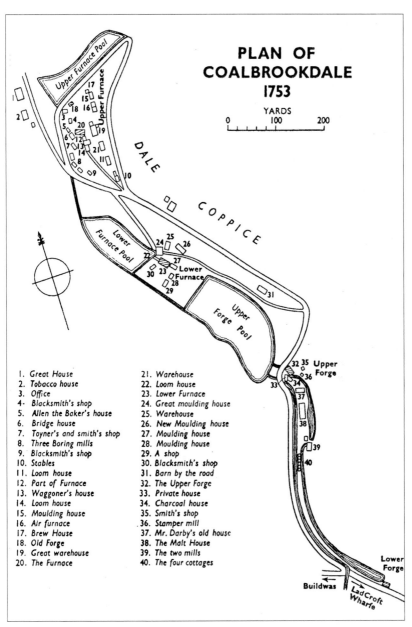

PLAN OF COALBROOKDALE 1753

YARDS

0   100   200

1. Great House
2. Tobacco house
3. Office
4. Blacksmith's shop
5. Allen the Baker's house
6. Bridge house
7. Toyner's and smith's shop
8. Three Boring mills
9. Blacksmith's shop
10. Stables
11. Loom house
12. Part of Furnace
13. Waggoner's house
14. Loom house
15. Moulding house
16. Air furnace
17. Brew House
18. Old Forge
19. Great warehouse
20. The Furnace
21. Warehouse
22. Loom house
23. Lower Furnace
24. Great moulding house
25. Warehouse
26. New Moulding house
27. Moulding house
28. Moulding house
29. A shop
30. Blacksmith's shop
31. Barn by the road
32. The Upper Forge
33. Private house
34. Charcoal house
35. Smith's shop
36. Stamper mill
37. Mr. Darby's old house
38. The Malt House
39. The two mills
40. The four cottages

Coalbrookdale in 1753. Based on map drawn by Thomas Slaughter, agent to the Manor of Madeley.

41

Sunniside, built 1750-51, by Abraham Darby II. Demolished 1856.

was so eminently suitable for Coalbrookdale's requirements had been obtained from mines in the adjoining Parish of Little Wenlock owned by the Forester and Hayward families. In 1726 Richard Ford had taken a lease of the Coalmoor mines (of William Hayward) for twenty-one years but they were abandoned in 1742 or 1743 because of drainage problems.[6] In 1740 this arrangement was overtaken by a new contract with William Forester and his son Brooke to sell all the clod coals from Huntington Heath and Smalley Hill to the Company. This was the situation when Abraham II took over management of the Company, and until this time, delivery of the coal was primarily by packhorse.

In 1749 Thomas Goldney, on behalf of the partnership, negotiated with George Dukesell of Furnace Bank Farm, an agreement for thirty-one years to *"lay rails on sleepers in such manner as is commonly used for drawing or waggoning coke, ironstone and other minerals"* to the ironworks in Coalbrookdale.[7] Although the agreement was very widely drawn, the railway was in fact built along the Rope Walk.[8] In 1750 the Company was also permitted to lay a railway from the Forester Pits at New Works to Coalbrookdale.[9] From that year therefore, the Company had a considerable railway from the Works to the source of supply, thus ensuring a continuity of resources.

While all this was going on Abraham and Abiah set about improving their living conditions. Abraham had already acquired five and a half acres of the northernmost portion of Glazebrook's Coppice[10] and had set out part of it as a garden. It was decided to build a fine new house at the very top of the hill, commensurate with their status as newly-emerging industrialists. This house was to become known as Sunniside, named after the Maude family home in Sunderland. The first brick was laid in June 1750 by Hannah, Abraham's daughter by his first marriage.[11] At that time Abiah was still "laying in" at Dale House after the birth of her first son Abraham.[12] Progress was rapid, as the house was roofed in by the following September. Two months later Abraham's sister, Mary Ford, died on 10 November 1750, aged 50,[13] survived by her four sons and three daughters. Abraham owed a great deal to his sister who had looked after him when their parents died, and later supported him and his daughter Hannah when his wife Margaret died in 1740.

Abraham and Abiah moved into their new home at Sunniside in the early part of 1751. Abiah makes no mention of her new surroundings in her journal, but Hannah as a young teenager was overjoyed. In a letter written to her aunt Rachel Thompson of Newcastle in 1753 she wrote:

"...Methinks how delightful it would be to walk with thee into fields and woods, then to go into the Dale to view the works; the stupendous Bellows whose alternate roars, like the foaming billows, is awful to hear; the mighty cylinders,

the wheels that carry on so many different Branches of the work, is curious to observe; the many other things which I cannot enumerate; but if thou wilt but come, I am sure thou would like it. It's really pleasant about our house, and so many comes and goes that we forget it's the Country till we look out at the window and see the woodland prospect".(14)

Apart from building Sunniside, which must have taken a great deal of his time, Abraham was applying himself to the major problem which confronted him in the Works – how to produce cast-iron which was acceptable to the great mass of the iron trade which needed iron suitable for conversion to wrought-iron.

Despite the success of the Coalbrookdale Works in producing iron for casting into pots, kettles, etc, including the parts needed for steam engines, iron produced by charcoal smelting was still being used for the production of nails and other small iron-ware in forges throughout the Black Country and the Midlands.

At about this time, probably between 1748 and 1754, Abraham succeeded in producing an iron acceptable for use in the forges. At this distance in time it is difficult to know whether the experiments which preceded success were of a purely technical nature or whether they were directed at the costings, but legend has it that at one time Abraham II stayed six days and nights on the bridge of the furnace, watching the experiments and waiting for satisfactory results. When at last he saw metal of an acceptable quality running from the tapping hole, he collapsed and was carried home by his workmen. Abiah, writing in 1763, shortly after Abraham's death, put this legend in its proper context:

"But all this time the making of Barr Iron at Forges from pit coal pigs were not thought of – about twenty-six years ago my Husband conceived this happy thought – that it might be possible to make bar from pit coal pigs. Upon this he sent some of our pigs to be tryed at the Forges, and that no prejudice might arise against them he did not discover from whence they came, or of what quality they were. And good account being given of their working, he erected Blast Furnaces for pig iron for Forges. Edward Knight Esq, a capital Iron Master urged my Husband to get a patent that he might reap the benefit for years of this happy discovery: but he said he would not deprive the public of such an acquisition which he was satisfyed it would be; and so it has proved, for it soon spread and many Furnaces both in this Neighbourhood and several other places have been erected for this purpose. Had not these discoveries been made, the Iron trade of our own produce would have dwindled away, for woods for charcoal became very scarce and landed gentlemen rose the prices of Cord Wood exceeding high – indeed it would not have been to be got. But from pit coal being introduced in its stead, the demand for wood charcoal is much lessened and in a few years I apprehend will set the use of that article aside".(15)

Abraham's new process was clearly a pivotal event in the Iron industry. When the ironmaster, Charles Wood, visited Coalbrookdale in 1754, he found that pit coal pigs were being used to make wrought-iron, and that there was such a demand for pig-iron of this sort that new furnaces were being erected to make it. [16]

During this period of the 1750s, Abraham was also deeply involved in the religious and domestic activities of the family. In 1752, Abiah gave birth to Sarah (known as Sally) who was the first child to be born in Sunniside. This did not prevent Abiah devoting herself to her commitments as a minister, with visits to a succession of Meetings.

Early in 1752, Abraham had developed a swelling in his breast, which necessitated him and Abiah staying six weeks in Shrewsbury. Abiah was dismayed by the wanton behaviour of the young men of the town and this prompted her to have printed "*A Serious Warning to the Inhabitants of Shrewsbury*" calling for their "sincere repentance and Amendment of Life, before the Night come upon you". [17] Abraham's abscess was cured by the Bishop of Cologne's Ficus. The visits to Meetings resumed, sometimes in Abraham's case combining business with his religious life. In 1753 on a visit to London for Yearly Meeting, Abraham was much involved with his London Agent. It may be that this was connected with the establishment of a foundry in Southwark which occurred at this period. [18]

The success of Abraham's experiments gave a greater impetus to his plans for expansion. For this purpose he needed capital, and to this end, he and Abiah mortgaged Sunniside in 1754 to raise £1000. [19] This enabled him to initiate a major development of the partnership at Horsehay in the Parish of Dawley, approximately one and a half miles in a northerly direction from Coalbrookdale. On 25 March 1754, he negotiated a lease of all veins of coal and ironstone under the lands of R A Slaney, the Lord of the Manor of Great Dawley, [20] and at the same time he rented from R A Slaney the Horsehay Farm with a corn mill, a dam pool and some adjoining land and obtained permission to build furnaces in the locality. He also leased mines at Ketley from Earl Gower, [21] and also a moiety of mines in Lawley from Robert Burton. In April 1754, he negotiated articles of agreement with John and Rose Giffard, with the concurrence of John Smitheman, Lords of the Manor for a wharfage at Loadcroft at Dale End on the River Severn. In the summer of 1754 he set about constructing the first Horsehay Furnace. The existing dam pool was too small and had to be enlarged, and despite very considerable difficulties the whole operation was in blast and making iron during May 1755.

This was a breakthrough of the highest importance. It marked the culmination of everything that had been done since 1708 to establish the new coke-fired process as markedly superior to the charcoal-fired process. It was achieved against the prejudices of many in the locality. Success was spectacular and the furnace was soon producing up to twenty-two tons of iron a week. The momentum of development was maintained. A railway was built from the new Furnace at Horsehay just north of the Little Dawley Manor to join at Cocks Wood, with the railway already constructed down the Dale along the Rope Walk. [22] In 1756 and 1757 the Slaney family granted extensive rights to Abraham to lay railways from Ketley and Dawley to Horsehay and Madeley Court, thus integrating the mineral resources with the Furnaces. [23] In fact the situation went much further than that because for the first time, the Company became directly involved in the coal industry and started to carry coal in excess of their own needs to the River Severn for sale down river.

The partnership between Abraham II and Thomas Goldney dated 12 June 1754 was extended on 24 April 1756 when it was agreed to erect another blast furnace at Horsehay for making pig iron. [24]

This represented a major gearing-up of the industrialisation of the Coalbrookdale Coalfield. One senses a measure of euphoria within the partnership – writing to Abraham II on 30 December 1756, Thomas Goldney stated *"Horsehay works may surely be said to be got to a top pinnacle of prosperity, 20 & 22 tons per week and sold off as fast as made, at profit enough, will soon find enough for another furnace and for the pocket too"*. [25]

Without doubt the partnership was riding the crest of a wave of success and prosperity. In the previous Spring of 1756 War had been declared between England and France. There is no direct evidence that the Coalbrookdale Company was involved in the armaments trade as they had been, previously, in the War of the Austrian Succession, but without question the Company shared in the increased prosperity resulting from the demands made on the nation's manufacturing ability.

The euphoria which accompanied this success was however severely affected by tragedies and misfortunes which afflicted the family during this same period. The family at this time consisted of the children of Richard Ford who had inherited four sixteenths of the Company's shares, and Abraham II and his unmarried brother Edmund, who owned three sixteenths of the shares. [26] After the death of Richard Ford in 1745, two of his four sons were for a time involved in lesser management roles. [27] After the death of the widow Mary Ford in 1750, Letters of Administration were granted to Richard Ford II, the eldest son who distributed the dividends to his brothers and sisters.

Shortly after Mary's death, one of the younger sons, Abraham Ford married Jane Burleigh of Sunderland, a niece of Abiah Darby and took up residence at Dale House in 1752. [28] However, despite this propitious event things started to go wrong for the Ford section of the family soon afterwards. In 1753, the behaviour of the youngest son Darby Ford, started to cause distress. The Broseley Meeting disassociated themselves from his behaviour, a very serious reprimand. [29] A few years later in 1756, he was found drowned in the New Pool, a few hundred yards from the Coalbrookdale Works. [30] A few months later, Edmund Darby, Abraham II's brother died as a result of a fall from a horse at Albrighton. [31] Also, the three Ford daughters, Mary, Hannah and Susannah left Coalbrookdale to live with cousins in Worcester. [32]

During the summer of 1756, industrial unrest occurred in the Coalfield. This was caused by the high price demanded by farmers for their corn. The trouble started at Wenlock Market, spread to Shifnal Market and finally to Wellington. A local armed levy met the mob at Ketley where they "*stood three fires before they fled*". Hannah Darby, Abraham II's daughter, recounted that that morning the men had agreed to plunder "*all our houses intending to begin with Sunniside,...but thro Divine favour was prevented*". The household had baked bread for three days, and most of the rioters had called at Sunniside where several hundred of them had meat and drink – "*but did not offer violence*". [33]

It was shortly after this episode that there arrived in the Dale one Richard Reynolds, sent there to represent the interests of the Goldney family. Thomas Goldney had been present in the Dale, during April 1756 [34] and had then indicated that he was considering sending someone to keep him more closely in touch with affairs, as he found with the increasing pace of events that he needed a deputy on the spot. His choice fell on Richard Reynolds, born in Bristol in 1735, the son of Richard and Jane Reynolds, members of the Society of Friends. The family firm of Daniels & Reynolds were customers of the Coalbrookdale Company, and Richard was nearing the end of his apprenticeship with William Fry, a grocer in Castle Street, Bristol. [35]

He was twenty-one years of age and on arrival in the Dale was appointed Manager of the new furnaces at Horsehay. He was described as "tall and handsome, of the true Saxon race, his hair light brown in flowing curls, his eyes blue, his complexion fair and ruddy, he formed a very striking figure." Very soon after arriving from Bristol he met Hannah Darby, the surviving child of Abraham II's first marriage to Margaret Smith of Shifnal. She was the same age as Richard Reynolds and the couple soon fell in love. They were married in 1757.

In the meantime, Abraham II had taken a lease on 28 October 1756 of fourteen acres of land in Ketley from Granville, Earl of Gower. He also leased one hundred and forty-four acres of land in Ketley, Donnington Wood and Wrockwardine, comprising several mines of coal and ironstone.

Bank House, Ketley Bank. Probably built by Richard Hartshorne in 1721. Residence of Richard Reynolds between 1757 and 1789 and then of his son William Reynolds from 1789 to 1800.

A partnership was established on 26 September 1757 between Abraham II, Thomas Goldney and Richard Reynolds with each contributing one-third of the capital of £10,000 to construct one or more blast furnaces in Ketley. Richard Reynolds was asked to oversee the start of the new furnaces, the first of which went into blast in 1757. Richard and Hannah, therefore, went to live at Bank House, Ketley, which had been built in 1721 by Richard Hartshorne. A second furnace was built in 1758, and by then the capital of £10,000 was overspent and so Abraham raised a further £3,585 from Richard Reynolds Senior, of Bristol, and mortgaged his one-third interest in the land and the blast furnaces. (36)

Within the space of a relatively few years after Abraham's discovery of the technology for producing coke-smelted pig iron suitable for conversion into wrought-iron, there had been a tremendous expansion of the Company's operations. Two furnaces had been brought into blast at Horsehay and two more at Ketley. Leases had been secured for supplies of coal and ironstone in Little Wenlock, Dawley, Lawley, Wombridge and Ketley. Railways had been constructed to bring these supplies to the furnaces at Ketley, Horsehay and Coalbrookdale and a wharfage had been established at Loadcroft on the River Severn. The final link in this network of operations covering over five square miles of territory, came with the construction of a railway from the Coalbrookdale furnaces down the Dale to the newly established wharfage at Loadcroft.

This was constructed within a few months at the end of 1755 and the beginning of 1756. In 1757, Abraham Darby took a lime works on the south side of the River Severn so that limestone could be brought across the River to a landing place at Loadcroft and thence by the railway to the works. In this way the Company's control of all its operations was virtually complete. (37)

The phenomenal success of the works at Coalbrookdale, Horsehay and Ketley, stimulated even more by the start of the Seven Years War (1756-63) quickly produced a highly competitive and very predatory situation. People who had previously been critical, not to say contemptuous of Abraham Darby's efforts, soon rushed to take advantage of the new technology. (38) Within a few years, new blast furnaces were constructed at Willey, Lightmoor and Madeley Wood. There is evidence that the price of coal was increasing and that a confederation of coal-owners in Madeley and Broseley were continuing to increase prices very considerably. (39)

It was against this volatile background that the Company approached its next major problem, which was the renewal of the lease (negotiated in 1734) and due to expire in September 1759. The 1734 lease had been granted by John Unett Smitheman and his wife Catherine, who owned one individual moiety (half) of the Manor of Madeley and John Giffard and Rose his wife who owned the other half. John Unett Smitheman and his wife Catherine had died and the ownership of their undivided moiety had passed to their son John Smitheman who came of age (twenty-one years) on 29 December 1755. The other half of the Manor was still in the hands of John and Rose Giffard.

In January 1756, the month after John Smitheman came of age, he attended a meeting at Sunniside and negotiations for a new lease started.[40] In March 1756 a meeting was arranged with John and Rose Giffard in Madeley, but no agreement was reached because the Giffards demanded what was deemed to be an 'extravagant rent'. This was because the transportation of coal on the recently constructed railway through Coalbrookdale to Loadcroft Wharf had had a considerable effect on the River Severn coal trade. The collieries at Madeley Wood, owned by the Manor, were greatly affected, and some had been closed. Understandably the Giffards were alarmed about the effect on their income and wished to be compensated for their loss. Notwithstanding this, in April 1756, the following month, John Smitheman who had been present at the meeting in March agreed to grant a lease of his half of the manor.[41] The rent was doubled from £100 a year to £200 a year, and it authorised the laying of the railway and the wharfage on the River Severn. This was a step forward towards the granting of the full lease and having agreed with John Smitheman on what appeared to be a fair rent, Abraham II hoped that an agreement for the other (and vital) half of the lease would follow. This, however, did not happen as John Giffard felt, either that the rent should be higher or that royalties should be paid on the passage of coal and iron etc, along the railway. Both sides displayed a measure of obduracy and no direct steps appear to have been taken to resolve the matter.

In July 1756 the contract with the Forester family to sell to the Coalbrookdale Company clod coals from their mines, in Little Wenlock, which had originally been negotiated in 1740, was renewed for a further twenty-one years.[42] During this year, a significant and potentially worrying event occurred with the arrival in the locality of John Wilkinson of Bersham, near Wrexham, who was in business at Bersham as a ironmaster with his father.[43] He became involved with Brooke Forester and during 1756 designed the erection of a new blast furnace at Willey, which was built the following year 1757, under the name of the New Willey Iron Works. John Wilkinson was to become one of the dominant ironmasters of the eighteenth century and made a considerable contribution to the development of the industry. He was, however, an aggressive and abrasive personality and although he was well remembered in the folk culture of the area he ended up by being almost universally disliked.

While the New Willey Works were being designed and built, John Wilkinson and Brooke Forester entered into negotiations with John and

Early cast iron rails, behind Rose Cottage, Coalbrookdale. These rails were laid on earlier wooden rails, laid in 1755/56.

Lincoln Hill and the Iron Bridge, 1788. In the middle distance is Loadcroft Wharf, leased by the Coalbrookdale Company from 1754. In the foreground is the wharf known as Stiches Wear.

Rose Giffard to take a twenty-one year lease of their half of the Coalbrookdale Works, and although they did not disclose it at the time, articles of agreement to that effect were completed on 12 September 1757 for a lease to take effect at Michaelmas 1759 (the termination of the lease of 1734).

With hindsight it is evident that Thomas Goldney and Abraham II were at fault in not pursuing negotiations with John and Rose Giffard after March 1756 and of underestimating the value, to the owner, of the Coalbrookdale site. On the other hand, the Giffards were badly advised about the likelihood of being able to superimpose a royalty charge on the use of the railway constructed under the auspices of the lease. These and many other matters came to a head when John and Rose Giffard filed a Bill of Complaint in the Court of Chancery on 4 November 1757 against Thomas Goldney, Abraham Darby II and Richard Ford II the principal partners in the Coalbrookdale Company.[44] This was a devastating blow which was to affect the partnership for the next five years. The Giffards sought an injunction from the Court to prevent the Coalbrookdale Company using the newly constructed railway through the Dale and to pay compensation for the loss to the Manor. Significantly no mention was made of the fact that they had agreed to lease their undivided moiety of the works to the New Willey Company.

The burden of their case was that it had been an understanding of the existing lease of 1734 that the Company would take their coal and iron-stone from mines in the Manor, that they had failed to do so and had obtained their supplies from elsewhere; that they had *artfully contrived to get John Smitheman in their power, so as to obtain from him what John and Rose Giffard would be more cautious of granting";* that John Smitheman had just come of age and but recently left college; that they had recently made a railway of great detriment to the Giffard's interests without making adequate compensation for their loss.

In May 1758 Goldney and his partners made full answer to the Bill of Complaint. They said, briefly, that the Company had taken all the iron-stone mined in the Manor of Madeley up to the limits imposed by the Giffard's desire to conserve supplies; that they had taken all the coal from the Manor's Paddock Pit until it was exhausted, and that since then the coal mined in the Manor was unsuitable for use in the Coalbrookdale Furnaces. They pointed out that their relationship with John Smitheman had been of long standing; that when his mother Catherine died in 1737, his father John Unett Smitheman had arranged for him to board with John and Mary Ford at their house in Coalbrookdale, that when his father died in 1744, his guardian had arranged for him to go to boarding school and subsequently university, but that throughout that period he had returned to the Ford's house during holiday periods; that he had been advised in the matter of the lease by his uncle Henry Rainsford, solicitor of Much Wenlock and by another uncle Henry Hallen, both of whom had lived in or near the area for forty years and were well acquainted with values in the area and were well satisfied with the terms agreed. They further maintained that they had a right to make a railway under the terms of the lease, which in no way restrained them from doing so; that some years before the present railway they had laid a railway between the furnace and the fire engine; that the present railway had been laid in part along the common highway and in part over cinder mounds and waste and barren land within their lease, except for one small piece of garden ground for which they had the tenant's permission.

The case then had to wait while evidence was taken from a considerable number of witnesses in support either of the Giffards or the Company. It was not until July 1759 that a hearing took place before the Lord Keeper of the Great Seal. It was then decided that the issue should stand over to enable the parties "*to adjust the same by compromise between them.*" The Court declined to grant an injunction against the railway and significantly ordered that the works should remain in the same condition as they then were. This at least was some consolation to the Coalbrookdale partnership .

Even so, attempts at compromise seemed ill-starred. The hitherto secret agreement between the Giffards and the New Willey Company came to the knowledge of the Coalbrookdale partnership. A meeting took place in 1758 between Thomas Goldney and Abraham Darby on behalf of the Coalbrookdale Company with Brooke Forester and John Wilkinson representing the New Willey Company, at which the Coalbrookdale parties offered to take over the moiety offered to the New Willey Company on the same terms i.e. £300 per annum. This was robustly rejected by John Wilkinson, who in turn offered to buy out the Coalbrookdale share. This was equally robustly rejected by Thomas Goldney. A proposal was subsequently made by John Wilkinson at a meeting held at Worcester that both companies should be jointly concerned in carrying on the Coalbrookdale Works. Thomas Goldney and Abraham Darby rejected this outright.

Matters once again came to a head in November 1759, when the Coalbrookdale partners counter-attacked . They filed their own Bill of Complaint against the Giffards and the other parties involved.[45] The Bill asserted that "*the works at Coalbrookdale are of very great public utility being one of the most capital if not the greatest iron foundries for cast-iron in the Kingdom*". They also asserted that Brooke Forester and his parties had entered into an agreement with the Giffards for their moiety and that this was the reason why the Bill of Complaint had been lodged by the Giffards in 1757 (a reference to the fact that they had by then already completed

Articles of Agreement which had not been disclosed); that the object was to interrupt and obstruct the Coalbrookdale Works, which would result in great injury, loss and detriment. They, therefore, proposed that the Furnaces and Works should be partitioned between the two parties, with common use of the fire engine and the railway. If this proposal was rejected it was proposed to withdraw the Works entirely from Coalbrookdale and to remove the operation elsewhere. This was no idle threat because during 1759 they had negotiated ninety-nine year leases of land in Lawley with associated coal and ironstone mines.[46] That year the Company established a small ironworks at Lawley, which they called Newdale (the title suggesting that it was built to succeed Coalbrookdale). It consisted of three purpose built ironworking buildings and a row of workers' houses and was connected by a railway to the Horsehay works.[47]

The proposal to withdraw from Coalbrookdale must have caused dismay in the Giffard family as it affected the inheritance by reducing the value of the Coalbrookdale site for the next twenty-one years. Consequently when their lengthy answer to the Bill was filed in January 1760 they urged repeatedly that the best solution would be for a joint company to be operated by the Coalbrookdale Company and the New Willey Company. This was totally unacceptable and the development of the Newdale site went ahead. Although the Bill of Complaint by Goldney and Abraham II appears to have been dismissed[48] their position in Coalbrookdale was safeguarded by the fact that the Court had made the Order that the Works should continue as it was in 1759. This in itself would have prevented any attempt by the Giffards or more particularly, by the New Willey Company from interfering in the operation of the Works. A stalemate situation had developed. The only way forward for the Giffards was to pursue a remedy at Common Law rather than in Chancery.[49] This they did at the Assizes in Shrewsbury in July 1762, by which time their action in Chancery had lapsed. The last act of the drama was, therefore, played out in Shrewsbury. Lady Labouchere in her book on Abiah Darby[50] states as follows:-

"Rose (Giffard) was being very difficult and Abiah finally decided to go and visit her herself to try and 'bring her to reason'. In this she did not succeed as on 31 July "The Tryal came on in Shrewsbury". The judgement was given to "desire my husband to sit down each with their own costs, and he sent an answer that he was ready to agree to whatever the Judge thought proper, the other party was hard to prevail upon but gave up at last."

And so the war of attrition which had lasted for six years was finally ended. No information has yet been discovered about the terms on which the matter was settled, but presumably the Company had to pay a higher rent than they originally intended. Certainly they continued to occupy the Coalbrookdale site and the threat from the New Willey Company was repulsed. The financial backing of Thomas Goldney was crucial as it is doubtful whether Abraham II would have had the resources to sustain the litigation. (On 1 January 1759 he had to mortgage his 3/16th share of the Works to raise £1000 from Thomas Goldney. [51] The Giffards also went into debt.) The Newdale Works continued in operation but only for a few years, certainly less than ten years. In 1768, one of the ironworking buildings was converted to a Quaker Meeting House while the cottages were occupied as miners' cottages and survived until recent times.

Apart from the limited expansion at Newdale, the Company also took a lease in July 1760 of the Waterborn Mill Buildings from the Corporation of Bridgnorth near the confluence of the River Worfe and the River Severn. [46] A forge was built there and Thomas Cranage, one of two sons of the Company's first forgemaster William Cranage, was sent there. Another employee of the Company, George Perry, left the Dale in 1758 and started a foundry called Coalbrookdale Foundry in Liverpool, which later became the business of Joseph Rathbone, soon to have close connections with the family. For a time, therefore, the Company was to have interests not only in Coalbrookdale, Horsehay and Ketley (with their associated coal and ironstone mines) but also in Southwark (London), Bridgnorth and Liverpool.

While the litigation with the Giffards was in progress the fortunes of the Darby and Ford families went through an enormous upheaval. Trouble started in or about April 1758 when a warrant for debt was issued against Abraham Ford who was living at Rosehill with his wife Jane and family. He heard about it from one of the Sheriff's bailiffs and escaped arrest. However, he incurred more debt and was arrested in December 1758. He was taken to Shrewsbury gaol where he remained for two months until a commission of bankruptcy was declared and his estate assigned to the commissioners. The partnership became involved because in May 1757 Abraham Ford had secured from his elder brother Richard Ford, his sixth part share of the Ford holdings in the partnership, [52] and also he received monies from Abraham II and from the Company which the Company sought to set off against dividends. [53] Quite apart from his financial embarrassment, all this had a terminal effect upon his marriage to Jane, who was living with her children in Rosehill. He left her, and Jane returned with her children back to Sunderland in 1760. [54]

The family's misfortunes did not end there. Richard Ford II the eldest son, who was involved in the litigation also ran into debt and a commission of bankruptcy was awarded against him in April 1758. As a result all the freehold properties belonging to the Ford family were transferred the following year to the commissioners.

56

This included the family home (Rosehill), Tea Kettle Row with the Quaker Meeting House and granary, and the garden orchard and arable or pasture land adjoining, with a summer house which Richard Ford had just converted into a dwellinghouse. *(55)* The following year 1760, all these properties were purchased from the commissioners by Abraham II. *(56)*

Richard Ford had little further involvement in the affairs of the Company. Having lost his newly-converted dwellinghouse behind Rosehill (the former summerhouse) he took a ninety-nine year lease in 1763 of an acre of land in Spring Coppice, east of the furnace and built a house there. This was the start of the development of Coalbrookdale in the direction of what eventually became the Lightmoor Road. There was at that time no road to Lightmoor nor to Horsehay. The only road was a track (still existing) up the hill over Vane Coppice leading to Dawley. *(57)*

The other brother Edmund Ford, prospered rather better. While Abraham and Richard were facing bankruptcy, he became involved in licences to explore and exploit mineral resources in Madeley Wood and other parts of Madeley, leading in 1760 to the setting up of a partnership in which he had a one-sixth share to establish the Madeley Wood Ironworks, which became known as Bedlam Furnaces. *(58)*

Despite this achievement, the two bankruptcies meant that the fortunes of the Ford family relative to Abraham II's family had received a major setback. From the 1760s onwards, although the Fords continued to be regarded and welcomed as full members of the family, their interests in the Company dwindled to relative insignificance. *(59)* They ceased to be involved in any further major activity.

During this entire period of business activity, including the family's trials and tribulations, Abiah carried on her pastoral duties as a Quaker minister with unremitting zeal. She travelled extensively and when at home entertained with the greatest hospitality the large number of visitors who came to the Works and were received at Sunniside. One significant event in her religious life was the arrival in 1760 of Reverend Fletcher as Vicar of Madeley. Until then the Quaker community, although small in number (in the 1750s still no more than a dozen families) undoubtedly provided the religious leadership of the locality. Soon after Reverend Fletcher's arrival, small groups of about twenty people calling themselves Methodists started to form and this brought Abiah into amicable conflict with the newly arrived vicar. The Quakers stood firmly outside the established church and many of them out of firm conviction spent many years in prison for non-payment of tithes. By contrast, John Wesley, although sharing much common ground with the Quakers, was seeking to change the Church from within. Reverend Fletcher as his heir-apparent was very charismatic and had an immense influence in Madeley and generally in the newly-industrialised areas. Indeed, it was the Methodists, and not the Quakers, who carried the gospel amongst the industrial population. The conflict with the Methodists came a little close to home when in October 1761, Abiah's nephew Samuel Maude married Ann (Nancy) Cranage and became a Methodist.

However, Abiah had greater things to worry about because Abraham II's health started to fail. He had always been prone to asthmatic attacks (inherited from his mother). During the early 1760s he started to get a succession of bronchial troubles. The supposed remedy was 'blooding' carried out by a surgeon. William Maude, writing in 1761 said *"My Uncle, through mercy, is better in his Health than he has been for some time past. He has got Blooded, which we think has done him good. He is a valuable man. I wish his life may be Preserv'd for his family's sake".*

Abraham II suffered a grievous loss the following year when his eldest child Hannah, who was married to Richard Reynolds, died quite suddenly after an attack of measles at Ketley Bank, aged twenty-seven years. Hannah had been the child of Abraham's first marriage to Margaret Smith and her death was a terrible blow to him, for her lovely and affectionate nature had made her one of the chief blessings of his life. She was buried on 29 June 1762 at the Friend's Burial Ground at Broseley, just one month before the Trial at Shrewsbury Assizes.

In the following September, Abiah left home on a long arduous itinerary not returning home until four months later, this despite her husband's failing health. It seems difficult to understand how she felt able to leave him for such a long time, but as Rachel Labouchere says in her book on Abiah,[60] *"Her life as a minister had become stronger than her role as a wife and mother and this could and did happen in the history of women ministers....Theirs was an equal partnership in a very modern sense, and Abraham was in complete agreement with this outlook, acknowledging the 'power of her concern', and the importance of her work in the ministry, without question".*

Abraham's health grew steadily worse and during February 1763 he set about the task of drafting and completing his Will, which was to establish the course of the family's relationships into the next century. After a period of deteriorating weakness he finally departed this life on 31 March 1763. He was then aged fifty-two. He was buried in a plot of land below Sunniside, which thereafter became the Friends burial ground for Coalbrookdale.

Abraham and Abiah had seven children:[61]

Rachel, born 1746, lived fifteen months – born at Dale House
Mary,* known as Mally, born 1748 – born at Dale House
Abraham,* known as Aby, born 1750 – born at Dale House

Sarah,* known as Sally, born 1752 – born at Sunniside
Samuel,* known as Sammy, born 1755 – born at Sunniside
William, born 1756, lived six months – born at Sunniside
Jane, born 1758, lived four months – born at Sunniside.
* Survived to adult years.

Abraham's son-in-law, Richard Reynolds, wrote that Abraham *"by his great exertions and spirit of enterprise had extended the concerns of Coalbrookdale Company far beyond the locality where those works were situated, having established foundries in London, Bristol and Liverpool, and agencies at Newcastle and Truro for the disposal of steam engines and other machinery made of cast-iron used in the deep mines of those districts"*.

Historically, he occupies a key position, perhaps a uniquely crucial position in the establishment of the modern iron industry in Great Britain. His role in extending the use of coke-fired iron into the wrought-iron industry was of critical importance and his success at Horsehay and Ketley established the superiority of the coke-fired process to the point at which the industrialisation of the nation was able to 'take off'.

In the process he met very powerful opposition. Abiah, writing after his death said of him that *"he had an extraordinary command over his own spirit, which with the assistance of Divine Grace enabled him to bear up with fortitude above all opposition, for it may seem strange, so valuable a man should have antagonists, yet he had those called Gentlemen with an envious spirit, could not bear to see him prosper, and others covetous strove to make every advantage by raising the Rents of their Collieries and lands in which he wanted to make roads and endeavoured to stop the works, but he surmounted all; and died in Peace, beloved and lamented by many".* (62)

He clearly had a powerful vision of a fully integrated iron producing industry controlling the sources of its own materials and the means of bringing those materials to the furnaces, the whole operation supported by strategically located foundries which would process the primary product into other uses including the all important manufacture of steam engines in which Coalbrookdale had been involved since 1718. In the pursuit of this vision, he clearly came up against the land-owning interests which heretofore had sought to profit from any such enterprise. He had a rough ride which may have prematurely affected his health. The lesson which was learned from this was that it was necessary to control not only the mineral resources but also the manorial holdings which had caused him so much trouble. It was to be another twenty years before this was accomplished.

Under Abraham II's Will his assets were carefully allocated. His business interests in the Company were placed in trust for the benefit of the family. An annuity of £300 was payable to Abiah with provision for the minority of the children. At the age of twenty-one each child was entitled to £2,000 together with a fifth share of the business. The same provision was made for the two children of Abraham's recently deceased daughter Hannah, who had been married to Richard Reynolds. A further sum of £2,000 was given to Abiah to dispose of by her Will.

The family home at Sunniside was left to Abiah for her lifetime and then by entailed interest to Abraham III and his heirs. This included certain lands held on lease in Little Wenlock and Madeley and in particular the piece of land known as Cockswood which was the railhead of the railway to the Works; but it excluded the schoolroom and two dwellings near Sunniside which Abraham had built. These were left to the two daughters Mary and Sarah for life, and then to Abraham III and his heirs. Abraham II had recently purchased an undivided half share in the Hay Farm, Madeley, and this he left to Abraham III. The lands which he had recently acquired from the assignees of Richard Ford, including Rosehill, Tea Kettle Row and the adjoining garden and Summer House, he left to his second son Samuel, but he excluded from that legacy the Quaker Meeting House and the land needed for the burial ground and any enlargement of the Meeting House. His trustees were required to discharge £500 of the £1,000 mortgage which he and Abiah had raised on the security of Sunniside in 1751.[63]

Abraham's death brought to an end an exciting and vitally important period in the development of the iron industry. It was left to others to carry on where he had left off.

"He was just in his dealings – of universal benevolence and Charity, living strictly to the Rectitude of the Divine and Moral Law, held forth by his great Lord and Saviour."

Abraham Darby II, written by his widow Abiah Darby in 1763.[64]

NOTES – CHAPTER V

1. For a full understanding of the pedigree of the Maude family see Abiah Darby by Rachel Labouchere viii - ix et seq).
2. Labouchere, *Abiah Darby*, p.12.
3. Labouchere, *Abiah Darby*, p.37.
4. Rachel Labouchere, *Abiah Darby*, p.15.
5. Rachel Labouchere, *Abiah Darby*, p.42.
6. S.R.O 1224/260 deed of 1740; VCH Vol IX Telford, p.85.
7. S.R.O 1987/58/14.
8. Author's report to IGMT – IGMT Archive.
9. S.R.O 1224/260; VCH Vol IX Telford, p.85.
10. The 5½ acres of land forming the site and grounds of Sunniside was acquired by Abraham II in two parts. The first comprising 2 acres

was purchased from George and Milborough Dukesell by Lease and Release dated 23/24 March 1738 and the second comprising 3½ acres was similarly acquired on 16/17 January 1743/4. It seems that Abraham had ambitions to extend his household during the period of his first marriage to Margaret Smith. SRO 1987/14/1-4.

11. Labouchere, *Abiah Darby*, p.50.
12. Abraham was destined to become Abraham Darby III the builder of the Iron Bridge.
13. Register of Shropshire Monthly Meeting.
14. Raistrick, *Dynasty of Ironfounders*, p.71.
15. S.R.O 1987/46/1/1-3.
16. Barrie Trinder, *The Darbys of Coalbrookdale*, p.19.
17. IGMT Archives.
18. Rachel Labouchere, *Abiah Darby*, p.63. There is also evidence that Thomas and George Cranage were involved in the Southwark works – see S.R.O 1987/4/1.
19. The mortgage of Sunniside was accomplished by a Lease and Release dated 2/3 May 1754 to Richard Case in the sum of £1000. Half of this sum was paid off by Abraham II's executors on 3 November 1766 and the balance was finally paid by Francis Darby, grandson of Abraham II, on 2/3 January 1804. See S.R.O/1987/14/6-18.
20. S.R.O 1681/118/4.
21. Rachel Labouchere, *Abiah Darby*, p.67. See also Bill of Complaint dated 4 November 1757 by John and Rose Giffard in the Court of Chancery and the answers thereto by Thomas Goldney, Abraham Darby and Richard Ford, dated 25 May 1758. P.R.O C12/1275/1. See also author's report to IGMT on these Chancery Proceedings, IGMT Archives.
22. See 1987/43/1. The line of the railway is shown in part on a survey map of Dawley Parva 1772.
23. S.R.O 1681/118/4.
24. S.R.O 1987/58/16.
25. S.R.O 1987/45/12.
26. The remaining 9 shares were owned by the Goldney family.
27. Richard Ford II, the eldest son was Clerk to the Company from 1745 to 1748, and subsequently as a partner He seems to have become involved in other activities in the locality. He took interests in three small ironworks at Caynton, Sambrook and Tibberton which did not prosper. He was declared bankrupt in 1759. Notice of a meeting of creditors was given in the London Gazette in February of that year and he was duly adjudged bankrupt.
28. Abiah Darby was the youngest child of Samuel and Rachel Maude. One of her sisters, Hannah, who was eighteen years older than Abiah, had married Mark Burleigh of Sunderland in 1721. It was their

daughter, Jane (Abiah's niece) who married Abraham Ford (Abraham Darby's nephew) in 1751/52, thus creating a second link between the two families.

29. *Abiah*, p.64.
30. *Abiah*, p.76. Darby Ford was aged twenty-two years.
31. *Abiah*, p.78. Edmund was aged forty-four years.
32. Friends Minutes 1756. The Ford daughters were the owners of 'Tony' the bullfinch, and wrote the epitaph poem to him which can be seen at Rosehill. Worcester became an outpost of the family and there are many occasions in Abiah's diaries when she records staying at the Fords in Worcester. Hannah went on to Bristol and became housekeeper to Thomas Goldney at Clifton.
33. *Abiah*, pp.78-79; Raistrick, *Dynasty of Ironfounders*, pp. 78, 79.
34. *Abiah*, p.77.
35. *Abiah*, p.77; Raistrick, pp. 83 and 84.
36. S.R.O 1987/25/6.
37. Chancery Proceedings. P.R.O C12/1275/1. See author's report to IGMT - IGMT Archives.
38. See Trinder: *Industrial Revolution in Shropshire*, p.34-35 and 40. William Ferriday, who was the agent for the Forester estates in Little Wenlock was highly derogatory of the development of the Horsehay Furnaces in 1754-55. Within a year he was a partner in the New Willey Company, building similar furnaces at Willey on the other side of the River Severn!
39. See Chancery Proceedings Giffard v. Goldney P.R.O. C12/1275/1. Several Answers of Thomas Goldney, Abraham Darby and Richard Ford – Author's report to IGMT.
40. *Abiah*, p.76.
41. S.R.O 1987/35/4.
42. S.R.O 1224/260. The contract was for the supply from New Works of 4000 stacks of Clod Coal per annum and 200 dozen of ball stone and 200 dozen of pinstone (Ironstone) per annum. In 1759 the contract was reaffirmed for eighteen years during the lifetime of Brooke Forester.
43. John Wilkinson lived at Wrexham Fechan. His wife Ann died in 1756 and is buried in the parish church.
44. Chancery Proceedings (Six Clerks Series II 1758-1800 Public Record office C12/1275/13. See author's report to IGMT.
45. Chancery Proceedings (Six Clerks Series II) 1758-1800 Public Record Office C12/1275/10. See author's report to IGMT.
46. See recitals to Dissolution of Partnership (1794) S.R.O 1681/179/2.
47. For more detailed information, refer to the archaeological survey undertaken in 1987 by IGMT sponsored by British Coal Opencast, Telford Development Corporation and English Heritage.

48. The orders of the Court of Chancery are confusing. See Decrees and Orders 1759 A Series Index No 1794 C33 413 Michaelmas 70 to Goldney -v- Forester 4 December 1759. Although the petition was dismissed, it appears again at Hilary 191 when the defendants were given six weeks to answer the petition. Also, the answers of John and Rose Giffard and John Smitheman were not filed until 17 January 1760. The dismissal of 4 December 1759 may, therefore, have been a procedural matter.

49. John and Rose Giffard kept their Chancery option open by reviving their official Bill of Complaint of 1757. See Decreees and Orders 1760 A Series Index No. 1796 C33 415 Hilary 160 Giffard -v- Smitheman (1761) when the Court ordered that the Bill be retained for six months. At the end of that time, by Summer 1761, it would have stood dismissed with costs.

50. *Abiah*, p.105.

51. S.R.O 1987/25/7.

52. i.e, one sixth of four sixteenths of the Company's value.

53. S.R.O 1987/53/4 and 1681/181/19.

54. Abiah explains in her diary that they "had had great distress on her account, her base husband had left her." She also added that "they lost many hundreds by her, had given her a great deal, kept her at our house a long time and gave her afterwards 15 pounds with her".

55. S.R.O 1987/25/8. All these properties are clearly shown on the engraving by Vivares dated 1758.

56. See Abstract of Title of Rev E Pryce Jones S.R.O 1681/179/3.

57. See S.R.O 1987/43/2/1 and 1987/43/1. Also see 1987/56/39 for memorandum dated 1772. See Articles of Partnership 5 September 1760, S.R.O 1681/132/24.

58. See S.R.O 1681/132/24. The Madeley Wood Furnaces were subsequently purchased by Abraham Darby III on 30 August 1776 See 1987/60/5. This was connected with the construction of the Iron Bridge.

59. The Fords appear in Company records from time to time. Richard Ford died in 1792. He was well-remembered. His funeral was attended by his kinswoman Hannah Mary Rathbone who referred to him as "my poor cousin, Richard Ford, formerly a kind associate in lovely and beloved scenes." He was recorded as having married Sarah and was succeeded by a number of children – Richard, Mary (1751), Thomas (1753), Edmund (1755), Darby (1757) and John. In her Will in 1821 Sarah Darby (then the last surviving child of Abraham II) left bequests of £100 each to "Richard Ford, Darby Ford, John Ford and Edmund Ford, sons of the testatrix's cousin, Richard Ford." Richard's sisters died in 1782 and 1784; Mary who had been living at Worcester died on 1 April 1782 and was buried at Broseley; Hannah

who moved to Bristol died in 1784, and the youngest daughter Susannah died in Worcester in the same year. Her remains were brought to Sunniside and she was buried in Shrewsbury next to her parents.

60. *Abiah*, p.122.
61. See Registers of Shropshire Monthly Meeting of Friends.
62. S.R.O 1987/46/1/3 Also *Abiah*, p.127.
63. The balance of £500 was paid off in 1804 by Francis Darby, grandson of Abraham II. (S.R.O 1987/14/17-18.
64. S.R.O 1987/46/1/3.

CHAPTER VI

Triumph and Nemesis –
Richard Reynolds and Abraham III

THREE WEEKS AFTER the death of Abraham II the trustees appointed under his Will to represent the family in the running of the works etc, decided to ask Richard Reynolds to undertake the management of the works on 6 June 1763 during the minority of Abraham II's eldest son, Abraham III, who was then aged thirteen and was still at James Fell's school in Worcester. Richard Reynolds left Bank House, Ketley, in August 1763[1] and took up residence in Dale House, bringing with him his two young children, William (five years) and Hannah Mary (two years) (their mother Hannah, Abraham II's eldest child, having died at Bank House the previous year in 1762).

The choice of Richard Reynolds made a great deal of sense as he was fully conversant with the furnaces at Ketley and Horsehay, and he owned a third share of the partnership at Ketley.[2] He proved to be an active and energetic manager.

Abiah, at Sunniside, was feeling very low following the loss of her husband and it took her some time to recover her zeal. Abraham had made provision in his Will for the enlargement of the Meeting House at the southern end of Tea Kettle Row and in September 1763 Abiah noted that the Meeting that month was held in the malthouse as *"we are enlarging our Meeting House, which my Dear Husband left to Friends"* and she added, *"he also left a graveyard which I have walled round".*[3]

In the meantime, Richard Reynolds was having difficulty in coping with his young family at Dale House. Over the years he had become acquainted with Rebecca Gulson of Coventry who had been an intimate friend of his late wife Hannah. Rebecca was described as a woman of great kindness of heart and because of her tranquil disposition and her regard for the memory of their mother, she was particularly qualified to take charge of the children.[4] She and Richard Reynolds were married at Coventry on 1 December 1763. It was to be a happy and loving marriage.

Another marriage of considerable significance within the still small community of Coalbrookdale took place in March 1764 between Hannah Thomas and Thomas Rose. Hannah was the only daughter of John Thomas, who came to the Dale with Abraham I in 1708 and was privy to his original patent.

The Rose family were likewise one of the original Quaker families. Hannah Rose, drawing on the recollections of her parents, wrote an account of the early days in the Dale. [5] Another resident of Coalbrookdale who featured considerably in Abiah's affairs at this time was Ann Summerland who had come to live in the Dale. She was a minister for many years and accompanied Abiah on many of her journeys during this period. [6] A special comfort to Abiah at this time was the return home of Mary (Mally) her eldest daughter, having completed her education. Soon afterwards Abraham III also completed his education and started his apprenticeship in the Works in accordance with his father's Will.

A sadder event in the family's history was the death in 1765 of Ann Hawkins, Abraham II's elder sister. She had been ten years older than Abraham and a year younger than Mary who married Richard Ford. She had married John Hawkins of Bersham and had been involved in the Bersham furnace which had been operated by the Ford/Goldney partnership until it was taken over by a Mr Harvey who in turn transferred them to Isaac Wilkinson, father of John Wilkinson, in 1753. Ann Hawkins had been a widow since 1739 and she had been supported financially by Abraham II and latterly by Abiah. She was buried at Bunhill Fields near London. [7] Ann Hawkins' son Robert was employed as a clerk in the Coalbrookdale Company from about 1746. [7]

On the industrial front, the executors of Abraham II's Will took a lease in 1764 of the ironstone mines in Donnington Wood from Earl Gower, the same year that Lord Gower formed Earl Gower & Co, the predecessor of the future Lilleshall Company. That year also Lord Gower set about the building of the first canal in Shropshire from Donnington Wood to the vicinity of Newport. [8]

By taking over the Donnington Wood lease, the Coalbrookdale Company finally established a comprehensive and predominant control over the mineral resources of the Coalfield as it then existed. The coal and iron measures lay in shallow strata west of the Lightmoor fault which extended from Coalbrookdale in a north-easterly direction to Donnington Wood. The resources to the east of the fault lay some six hundred feet below the surface and could only be reached by deep mining which became technically possible in the following century. The Company's leases of the known resources in Dawley, Lawley, Ketley, Wrockwardine Wood and

Donnington Wood were essential to assure a continuity of supply to the furnaces at Coalbrookdale, Horsehay and Ketley.

Abraham I had shown the world how to use pit coal to produce pig iron for cast-iron, and his son Abraham II had shown how to produce pig iron suitable for conversion into wrought-iron. The only process which still used charcoal was in a 'Finery' at the Forge where the pig iron was heated and stirred to produce wrought-iron. Attempts had been made to use pit-coal instead of charcoal in this final process but without success until 1766 when Thomas and George Cranage discovered a way of doing so in a reverberatory furnace where only the flames from the coals came into contact with the pig iron. Thomas and George Cranage were the sons of William Cranage, who was the first forgemaster of the Company appointed in 1722.[9] Thomas had been put in charge of the Bridgnorth Forge between 1760-63 leaving his brother as a foreman in the Dale.[10] The brothers had previously raised with Richard Reynolds the possibility of producing wrought-iron through the application of heat in a specially designed furnace and in 1766 he agreed to their proposals, which met with great success. At his insistence a patent was taken out in their joint names.[11] This led to the extension of the forges at Bridgnorth and Liverpool. Their process proved wasteful however, and was eventually overtaken by the much improved puddling process introduced by Henry Cort in 1784, which finally brought about the end of charcoal as a fuel.

Despite this technological advance, the industry was facing a down-turn following the end of the Seven Years War and there was a drop in prices and markets in 1767 and 1768. This caused serious distress through hunger. Abiah in her Journal recorded in January 1767 that *"above a hundred people served at my Door this day and great numbers daily"*.[12] Richard Reynolds was determined to keep the furnaces in work even though this meant accumulating iron in stock. One of the methods he devised to retain the iron was to fashion it into strips of iron to be placed on the wooden railways, in expectation that they could be lifted and re-used later. In the event, the newly-laid iron rails proved a great success and within a few years the Company had laid some twenty miles of rails and these proved to be the true forerunners of all the world's metal railways.

Progress was also being made elsewhere in the iron industry. In 1769, James Watt took out his patent which was in due time to transform the development of the steam engine, in which the Coalbrookdale Company was destined to play its part.

During this period, Richard Reynolds had been living at Dale House, where two children, Richard (1765) and Michael (1766) were born.[13] During the three years to 1768, Abraham III had been serving a much reduced apprenticeship with Richard Reynolds in the Works and he attained his eighteenth birthday on 24 April 1768. He thereupon took over management of the Dale works from Richard Reynolds, who on 5 June of that year returned to Ketley with his family to resume management of the Ketley works. A third child, Joseph was born at Ketley soon after. [14]

The establishment of the Ketley and Horsehay works had produced difficulties for those Quaker families who had moved there as Meetings continued to be held at Coalbrookdale. It was, therefore, decided to establish a new Meeting House at New Dale by converting one of the iron-working buildings which had been built some ten years earlier and were now no longer required. [15]

Over the years one visitor among the many who called at Sunniside was Joseph Rathbone of Liverpool. He was a partner, with his cousin William Fawcett in the foundry which the Coalbrookdale Company had established near Liverpool in 1759. George Perry [16] had been sent to establish the foundry which was named Coalbrookdale Foundry. After he died, the business was managed by Joseph Rathbone and William Fawcett. It was during his visits to Sunniside that Joseph Rathbone came to know Mary Darby and in July 1769 the couple were married. [17] Mary and Joseph then left the Dale to set up home in Liverpool. Mary had been a great comfort to her mother and Abiah missed her company, although Abraham III and Sarah (Sally) remained at home with her.

As 1768 came to a close, news arrived of the death of Thomas Goldney III who had been a partner in the Company since the death of Abraham I. [18] He had given unfailing support to the enterprise for over fifty years. Whenever there was a crisis, as for example with John and Rose Giffard in the recent Chancery Proceedings, he had always taken the lead as the principal partner. He also looked after the affairs of the Company in Bristol. Above all he acted as banker and financial guide to the enterprise and during his lifetime saw it progress from a rather unsteady start to become a remarkably successful operation. His shares in the Company passed to his brother Gabriel and his sister Ann, but almost inevitably with his death, the connection with the Goldney family was drawing to a close.

A few months later in 1769 the death occurred of Richard Reynolds' father (also named Richard Reynolds) at Frenchay, Bristol. His company Daniel & Reynolds had long been a customer of the Coalbrookdale Company and there is no doubt that he had underwritten the interest of his son in the Ketley undertaking. Richard Reynolds, free from his responsibilities for superintending the Dale Works, and having inherited his father's wealth and industrial connections, turned his attention more towards his commercial and financial interests. He had since 1762, been a partner in the Redbrook Furnace & Lydbrook Forge.[19] He had also in 1768 formed the Bristol Company of Ironmasters and entered into many other partnerships including Reynolds Getley & Company. Through his father's company he had many connections with the iron and tin plate industry in South Wales as far west as Carmarthen. The result of all these activities was that he soon became an immensely wealthy man. Even so he continued to live at Ketley, to look after the Ketley furnaces and, jointly with Abraham III, the Horsehay furnaces also. As the Goldney influence receded, so his increased and eventually became dominant.

Within this changing context, the young eighteen year old, Abraham III, was taking command of the fortunes of the Company. This continued in the same manner as before. Shortly after Abraham took over, he began the installation of two steam engines at Horsehay and Ketley to supplement two engines installed by his father for the purpose of pumping water needed to turn the water wheels for the blast.[20] He seemed determined to carry on where his father had left off. Even so, conditions in the iron industry continued to be affected by the depression which followed the end of the Seven Years War, and he made the mistake of trying to do too much, too soon.

In 1771 Abraham III became twenty-one and received the legacy of £2,000 under Abraham II's Will. He also started to keep a journal of his accounts, which included not just his personal outgoings but also other dealings such as the building of the Iron Bridge. From these accounts we gather that he borrowed £3,000 from his mother Abiah in 1771. In the following year he borrowed money from Richard Reynolds, thus starting a financial dependency which was to increase over the years. He was guilty of considerable imprudence and within the family, he was remembered as having 'failed in business'.

There were a number of matters for which Abraham required finance. The first arose from his father's Will, under which he had been bequeathed the Hay Farm. This had been purchased by Abraham II in 1761[21] but had been subject to a mortgage back of half the purchase price. Abraham III although he was the owner of the property, was not in a position to take possession, and did not do so until after he paid off the mortgage in 1778.[21] In the meantime he undertook a programme of improvements and extension of the premises until it became a fine home suitable for his occupation in the autumn of 1780.

A second drain on his resources came in 1773 when the opportunity of purchasing the Goldney family shares arose. After Thomas Goldney's death in 1768, these were held by Gabriel Goldney and his sister Ann, both of whom were elderly. In 1773, therefore, Abraham III agreed to purchase the Goldney shares for £10,000 to be paid in equal instalments over five years. This finally brought all the Coalbrookdale partnership shares for the first time into the family's hands. Two years later in 1775, Richard Reynolds purchased the Goldney shares in the Horsehay and Ketley partnerships. In this way, Richard Reynolds became the owner of half of the Horsehay business and two-thirds of the Ketley business. [22]

An even greater drain of Abraham's finances came in 1774 during the negotiations of a new lease for the Coalbrookdale Furnaces, etc. The previous lease, which had caused the litigation with John and Rose Giffard, was for twenty-one years from 1759 [23] and was due to run out in 1780. Rose Giffard had died within a month or so of Abraham II in 1763 [24] and her half of the manor house devolved to her four daughters, Rose, Ann, Mary and Barbara. They now joined with John Smitheman who owned the other half of the manor in agreeing a lease of the Works dated 24 March 1774 for forty-two years at £400 per annum. [25] This was eminently satisfactory, but six months later in September 1774, John Smitheman agreed to sell his half of the manor to Abraham III for the sum of £26,500. [26] In the meantime, one of the four Giffard daughters, Rose, had sold her one-eighth share to her two unmarried sisters, Ann and Mary who in 1774 agreed to sell the resulting three-eighth share to Abraham III. [27] This left the final one-eighth share in the hands of the fourth daughter, Barbara, who had married Thomas Slaughter, the family's agent and steward, and was widowed. [28] For some reason which is not apparent, Barbara Slaughter in 1775 sold her one-eighth share to William and Edward Elwell, Ironfounders of West Bromwich. Abraham III's overall objective was to secure the complete ownership of the manor, thereby safeguarding the future of the Coalbrookdale Works [29] and in 1776 he appeared to be close to success when he agreed with Messrs Elwell to purchase their one-eighth share for £2,000 with the remainder of the purchase, £4,700 to be paid in grey melting pig iron from the Madeley Wood Furnaces. [30]

The deal was finalised in 1778. [31] Full ownership of the manor was therefore tantalisingly close except for the settlement of the 1774 agreement with Anne and Mary Giffard for the acquisition of their three-eighth share. This was held up probably by Abraham's other major burden of expenditure, the building of the world's first Iron Bridge, the achievement for which Abraham III is best remembered. This is the monument which ensures Abraham III's place in history. It was a triumph of technology and deservedly is seen as a great emblem of the Industrial Revolution. Its building, however, left its mark on Abraham's fortunes, as he was running out of finance.

The story of the Bridge goes back to an earlier period, because the need for a bridge had been evident for a long time. Randall, the historian

Georgii III. Regis.

C A P. XVII.

An Act for building a Bridge across the River *Severn* from *Benthall*, in the County of *Salop*, to the opposite Shore at *Madeley Wood*, in the said County; and for making proper Avenues or Roads to and from the same.

Preamble.

𝔚𝔈ℜ𝔈𝔄𝔖 a very considerable Traffick is carried on at Coalbrook Dale, Madeley Wood, Benthall, and Broseley, in the County of Salop, and the Places adjacent, in Iron, Lime, Potters Clay, and Coals, and the Persons carrying on the same are frequently put to great Inconveniencies, Delays, and Obstructions, by reason of the Insufficiency of the present Ferry over the River Severn from Benthall to Madeley Wood, commonly called Benthall Ferry, particularly in the Winter Season, in which Time it is frequently dangerous, and sometimes impassable: And whereas the Reverend Edward Harries and Abraham Darby are Owners of the said Ferry, who, with the several Persons herein-after named, are willing and

5 L 2

desirous,

Act of Parliament for the Iron Bridge.

The study in the restored Dale House, Coalbrookdale where Abraham Darby III did much of the planning for the building of the world's first Iron Bridge.

Iron Bridge, near Coalbrookdale (William Williams).

of Madeley, maintains that it was even in the contemplation of Abraham's father, Abraham II, and so Abraham may have been carrying out his father's wishes.

Abraham had become a trustee of the Turnpike Trusts in and around the Gorge[32] and was, therefore, much acquainted with the problems of transporting goods through the Gorge and across the river. The only river crossing, an inconvenient one, was at Buildwas. All goods, including heavy material had to cross the river by ferry. A meeting of interested parties met in Broseley in September 1775 and Abraham was appointed Treasurer. It is evident that discussions had taken place before that date, as Abraham III's journals start referring to the Bridge from 1773. The principal subscribers at that time were Abraham III and Edward Harries the proprietor of the Benthall estate on the south side of the river, but they were joined by John Wilkinson, Edward Blakeway and John Matthews and twelve other supporters.[33]

A decision was made to appoint Thomas Farnolls Pritchard, the Shrewsbury Architect to design the Bridge and arrangements were made to obtain an Act of Parliament. It is not known who has the credit for making the Bridge in iron, although Pritchard had shown an interest in using iron in bridge making before that time. However, from the outset,

Madeley Wood Furnaces (Edward Dayes)
COURTESY OF BRITISH MUSEUM, TURNER BEQUEST

73

Abraham III and John Wilkinson were firmly in favour of the use of iron, and when in 1776 the other subscribers asked for alternatives to be sought for a bridge "of stone, brick or timber", it was Abraham's views and those of Pritchard and Wilkinson which prevailed, so that in 1776 a firm decision to proceed in iron, with stone abutments had been made. [34]

An Act of Parliament was obtained that year. [35] The estimate for the construction of the Bridge was £3,200 and any cost above that fell on Abraham III. In the end the Bridge cost £6,018, so the additional sum of nearly £3,000 had to be added to Abraham's already over-stretched finances. [36]

By the time the Bridge came to be built, Abraham III held thirty-seven shares and his brother Samuel had four, so that the Darbys held forty-one out of sixty-four shares. The furnace at Coalbrookdale was expanded in 1777 but it seems probable that even this was insufficient for the task of casting the iron for the ribs of the Bridge. In 1776 Abraham III acquired the lease of Madeley Wood Company which owned the Bedlam Furnaces [37] and it seems probable that these were also used.

It is also a reasonable speculation that the flat area of land, known today as the market square in Ironbridge was levelled for the purpose of casting the Bridge on the spot. [38] After preparatory work during 1777-8 the actual work of erecting the Bridge took place during a three month period in the summer of 1779. Thomas Farnolls Pritchard, the architect, died in 1777 and did not, therefore, see his work completed. Even then much work was needed on the approach roads and the Bridge was not finally opened to traffic until New Year's Day 1781.

The Bridge was without doubt one of the wonders of the world and attracted enormous interest. Although the term 'public relations' had not been invented at that time, the construction and opening of the Bridge was publicised in a curiously modern way. Paintings by William Williams, a Shrewsbury artist, and by Michael Angelo Rooker, scene painter at the Haymarket Theatre, were commissioned and engravings were widely available. [39] The Bridge seems therefore to have become a widely publicised advertisement for Coalbrookdale far beyond its significance as a river crossing. Indeed it can be seen as a pinnacle of achievement as the Company, under Abraham III's guidance became the largest iron-producing company in the country and therefore in the world.

While this saga of spectacular progress was unfolding, important events were also occurring on the domestic scene. Abraham's younger brother, Samuel, had left school in 1771 and entered apprenticeship. It was decided that this would take place not in Coalbrookdale but at the foundry in Liverpool. Samuel went to live with his sister Mary Rathbone.

During this period, the Rathbones became much more closely associated with the Darbys. They remained in the maritime industry which was the source of their wealth but they increased their involvement in the Dale, principally in a financial way. The Darbys for their part became briefly involved in the maritime business. [40]

Samuel was subject to the trusts under his father's Will (Abraham II) until he came of age in 1776. Abiah was trustee and was zealous in her duty towards him. In 1773 she submitted a case for the opinion of Alexander Wedderburn, Solicitor General, about the conduct of Richard Reynolds under an agreement made by Abraham II and Richard Reynolds just before Abraham's death in 1763 for the management of the Dawley and Lawley mines. The agreement appeared to require Reynolds' personal involvement but he had appointed John Young (one of Abraham II's executors) as Manager instead of himself on terms which appeared to be advantageous to Young and himself. The Solicitor General clearly supported Abiah's view that this was to the detriment of the children and awarded accordingly.

At this time, Abraham III was spending some time in London, in connection with the passing of the Bill for the Iron Bridge, and also in relation to the Company's foundry in Southwark. The family was fairly familiar with the London scene through regular attendance at the Friends Yearly Meetings which took place there. At some stage, a foundry had been established in Southwark. As early as 1735, Richard Ford mentions in correspondence with Thomas Goldney, '*a Modell which is Erected near ye Faulcon Stairs in Southwark Facing St Pauls.*'[41] Also Thomas Cranage later spent some time at the London Foundry. [42] The premises were in Storey Lane, in Southwark to the east of London Bridge between Battle Bridge Stairs and Pickle Herring Stairs. This lane ran north from Tooley Street to the Thames. [43]

Another property in which the Company had an interest was on the other side of the River Thames in George Yard south of Upper Thames Street. [44] Various payments appear in Abraham's ledger for the setting up of an office and counting house. [45] Samuel, having completed his apprenticeship in Liverpool, was established in George Yard to undertake the Company's business there. He was accompanied by his sister Sarah, who went there to do the housekeeping. It was there that Sarah became acquainted with Susannah (Sukey) Appleby who became her friend and companion and returned to Coalbrookdale with her to live the greater part of her life at Sunniside. Samuel settled down in George Yard to run the London business.

For the past few years a visitor to Richard Reynolds' home had been Rebecca Smith from Doncaster who was a niece of Richard's wife, Rebecca (née Gulson) and in this way she had become acquainted with Abraham III. Marriage was in contemplation. Although he owned the Haye, he had not discharged the mortgage back to the Worrall family from whom the property had been bought. He, therefore, decided to upgrade and modernise Dale House which had been vacated by Richard Reynolds in 1768. At this time, it was a two storey house with bedroom accommodation in the roof space with dormer windows. It was much as it had been built by Abraham I in 1717. Abraham III decided to add a third storey, and the house was extended to the rear replacing a previous two storey wing. In March 1776 Abraham gave notice of intention to marry and the wedding took place at the Meeting House, Warnsworth in the County of York on 3 May 1776.[46]

Carpets worth £25 were purchased and over £60 of plate, together with pewter, various silver items, glass salvers and a glass lamp. This was at a time when the Iron Bridge was being planned, and so Abraham's study at Dale House became the scene of many discussions and meetings leading up to the construction of the Bridge and Rebecca the young wife became involved as hostess to the many visitors.

Romance was clearly in the air, because three months later in August 1776, Samuel, although five years younger than Abraham, married Deborah Barnard at Sheffield. Samuel had met Deborah in the London society which he had joined at George Yard in London. Deborah's family was known to Abiah, as Deborah was a granddaughter of an old friend Deborah Wilson. After the wedding, Samuel and Deborah returned to London to continue the task of running the London business. Their first born, named Abraham, was born in 1777 but he died in childhood.

Although the building of the Iron Bridge was claiming attention centre stage, the work of the Company in Coalbrookdale, Horsehay and Ketley continued to be developed. As has been mentioned, the lease of the Madeley Wood Company with its Bedlam Furnaces alongside the River Severn was acquired by Abraham III in 1776.[47] Elsewhere technology had been moving ahead very fast. James Watt had teamed up with Mathew Boulton to develop his improved steam engine and one of the first two engines produced by their partnership was installed in 1776 at the New Willey Furnaces in Broseley. Two years later, Richard Reynolds, made an agreement with Boulton and Watt for the erection of an engine at the Ketley Furnaces for which Reynolds was to supply the cast-iron parts.

This was installed in 1779 and a second similar engine the following year.[48] During this same period Abraham III was further securing the mineral resources of the Company by agreements with George Forester and Plowden Slaney for coal and ironstone mines in land at Little Wenlock and in the Manor of Dawley.[49]

A morning view of Coalbrookdale (William Williams, 1777).
COURTESY OF CLIVE HOUSE MUSEUM, SHREWSBURY

An afternoon view of Coalbrookdale (William Williams, 1777).
COURTESY OF CLIVE HOUSE MUSEUM, SHREWSBURY

In 1774 Wilkinson had taken out a patent for boring cannon but this had been revoked in 1779.[50] The next year in 1780, a boring mill for steam engines on Wilkinson's plan was installed at Coalbrookdale.[51] The following year in 1781 a massive Boulton & Watt engine which became known as 'Resolution' was installed at the head of Coalbrookdale to replace the old Newcomen engine installed in 1742 by Richard Ford and Abraham II.[52]

To all outward appearances, the Coalbrookdale Company with its furnaces at Madeley Wood, Coalbrookdale, Horsehay and Ketley and its vast mineral resources covering the whole of the known coalfield, was an outstanding success. But behind the story of undoubted triumph a picture of personal tragedy and of financial nemesis was unfolding. The personal tragedy revolved around the personality of Samuel Darby. He had taken over the London business in 1776 and had become a member of the Gracechurch Street Meeting. He was highly regarded within his circle of friends and was described as *'wealthy and handsome, sensible and religious, dutiful to his Parent, affectionate to his relations, kind and liberal to mankind in general.'*[53] Three years later, however, as the Iron Bridge was being constructed, Abiah wrote *"I have witnessed a time of great distress of mind upon my son Sammy's account who was to outward appearances near Death in a violent fever."*[54] He recovered and was brought back to Sunniside with his wife Deborah, who was close to having her second child Samuel.[55] Abiah concluded that *"London air does not agree with him"* and she wanted the couple to live in the country.

Samuel recovered well enough to return to London where it was evident that the Southwark Foundry under his guidance was near to failure. In October 1779 just as the Iron Bridge was nearing completion, Abraham III went to London, closely followed by Joseph Rathbone and Richard Reynolds. The decision was made *"to part with our concerns in London"* and the foundry was duly sold at the end of November 1779.[56] The tragedy was not just the failure of the Southwark foundry, but the fact that Samuel's illness led to recurring attacks of a *"nervous illness of a mental nature"* and the decision that Samuel and Deborah would thereafter live the rest of their lives at Sunniside. Samuel was a spent force and became a continuing problem to the family during the next fifteen years.

By this time, Abraham III's financial commitments were hopelessly overstretched. He had been spending regularly on The Haye and also on Dale House; he had spent £10,000 in the acquisition of the Goldney shares; he had expended even greater sums in his bid to acquire the Manor of Madeley; he had acquired the lease of Madeley Wood Furnaces, and he had incurred losses of the order of £3,000 on the building of the Iron Bridge. In order to meet these and other commitments he had to borrow money. On 24 November 1777 he and Samuel mortgaged their four-twentieth share of the Horsehay and Ketley furnaces to Richard Reynolds for £8,000. In February 1788, they gave a bond to their sister Sarah for £200 and in June they gave another bond to Joseph Rathbone for £500. Thereafter the calls for money escalated and by June 1781, Abraham and Samuel were jointly indebted to Joseph Rathbone in the sum of £60,000.[57] Abraham also agreed to transfer to Richard Reynolds all his transactions relating to the acquisition of the Manor of Madeley with the result that it was Richard Reynolds, rather than Abraham III, who became Lord of the Manor and the owner of the freehold of the Coalbrookdale site.

Matters came to a head in June 1781 when the affairs of the enterprise were completely restructured. First, the lease of the Coalbrookdale Works granted to Abraham III by John Smitheman and the Giffard sisters in 1774 was surrendered and a new lease for twenty-six years from 1 July 1781 was granted to (1) Joseph Rathbone (husband of Mary Rathbone, née Darby), (2) Abraham Darby, (3) Samuel Darby, (4) Sarah Darby and (5) William Reynolds (son of Richard Reynolds by his first wife, Hannah Darby). This lease was granted by Richard Reynolds who as already stated had acquired all the interests in the Manor of Madeley and had become Lord of the Manor.[58] This lease included all the Coalbrookdale furnaces, forges and malthouses, together with all railways, watercourses, waste land and the newly-erected engine at the head of the Dale, extending from these to the River Severn and including wharfages up to Madeley Wood. The lease also included the Madeley Wood Furnace, which had been transferred to Richard Reynolds by Abraham III and nearby engines, gins and other buildings comprising the Mallets Pit Company, the New Jacobite Pit Company and the Hollands Footroad Company with rough ground known as the Upper Lloyds. The rent was increased to £1,600 per annum (four times the 1774 rent).

On 22 June 1782, Articles of Partnership were entered into between the five parties to the lease with each entitled to one-fifth share of the various leasehold lands, collieries, ironstone works, roads, railways etc, ironworks, furnaces, foundries and forges in Dawley, Wellington, Little Wenlock Bridgnorth, Madeley and Liverpool. On account of the £60,000 paid to Abraham and Samuel and also on account of the £8,000 paid by Richard Reynolds, two-fifths of the shares in the partnership (i.e., Abraham and Samuel Darby) and four-twentieths of the shares in the Horsehay and Ketley furnaces, etc, were assigned to Joseph Rathbone as security, but subject to equity of redemption.

In many ways this reflected and respected the wishes of Abraham II set out in his Will, but now the shares of the two sons, Abraham III and Samuel were severely constrained by the large debts incurred in the 1770s. Insofar as there was a balance of power within the partnership, there can be no doubt that Joseph Rathbone had emerged as the senior partner, and for the first time, William Reynolds (son of Richard Reynolds and grandson of Abraham II) had emerged as a full and unfettered partner.

The impressive feature of this whole unhappy episode is that the family, including its in-laws, stuck together as a group. They overcame their problems by acting as their own bankers, with particular credit to Joseph Rathbone, whose involvement in the Company at that stage was limited to the Liverpool foundry. If there were recriminations, none were evident, as they continued to visit each other at their respective homes and continued their lives as before. The bond between them, apart from their family relationships was their strong commitment to their Quaker faith.

In the few years encompassing the end of the 1770s and the beginning of the 1780s, nemesis had closely accompanied triumph, and success must have been a close run thing. In the end the enterprise emerged intact, although the burden of the huge debt hung like a shadow over the fortunes of the Darby family for the next twenty years. The £8,000 due to Richard Reynolds was paid off, and the debt to Joseph Reynolds was reduced, until in the 1790s the indebtedness was finally cleared in another major restructuring of the Company.

Although all the turmoil was essentially a Coalbrookdale affair, repercussions were noted throughout the industry. In 1782, Matthew Boulton told James Watt *"the last Prime Minister of Coalbrookdale was very near settling fast the whole concern. It would have been the case had Mr Reynolds not strained every power to raise money"*. [59] Despite everything, the Iron Bridge has survived to this day when much else associated with its birth has disappeared or faded.

NOTES – CHAPTER VI

1. *Abiah*, p.128.
2. The enterprise was run as a single operation, although in fact there were three separate partnerships. The original partnership in Coalbrookdale comprised the Old Furnace and the new furnace, with the three forges, malthouse and waste land associated with them, together with right of wharfage on manorial land adjoining the River Severn up to Madeley Wood. The Goldney family held nine shares out of sixteen and the Darby family had the remaining seven shares. The Horsehay partnership comprised the two furnaces and pools at Horsehay Farm together with coalmines and ironstone mines in Great Dawley and Ketley, with railways between the works and Coalbrookdale. This partnership was held by Thomas Goldney and the Darby family. The third partnership consisted of two furnaces at

Ketley held on lease from Lord Gower together with land in Ketley, Donnington Wood and Wrockwardine Wood. This partnership was owned by Thomas Goldney, Richard Reynolds and the Darby family in equal parts. Under Abraham II's Will his Trustees also held the land at Lawley (Newdale) and Littlehales Tenement, Dawley, and the Town Mills in Bridgnorth for the benefit of the Coalbrookdale Company.

3. *Abiah*, p.130.
4. *Abiah*, p.132.
5. Hannah Rose's account – IGMT archives.
6. Ann Summerland 1709-1798. Daughter of Joshua and Rebecca Waterhouse of Dronfield, Derby. Married John Summerland and resided at Coalbrookdale.
7. *Abiah*, p.145. Also see interrogatories in Chancery Proceedings Giffard v Goldney IGMT Archives.
8. *The Lilleshall Company Limited* – a history 1764-1964. W K V Gale and C R Nicholls p.16.
9. Raistrick, p.54.
10. In moving to Bridgnorth, Thomas Cranage had transferred four cottages in Coalbrookdale to his brother George (S.R.O 1987/4/1). These formed part of the settlement at the head of the Rope Walk which was acquired by Francis Darby between 1821 and 1841 and then demolished between 1841 and 1850. George Cranage had also purchased, in 1748, an area of land on the west side of Darby Road, subsequently the site of the Chesnuts (S.R.O 1987/31/1-2).

   The Cranage family were a Quaker family who came to the Dale from the village of Cranage in Cheshire. They prospered well and their descendants moved to Ketley and Wellington, where they became ironmasters, accountants and solicitors. A Thomas Cranage, probably the grandson of George Cranage, married Henrietta Thomas, granddaughter of John and Grace Thomas in the 1790s. Their grandson became the distinguished Dr Joseph Edward Cranage, founder of The Old Hall School, Watling Street in Wellington which celebrated its 150th anniversary in 1995 (see *Memories of The Old Hall School*, published by The Old Hall School 1995).
11. Patent No. 815, June 1766, "Making pig iron or cast iron malleable in a reverberatory furnace or air furnace with pit coal only" – See Raistrick pp 85-87.
12. *Abiah*, p.151.
13. Raistrick, p.85.
14. *Abiah*, p.156.
15. *Abiah*, p.153.
16. George Perry was joint publisher of the engravings by Vivares of the Views of Coalbrookdale, 1758.

17. *Abiah*, p.155.
18. *Abiah*, p.158.
19. Raistrick, p.87.
20. Raistrick, p.91.
21. See Abstract of Title S.R.O 1987/29/9.
22. *Abiah*, p.168. In 1775 Richard Reynolds also purchased the Manor of Sutton in Wiltshire for £20,800.
23. S.R.O 1987/35/4.
24. S.R.O 1681/136/8.
25. S.R.O 1681/139/7.
26. S.R.O 1681/133/3,4,5,6, and S.R.O 1681/131/12.
27. VCH Vol XI (Telford) p.36. See also S.R.O 1681/136/8, 1681/134/10, 11, 12, 13, 14, 15; 1681/132/28.
28. S.R.O 1681/135/1.
29. S.R.O 1681/135/2, 3, 4, and 5.
30. S.R.O 1987/60/4.
31. S.R.O 1681/135/6, 7-8, 9-10.
32. These were the Madeley turnpike, the Wenlock turnpike trust and the Leighton turnpike. See Trinder, The Darbys of Coalbrookdale, pp 36 and 37.
33. The original subscribers of the Bridge as shown in the Minutes were:

John Wilkinson	£2. 0.0	Abraham Darby	£5. 0.0
Edward Blakeway	£2. 0.0	Edward Harries	£5. 0.0
Leonard Jennings	£1. 0.0	John Matthews	£2. 0.0
Thomas Slaughter	4.2½	Sergeant Roden	10.6
Robert Gilpin	4.2½	John Guest	1.0
John Morris	£1. 0.0	Charles Guest	£1. 0.0
John Thursfield	10.6	John Corbel	10.6
John Hartshorne	£1. 1.0	Daniel Boden	10.6
John Nicholson	10.6		

34. For more detail see Raistrick, pp.193-200 and Trinder, pp.32-35.
35. Statute 16 Geo. III C.XVII 1776.
36. For an analysis see paper by David de Haan, Deputy Director, IGMT, given to the International Bridge Conference, Columbus, Ohio on 27 August 1992.
37. S.R.O 1987/60/5.
38. See Note 36.
39. An engraving was purchased by Thomas Jefferson's London agent while he was in Paris, and was eventually displayed in Monticello, Jefferson's home in Virginia.
40. *Abiah*, p.164. Abraham III paid £400 in August 1771 for a share in William Rathbone's ship 'Darby'. Two years later he received £200 from underwriters on the loss of the ship, and a further payment of £200 in 1775.

41. Raistrick, p.111.
42. See S.R.O 1987/4/1.
43. *Abiah*, p.174.
44. It is possible that this was the subject of the agreement signed in 1772 and referred to in *Abiah*, p.167.
45. *Abiah*, p.174.
46. *Abiah*, pp 182 and 183.
47. S.R.O 1987/60/5: The Madeley Wood Company was established as a partnership in 1757. Edmund Ford was one of the partners. See S.R.O 1681/183/14 and also S.R.O. 1681/132/24.
48. Trinder: *Industrial Revolution in Shropshire*, p.163.
49. S.R.O 1681/179/2 and 1681/118/4 and 7-8 and 1681/120/3.
50. Trinder: *Industrial Revolution in Shropshire*, p.162.
51. Trinder: *Industrial Revolution in Shropshire*, p.66.
52. Raistrick Plate XI and Plate VIII.
53. *Abiah*, p.181.
54. *Abiah*, p.198.
55. Samuel, born at Sunniside 30 May 1779. Abiah p.200.
56. *Abiah*, p.204 and 205.
57. The sorry story of the financial decline of Abraham and Samuel's financial fortunes is set out in a complex document dated 4 February 1794 in which Samuel Darby's shares were placed in trust. S.R.O 1987/35/1.
58. Richard Reynolds acquired the 3/8th interest of Anne and Mary Giffard on 18 December 1780. See VCH Vol XI Telford p.36 and S.R.O 1681/134. The remaining 5/8th were transferred to Richard Reynolds by Abraham III and Rebecca his wife on 18 and 19 June 1781. See S.R.O 1681/135/2-12 and S.R.O 1987/60/4 (the Elwell portion) and S.R.O 1681/133/7, 8 and 9 (the former Smitheman portion).
59. See Trinder, *Industrial Revolution in Shropshire*, p.66. Matthew Boulton, James Watt 13 April 1782, B.R.L., B & W Colln, Parcel D.

CHAPTER VII

The Reynolds and the Rathbones

AFTER THE UPHEAVAL of 1782, leadership within the partnership shifted almost inevitably to the Reynolds and Rathbone families. For a time the Company became known as Joseph Rathbone and the Dale Company.

When Abraham III and Rebecca with their three children moved from Dale House to The Haye in September 1780,[1] Joseph Rathbone and his wife Mary (née Darby) moved into Dale House. They were, therefore, present in the Dale throughout the transactions of 1781-82. Richard Reynolds and Rebecca with their three children were living at Bank House, Ketley.[2]

The three families were closely connected by marriage, as well as by their Quaker beliefs and mutual business interests. The Rathbones had been business partners of the Darbys since the late 1750s and Joseph Rathbone had married Mary Darby (Abraham II's first daughter by his second marriage to Abiah).[3] The Reynolds had even longer business dealings with the Darbys and their relationship was even more strongly cemented when Richard Reynolds married Hannah Darby (Abraham Darby II's daughter by his first marriage). The children of that marriage – William Reynolds and Hannah Darby – were, therefore, grandchildren of Abraham II; indeed they were his first grandchildren and the only ones he knew during his lifetime. They ranked equally with his other children in his Will, and were always treated as Darbys despite being named Reynolds.[4]

The Reynolds and Rathbones were to become even more closely related during the 1780s. Joseph Rathbone's half brother, William Rathbone III, had two children, Elizabeth and William Rathbone IV.[3] They became friends with Richard Reynold's children, William Reynolds and Hannah Mary. This friendship led to the marriage in 1786 between Hannah Mary Reynolds and William Rathbone IV. They moved to Liverpool where William Rathbone was the first to import American cotton to Britain.[5] It was hoped that there would also be a marriage between Elizabeth Rathbone and William Reynolds, but sadly this was not to be, because Elizabeth's love for William was not reciprocated and William instead married his first cousin, Hannah Ball, in 1789. Elizabeth remained unmarried. *(6)*

(Some fifty years later a similar situation was to occur again in the Darby family, when Abraham IV and his brother Alfred sought to marry Matilda and Adelaide, daughters of Francis Darby, with similar results.)

At Sunniside, Abiah was approaching her seventieth birthday and reducing her activities as a minister. Resident with her were her daughter Sarah with her companion Susannah Appleby. Also in another part of the house lived her son Samuel and his wife Deborah with their children, Samuel and Edmund. It had been finally accepted that Samuel would no longer be active in business as his mental illness continued to cause great concern. There were overtones of marital stress first noted in 1779, when Deborah recorded *"My dearest friend differing from me in sentiment"*. *(7)* The situation was compounded in 1782 when Samuel suddenly departed for London. Sarah and Deborah followed and although Sarah visited Samuel, Deborah was *"not permitted to do so for fear of making him worse"*. *(8)* Some eighteen months later Samuel returned home to everyone's relief. *(9)* Unfortunately Deborah's worries had been worsened in the meantime by the failure in business of her father John Barnard, who then moved to the Dale with his wife to reside until his death in 1789. *(10)*

The effect of all this pressure on Deborah was to divert her energies even further into her commitments as a minister. As Abiah declined, so Deborah's involvement in the ministry increased. From 1783 she started a series of itineraries which took her to many parts of the country including Scotland and Ireland. Abiah for her part, although more constrained by her age and approaching infirmity continued to dominate the scene at Sunniside. Over the years she had continued her confrontation with Reverend Fletcher the parish priest, but this mellowed to a state of mutual respect. Methodism which Reverend Fletcher espoused had spread throughout the district, aided no doubt by John Wesley himself who was a frequent visitor. *(11)* A Methodist chapel had been built at The Rock in Madeley Wood in 1776 and a small chapel was built in Coalbrookdale in 1785. *(12)*

The year before in 1784, Abiah wrote to Reverend Fletcher suggesting the establishment of Sunday Schools and this led to the setting up of Sunday Schools for boys and girls in Coalbrookdale, Madeley Wood and Madeley, a cause of mutual satisfaction. The last public function of Reverend Fletcher was to lay the foundation stone of the Sunday School in Madeley. He died in August 1785. Deborah Darby recorded *"this*

The Haye Farm stands on high ground above Coalport. Five years before his death Abraham Darby II purchased half of the Haye Farm. In 1771 his son Abraham III purchased the other half. He lived there from 1780 until his death in 1789.

Richard Reynolds.

William Reynolds.

evening our Valuable Neighbour John Fletcher was removed by death – made a peaceful close. (13)

During this decade, Abraham III, after the triumph of the Iron Bridge, was living at The Haye, whence he could see the Bridge in its dramatic setting. He was of course deeply in debt to Joseph Rathbone and Richard Reynolds. It must have been galling for a man of his spirit to look at the Bridge and to reflect that in 1782 he had been obliged to transfer almost all his now profitable shareholding to Richard Reynolds, (14) who had taken virtually no part in its building.

The driving force within the partnership had now passed to Richard Reynolds who had brought his son William into full management. William had become a partner of the Coalbrookdale Company in 1781. (15) In 1783 William Reynolds and Joseph Rathbone leased thirty-six acres of land at Donnington Wood from Earl Gower for the building of furnaces to smelt iron from Wrockwardine Wood. The furnaces came into blast in 1785. (16) Although this came within the overall orbit of the Coalbrookdale Company, it appears nevertheless to have been a separate Rathbone/Reynolds initiative. (17)

William Reynolds was the first member of the fourth generation of the Darby Family to come into active management of the Company. His mother was Hannah Darby who was Abraham II's eldest child, and William clearly inherited from her the Darby family genius. From his father, Richard Reynolds, he inherited the Reynolds prudence and compassion and their business acumen. He shared with Abraham III an interest in scientific matters. His combination of talents made him into one of the leading ironmasters of his age, able to deal on equal terms with James Watt, Matthew Boulton and Thomas Telford, and the new rising generation of industrialists.

He first made his mark in the construction of the canal system within the Coalfield with its distinctive system of inclined planes. It was his father who had first shown an interest in canals following a visit to the Duke of Bridgewater's canal in 1769. This prompted the building of a private canal to the Ketley furnaces, but because of the difficulties of the terrain, the canal was brought close to the works and the goods were then transported to their destination down an incline which descended a height of seventy-three feet, the first time that this device had been tried.

Encouraged by this experience, Richard Reynolds sought and obtained an Act of Parliament for the construction of a canal from the iron works in Shropshire to the River Severn. It was his son, William Reynolds, who became the prime mover in the construction of this canal. It ran from Donnington Wood in the north in a generally southerly direction past Oakengates, connecting up with the private canal to Ketley and then proceeding to a point at Southall, south of Dawley, where it split into two branches, the western branch proceeding south of Horsehay to a point above Coalbrookdale, and the eastern branch, going through Madeley to a point above the River Severn at the area now known as Coalport, to which it descended by a spectacular inclined plane which still exists. The system eventually incorporated six inclined planes which became a distinctive feature of what became known as the Shropshire Canal Company. The two largest shareholders were Richard Reynolds and Joseph Rathbone, but its other shareholders included most of the ironmasters and landowners in the Coalfield. [18] Construction of the canal was by the Coalbrookdale Company and started in 1788. It became fully operational in 1793.

In the same year that the Act was obtained, Richard Reynolds bought from Abraham III the meadows adjoining the River Severn which were part of Haye Farm. It was to these meadows leased by Richard Reynolds to his son William in 1793, that the Hay Inclined Plane descended and which were developed by William Reynolds to become the '*new town*' of Coalport. It was also where, in 1787, he engineered a horizontal adit from the riverside under Blists Hill where in 1790 a new coalpit was sunk. [19] A vein of mineral bitumen was encountered on the way and this became in due course, the Tar Tunnel.

It was quite evident by the late 1780s that William Reynolds was in full command of all the operations not only at Ketley, but also elsewhere throughout the Company's sphere of operations. In 1789, Joseph Reynolds, Richard's second son by his marriage to Rebecca (Gulson), became twenty-one and took over some of the management operations. This prompted Richard Reynolds in February of that year to withdraw from management and to hand over his operational responsibilities to his two sons. He and Rebecca, therefore, moved back to Dale House which had recently been vacated by Joseph Rathbone and Mary who had moved back to Liverpool because Joseph was suffering ill-health. [20] This arrangement left Bank House, Ketley, free for the sole occupation of William Reynolds, who then married his first cousin Hannah Ball [4] in the following November. [21]

Sadly the Reynolds removal to Dale House was followed within the month by the sudden death of Abraham III from Scarlet Fever, the disease which had killed his eldest son Abraham the previous year. By misfortune his wife Rebecca was also seriously ill with an ulcerated throat and could not look after him.

So Susannah (Sukey) Appleby went to The Haye followed by Abraham's sister Sarah, who in turn caught the fever and became extremely ill. Against the odds, Abraham seemed to get better and insisted upon going out riding, which brought on a relapse from which he did not recover. He died on 20 March 1789. Sarah his sister remained delirious but thereafter made a slow recovery.

Abraham's death at the age of thirty-eight was a tragedy and put the affairs of the family once again into turmoil. He had paid off the £8,000 owing to Richard Reynolds and had started to decrease the loan from Joseph Rathbone which had been reduced from £60,000 to £46,400. If he had lived longer, he would no doubt have cleared his debts, but as it was, he was at the time of his death overstretched financially. It was, therefore, necessary to sell all the farm stock and implements as well as most of the contents of the House, including his valuable library. The sale lasted five days. This left his widow Rebecca and six children *(22)* without a home. Arrangements were made, therefore, for them to move to Sunniside where property nearby, which in due course became known as the White House, was made available for them. It seems probable that this was made from the two dwelling houses and schoolroom buildings built by Abraham II and referred to in his Will. *(23)*

It was a pity that Abraham's life should have ended in this way. He had shown tremendous energy and initiative after taking over management of the Company at the age of eighteen years. His strategic objectives were sound although he lacked the capital to carry them through. The Company, under his leadership, became the largest iron making Company in the country. He was strict and diligent in his devotion to his Quaker faith, although one senses that he was perhaps more flamboyant and maybe more sophisticated than his father and grandfather. He was well remembered. Adam Luccock, whose father had been apprenticed under Abraham I and who had himself worked under Abraham II and Abraham III, said of the Darbys *"they all liked a joke right well, and as for kindness, it seemed as if they thought it a favour to be allowed to assist you"*. In the end it was the Iron Bridge which was to be his enduring monument.

At the time of his death, Abraham III had started to resume his activities at Coalbrookdale. A new Boulton & Watt engine had been installed in the Dale in 1789. *(24)* Also a lease of lands in Madeley had been negotiated and was executed after Abraham's death in April 1789. *(25)* Soon, however, it was Joseph Rathbone's health which was causing concern after his return to Liverpool, and early in 1790 he started to put his affairs in order.

He and Mary had no children, although they had earlier had a son who died in infancy. In February of 1790 he placed the debt owing to him by Abraham and Samuel on trust for the Coalbrookdale Company. This in effect converted the debt into part of the equity of the Company, so

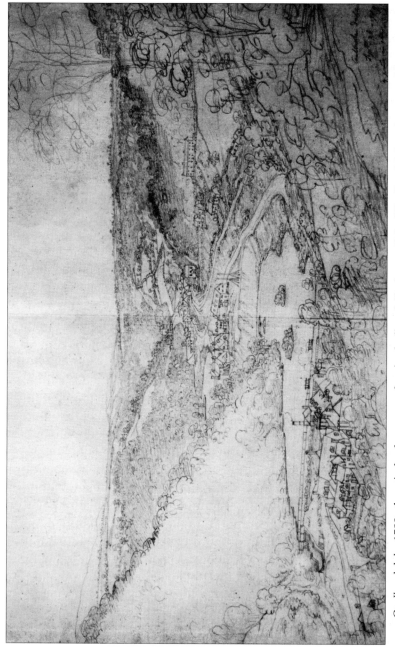

Coalbrookdale, 1789. A meticulously accurate drawing by Joseph Farington, RA of Coalbrookdale as it appeared in 1789.

that he with Samuel, Rebecca and Sarah each had a one-fifth share and William and Hannah Mary Reynolds had the other one-fifth share.*(26)* In June 1790 he made his Will, which after legacies left the residue of his estate to Mary his wife. He died at the end of August 1790.*(27)* Soon afterwards Mary returned to live at Sunniside, her childhood home, where Abiah was glad to have her company in her advancing years.*(28)*

Once again the affairs of the partnership were put into disarray. Within a period of eighteen months, Abraham III and Joseph Rathbone had died and Richard Reynolds had withdrawn from active management. This effectively left William Reynolds in charge, assisted by his brother Joseph. The first instinct of the partners was to consolidate the various operations under the parent firm to be known as the Coalbrookdale Company, and staffing was restructured with heads of department appointed for various functions. But the most important decision taken shortly after the death of Joseph Rathbone was to invite Richard Dearman of Birmingham to become Agent-Manager of the Company.*(29)*

Richard Dearman was from old Quaker stock linked by marriage to many of the Quaker banking families. His experience was, however, in the Iron trade, and he was married to Elizabeth Freeth of the Birmingham family of Freeth, to whom Abraham I had been apprenticed in the 1690s. Before moving to Coalbrookdale he was manager of the Eagle Foundry in Birmingham, a position which he then passed on to his son.*(30)* To provide accommodation for him, the Coalbrookdale Company took a lease of Rosehill (built by Richard Ford in 1738) from Samuel Darby for twenty-one years from 1791, and spent £800 – a considerable sum in renovating it.*(31)*

During this period the Company continued its activities unabated. A decision was made to manufacture bricks and other clay goods and this soon became a major part of the Company's work. Also it was agreed to build an incline from the canal at Brierly Hill above Coalbrookdale to a railway in the Dale to take goods to the wharf at Severnside. A visit by Richard Dearman to collect outstanding debts in Cornwall resulted in a decision to write off a considerable sum. A resulting cash shortage led to a decision to contract and consolidate the Company's operations. As a result the Liverpool Foundry was sold to William Fawcett and the Bridgnorth Forge was leased. A decision was made to sell Madeley Fields, the Lloyds and the Madeley Wood furnaces.*(32)*

At some stage the parties started to think in terms of separating the Company into its constituent parts. It is difficult to know whether any person was the prime mover in this situation, but Richard Dearman reported to the partners two letters, one from William Reynolds and the other on behalf of Hannah Mary Rathbone (the two grandchildren of

Abraham II who between them held one-fifth share of the Coalbrookdale Company) offering to sell their respective shares in the Company.[33] This led to a formal dissolution of the existing partnership[33] and a series of negotiations which resulted finally in a decision to sell the Madeley Wood and Madeley Fields concerns to William Reynolds and Hannah Mary Rathbone in exchange for their shares in the Coalbrookdale Company.[34]

As a result of this transaction the shareholders of the Coalbrookdale Company became the four members of the family who held the shares under Abraham II's Will:[35]

> Mary Rathbone (née Darby)
> Rebecca Darby (widow of Abraham III)
> Samuel Darby
> Sarah Darby

In order to facilitate the execution of this situation, it became necessary finally to deal with the outstanding debt to the Company of Abraham III and Samuel. It will be remembered that this had been converted into a trust for the Company by Joseph Rathbone before he died in 1790. Mary Rathbone and Sarah Darby, therefore, agreed to transfer to the Company £6,400 each out of monies payable to them which together with dividends, would discharge the outstanding debts due from Abraham and Samuel.[36] The two sisters also created a trust which ensured that a sum of £300 per annum would be available to Samuel, his wife Deborah and their children.[37]

In the developing situation, Richard Reynolds agreed to rebate the high rent which he had charged the Company in 1781 from £1,600 to £700. The 1781 lease was, therefore, surrendered and in June 1794 a new lease of the Coalbrookdale Works at the new rent was granted to Samuel, Rebecca, Mary and Sarah.[37a]

There remained the final decision about the future of the Horsehay and Ketley Works and the Donnington Wood Furnaces. The way ahead was cleared when William Reynolds offered to exchange the Coalbrookdale Company's half share of the Ketley Works for his share in the Horsehay Works.

Valuations of the respective shares were made and accepted as a basis. As a result in September 1794 the partnership entered into in 1781, was dissolved[38] and new agreements were signed in 1796.[39] The transactions were finalised and public notice was given in February 1797 of the creation of two new companies:-[40]

1. The Coalbrook Dale Company carried on by Rebecca Darby (widow of Abraham III), Mary Rathbone (née Darby), Sarah Darby and the executors of Samuel Darby deceased. This Company operated the Coalbrookdale and Horsehay Works.

2. W Reynolds & Company carried on by William Reynolds and Joseph Reynolds. This operated the Ketley Works.

In 1797 the Donnington Wood Furnaces were sold to John Bishton and shortly afterwards they became part of the Lilleshall Company.[41] In this way, the vast empire built by Abraham II and Abraham III, with help from Richard Reynolds and Joseph Rathbone, was curtailed in extent and divided into two manageable portions. The mainstream of the Darby family was now back in sole charge of its original holding while the Reynolds family concentrated on the Ketley operations.

While this complicated reconstruction of the two companies had been taking place, important events had been occurring within the domestic scene. The first and most important event was the death of Abiah, Abraham's widow on 26 June 1794 aged seventy-eight years. She had been the dominant personality in the family since the death of her husband in 1763 over thirty years before. It was of course her absolute commitment to her life as a minister which distinguished her, but in the process she acquired matriarchal status which continued to influence the family well into the next century. Her later years had been clouded by the death of her elder son Abraham III in 1789 and the illness of her younger son Samuel. However, she had been greatly supported by the devotion of her daughters Mary Rathbone and Sarah, and her daughters-in law, Rebecca and Deborah. This family group, lately all domiciled at Sunniside and the White House exemplified Abiah's oft-repeated advocacy of "*Love, it being the foundation of Unity*". She was buried beside her husband in the burial ground which he had given to the Friends on his death. By her Will[42] she divided the £2,000 which she had been given in her husband's Will into equal shares of £400 to be divided between her children and the two grandchildren, William and Hannah (Mary) Reynolds.

Her role as a minister had already passed to Deborah, while the task of managing the family's affairs passed, seamlessly, to Sarah who continued her dominance of Sunniside until Sarah's own death in 1821.

Deborah was not present at Abiah's death. Her devotion to her work as a minister seemed to equal Abiah's. Indeed her capacity to travel seemed to exceed even Abiah's sterling example. The year before Abiah's death, she had been called to visit America, an eventful journey which lasted from August 1793 to June 1796. She was accompanied by her young friend, Rebecca Young of Shrewsbury. They were away for nearly three years, during which time they visited Friends in New York and Philadelphia, crossed the Alleghenies and did much for the welfare of Negro slaves.[43]

On Deborah's return in 1796 Samuel was away from home, probably through a recurrence of his illness. He returned a month later, but was soon away again. He died at Bilston on 1 September 1796 aged forty-one. After his apprenticeship in Liverpool as a young man, he had taken on the responsibility of the Southwark foundry. His promising career was blighted by the failure of the enterprise and he did little active work afterwards. He was appointed Treasurer of the Shropshire Canal Company in the late 1780s but otherwise his mental illness caused him and his family great distress and concern. He made a Will on 4 February 1794.[44] He had inherited from his father the property now known as Rosehill together with Tea Kettle Row and the adjoining land. This property was entailed under Abraham II's Will to pass to Samuel's eldest son Samuel II, although he purported to give to Deborah the 'summer house' behind Dale House with an acre of land. This may have been to ensure that she had a house of her own, because her continued residence at Sunniside was perhaps uncertain after his death. The rest of his property, after legacies, etc, including his shares in the Company was placed on trust for Deborah and the children.

After Samuel's death the situation in the Company was highly unusual, if not unique, because all the partners were women, Mary Rathbone, Deborah, Rebecca and Sarah. They were assisted by Richard Dearman, but he was Agent-Manager and not a partner. This became known as the period of 'petticoat government', and was marked by a revival in the fortunes of the Company.

At the time the omens were not particularly encouraging because during 1795 and 1796, Britain was afflicted by a shortage of food leading to high prices and great distress.

A meeting was held at the Tontine Inn, Ironbridge, at which a subscription was raised which led to a scheme supported by all the leading companies, under which rice and corn was purchased in bulk and sold to the work people at three-quarters of the cost price.[45] In 1797 a large sum of money was subscribed to enable the Shrewsbury Bank to continue in business.[45] Despite these difficulties visitors continued to come to see the Iron Bridge, including, on 12 August 1796, the Prince and Princess of Orange.[46]

At this time of depression, it was another disaster which turned the fortunes of the Company for the better. In 1795 a very high flood occurred in the River Severn, which had the effect of carrying away or severely damaging all the bridges in Shropshire except the Iron Bridge. Thomas Telford, who was County Surveyor of Shropshire, was commissioned to design a new bridge at Buildwas two miles upstream from the Iron Bridge. He designed it as a cast-iron bridge and as he subsequently reported "*it was executed in a masterly fashion by the Coalbrookdale Company, and finished in 1796*".[47] Fifteen years had passed since the building of the

Buildwas Bridge, built 1796.

Thomas Telford.
The first County Surveyor
of Shropshire.

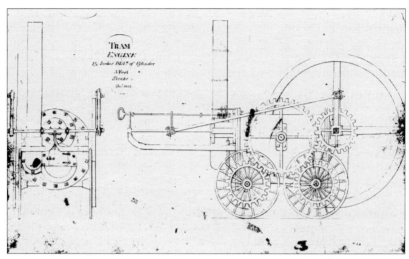

The world's first steam railway locomotive, designed by Richard Trevithick and built at Coalbrookdale in 1802.

COURTESY OF THE SCIENCE MUSEUM

Ketley Hall, Red Lees, Ketley. Originally a farmhouse, Ketley Hall was altered and enlarged in the late 18th century. Residence of Joseph Reynolds (son of Richard Reynolds) from 1793 to 1818.

Iron Bridge, and no previous attempts had been made to emulate the experiment, but after the building of the Buildwas Bridge the Company developed a considerable trade in heavy engineering. This led to the rebuilding of the No.2 Furnace at Horsehay in 1799 and subsequently to the construction of a third Furnace in 1805. *(48)*

It was the Company's immense reputation which drew another great engineer, Richard Trevithick, to Coalbrookdale in 1796. Trevithick was developing his ideas for applying a high pressure steam engine to the propulsion of a road carriage. On Christmas Eve 1801, a road trial was carried out at Camborne and in the following year he was back at Coalbrookdale. In August of that year he wrote *"The Dale Company have begun a carriage at their own cost for the railroads and are forcing it with all expedition". (49)* This became the world's first steam railway locomotive and was one of the greatest achievements of the Company throughout its long and distinguished existence. It was not just the Company's great reputation which produced these results, but also their willingness to foster, often at their own cost as in Trevithick's case, the latest experiments and advances in technology.

The same philosophy applied to the sister company of W Reynolds and Company at Ketley, which was very much concerned in the development of the steam engine in conjunction with Matthew Boulton and James Watt. Despite this involvement they supported a local man, Adam Heslop, in 1790, in developing an engine derived independently from the previous Newcomen engine.

A patent was taken out in 1790 and a number of these engines were built in the Coalfield, some even surviving into the present century. *(50)* Similarly, they supported the ideas of James Sadler who came to Ketley and took out a patent for a small engine in 1791. Again a number of Sadler's engines were built in and around the locality before Sadler left Coalbrookdale for Portsmouth dockyard. *(51)*

In 1793 Joseph Reynolds married Deborah Dearman, a niece of Richard Dearman. They went to live in a former farmhouse at Red Lees, Ketley, which was doubled in size and became known as Ketley Hill Hall or simply Ketley Hall. *(52)* Joseph Reynolds was already involved in the management of the Works and the following year, 1794, Richard Reynolds handed over his shares in the Company to his two sons, William and Joseph. When it separated from the Coalbrookdale Company in 1796/97 it was known as William Reynolds and Company. Increasingly, responsibility for Ketley started to move to Joseph while William was more and more involved in developing the canal system and Coalport.

In 1793 as the Shropshire Canal was nearing completion, an Act of Parliament was passed authorising the construction of the Shrewsbury

Canal to connect the Shropshire system to the County Town. Josiah Clowes was the engineer but on his death in 1795, Thomas Telford was appointed. When the need for an aqueduct at Longden-on-Tern became evident, Telford consulted William Reynolds and the result was the construction by the Company at Ketley of the Longden aqueduct in cast-iron, the world's first iron aqueduct. This led to the building of the Chirk aqueduct and the world famous aqueduct at Pontcysyllte on the Llangollen canal. *(53)*

The development of the new town at Coalport was absorbing more of William Reynolds' time, as well as his involvement in the Madeley Wood Company, which he had taken over from the Coalbrookdale Company in the big reconstruction of 1796. This prompted William Reynolds to move his home in 1800 from Bank House, Ketley, to The Tuckies on the south side of the River Severn opposite Coalport. *(54)* Shortly afterwards the partnership of the Madeley Wood Company was reconstituted with William Reynolds taking three-quarters of the shares and the remaining quarter going to his nephew, William Anstice. *(55)*

The last decade of the eighteenth century had seen exciting and sometimes tempestuous times. The Company had split into two, but the two separated companies had prospered and had continued to grow.

It might be thought that in the midst of all this activity the role of Richard Reynolds had diminished. This was not so. Although he had retired from active management in 1789 when he moved back to Dale House, he remained as ever a deeply influential figure.

There can be little doubt that he was very much involved in the negotiations leading to the reconstruction of the Company in 1796-97. Above all, he was the Lord of the Manor and as such was the landlord of the Coalbrookdale Company. He also lived next door to Richard Dearman, the Manager of the Company, who was resident at Rosehill. Clearly he retained a powerful stake in everything that was going on.

In his new role, however, he was able to take a wider interest in the community at large. Increasingly he became involved in benevolent and community activities. He shared with the Darby family a concern for the provision of housing and schools. Much of the housing that has survived to this day such as Carpenters Row and Charity Row in Coalbrookdale and Old Row in Horsehay date back to this period. Building leases of one-eighth of an acre of land for ninety-nine years at five shillings a year ground rent were arranged. Schools were built at Coalbrookdale, Ketley and Madeley. *(56)*

In 1788 he purchased Cawbrook (Stanley's) Farm, part of which had been sold out of the Manor in 1704. This followed litigation which had taken place in 1786/87 between the partners of the Coalbrookdale

Company and John Powys Stanley, the owner of Cawbrook Farm. The cause of the litigation was the re-building in 1783/84 of the Upper Forge on land which the Company considered was part of their lease, but which John Powys Stanley maintained was his. Judgment in the case went in favour of the Company and against Stanley. Within twelve months he had sold the whole of Cawbrook Farm to Richard Reynolds. [57] This, with the manorial land on the eastern flank of the Dale, consolidated his ownership of virtually all the land in Coalbrookdale, except Furnace Bank Farm at the head of the Dale, and the lands formerly known as Glazebrooks Coppice acquired by the Darbys and others earlier in the century. Richard Reynolds was, therefore, enabled to carry out extensive planting of woodlands. [58] What he did, established the wooded landscape of Coalbrookdale which has survived to the present day. In this landscaping he was much influenced by Shenstone's work at The Leasowes near Halesowen with which he was familiar. This led him to lay out walks through the woods on Lincoln Hill for the pleasure and benefit of the workmen. They were called 'Workmens' Walks' and were much frequented by the men and their families.

Having moved into Dale House in 1789, he purchased a strip of land at the rear of Dale House which enabled him to gain access to the house from the back. [59] In 1791 he took a surrender of land part of Spring Coppice granted to Richard Ford in 1763 so as to continue the development along the Lightmoor track initiated by Richard Ford and continued by Abraham Darby in 1779. [60]

After this spurt of activity, Richard Reynolds and Rebecca settled into an orderly existence at Dale House, frequently visiting Sunniside and the other family homes, and helping to entertain the many visitors to the area.

In 1791 he and Rebecca gave a home at Dale House to a young lady named Priscilla Hannah Gurney, a member of a Norfolk family of Quakers who were well known to the Darbys. Priscilla was born a Friend, but after the death of her father, her mother married Sir William Watson and for a time Priscilla entered into the fellowship of the Church of England. However, she felt herself drawn back to the Society of Friends and it was during this period that she accepted the offer of the Reynolds to make her home with them. She helped to fill the void in the family left when their daughter Hannah Mary Reynolds left to marry William Rathbone in 1786. She was given a suite of rooms at Dale House. She had her own maid and horse and carriage.

It was Priscilla's presence in Coalbrookdale that led to the visit of her cousin, Elizabeth Gurney, in 1798. Later that cousin was to become better known as Elizabeth Fry, but at the time of her visit to Coalbrookdale she was much troubled about the direction her life was to take. The 4th of

101

September 1798 was to be the turning point in her life. She records in her journal that after tea, she and Priscilla, accompanied by Richard Reynolds, went over to the Darbys at Sunniside. After a pleasant evening together, Deborah Darby spoke as a minister and addressed part of her talk to Elizabeth whom she called to be '*a light to the blind, speech to the dumb and feet to the lame*". *(60a)* This had a most powerful effect on Elizabeth, for as she said in her journal – "*Here I am now in Cousin Prissy's little room – never to forget this day while life is in my body. I know now what the mountain is I have to climb. I am to be a Quaker.*" Time and again throughout her life Elizabeth Fry was to speak of those vital days in Coalbrookdale, which launched her on her task of reform and reconciliation which made her into the great Quaker philanthropist that she was to become.

This event could perhaps only have occurred against the background of the deeply religious beliefs which characterised the life of the Darby and Reynolds families as the eighteenth century was nearing its close. Richard Reynolds himself was an immensely wealthy man, but he followed a plain and frugal lifestyle without adornment or any sense of pretension, and he diligently took part in the Meetings of the Society. Sadly his long residence in the locality was soon to come to an end. In March 1803 a bout of influenza spread through Coalbrookdale, and Mary Rathbone and Richard and Rebecca Reynolds were all affected by it. At the beginning of April Rebecca died of the illness, leaving Richard and the family devastated. *(61)* Two months later Richard suffered another crippling blow in the death of his son William Reynolds, at The Tuckies on 10 June 1803. *(62)*

William was only forty-five years of age and his death was a dreadful loss, not only personally, but to the future of the whole Coalfield. He was virtually the only one of the Shropshire ironmasters who applied science to the development of industry. He was the peer of all the leading industrialists of the age, and would undoubtedly have continued to make his mark.

With the loss of his wife and of his son in such a short space of time, Richard Reynolds' thoughts turned away from Coalbrookdale and back to his home town of Bristol. He left the Dale on 14 February 1804, having lived in the Dale or in Ketley for nearly fifty years. He moved to a house he owned in James's Square, Bristol, accompanied by his cousin Sarah Allen, who had been housekeeping for him since Rebecca's death. *(63)* Priscilla Hannah Gurney left a month later to live in Bath.

Richard Reynolds lived on in Bristol for another twelve years. He died in 1816, having made a Will under which all his property, after legacies, were devised to his daughter Hannah Mary Rathbone and his son Joseph Reynolds equally as tenants in common. *(64)* In 1818 Hannah Mary and

Joseph agreed to partition the property so that Hannah Mary became the absolute owner of Reynolds' properties in Somerset and Joseph Reynolds became the absolute owner of the Manor of Madeley together with Cawbrook (Stanley's) Farm in Coalbrookdale.[(65)]

In the same year, 1818, Joseph Reynolds relinquished control of Reynolds & Company and the Ketley Ironworks. He and his wife Deborah left their home at Ketley Hall, and moved to Bristol. He and his family remained as Lords of the Manor for the rest of the century, but the lease to the Coalbrookdale Company was finally bought out by the then partners in 1845.[(66)] Joseph Reynolds lacked the inventive flair of his half-brother William, and the contribution of the Reynolds family to the Coalbrookdale story effectively ended with the death of William Reynolds in 1803 and the departure of his father Richard Reynolds from the Dale in 1804.

NOTES – CHAPTER VII

1. *Abiah*, p.212. Abraham III and Rebecca had three children by 1780 – Abraham born 1778, Ann born 1779 and Mary born 1780. Abraham the eldest died of Scarlet Fever in 1788 at Sunniside where he had been sent from The Haye to attend school. Ann grew to adult years and married Barnard Dickinson who managed the Works from 1810 to 1830. Mary died in 1801 aged twenty-one years.

2. Richard Reynolds had three surviving children – William Reynolds, born 1758 and Hannah Mary, born 1761, were the children of Richard's first marriage to Hannah (Darby) Abraham II's daughter. Joseph Reynolds (born 1768) was the child of Richard's second marriage to Rebecca (Gulson). There had been two other sons of this second marriage – Richard, born 1765 and Michael, born 1766, but these died in infancy.

3. The family tree of the Rathbones is as follows:

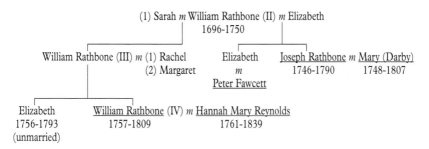

103

4. The family tree of the Reynolds is as follows:

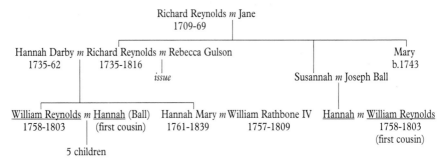

Richard Reynolds *m* Jane
1709-69

Hannah Darby *m* Richard Reynolds *m* Rebecca Gulson
1735-62   1735-1816
issue

Mary
b.1743

Susannah *m* Joseph Ball

William Reynolds *m* Hannah (Ball)   Hannah Mary *m* William Rathbone IV   Hannah *m* William Reynolds
1758-1803   (first cousin)   1761-1839   1757-1809   1758-1803
(first cousin)

5 children

5. William Rathbone IV and Hannah Mary had eight children. In 1804 William published a *"Narrative of Events that have recently taken place in Ireland"*. This led to him being disowned by Irish Friends. His descendants became well-known Unitarians.

6. *Deborah*, p.36.

7. *Deborah*, p.31.

8. *Deborah*, pp.52-53.

9. *Deborah*, p.63.

10. *Deborah*, p. 50 and 51.

11. John Wesley was at Madeley in 1771, 73, 74, 79 and 89.

12. The chapel was enlarged in 1789 and rebuilt in 1828. See VCH Vol XI (Telford) p.69.

13. *Abiah*, p.228. Also *Trinder, Industrial Revolution in Shropshire*, pp.370-371.

14. Raistrick, p.200. After Richard Reynolds' death, the shares were inherited by Hannah Mary Rathbone in whose family they remained until 1950 when the Bridge was handed over to Shropshire County Council, who in 1998 transferred ownership to Telford & Wrekin Council. The Bridge is designated as an ancient monument under the guardianship of English Heritage.

15. S.R.O 1987/33/1.

16. Trinder, *Industrial Revolution in Shropshire*, p.67.

17. In 1797 the Donnington Wood Furnaces were conveyed by William Reynolds to John Bishton, and shortly afterwards they became part of the Lilleshall Company.

18. See Trinder, *Industrial Revolution in Shropshire*, pp.126-142 and Raistrick, pp.182-192.

19. V.C.H Vol XI (Telford), pp.46-47.

20. *Deborah*, p.86. *Abiah*, p.239.

21. *Abiah*, p.241.

22. The children were Ann, Mary, Francis, Joseph, Hannah and Richard. Of these, Ann, Francis, Hannah and Richard lived to adult years.

23. S.R.O 1487/34/1. It also seems probable that the schoolroom had been moved elsewhere in the Dale during the 1780s, possibly to the enlarged Meeting House. There is, however, no record of this.

24. Raistrick, p.153.

25. See S.R.O 1681/138/4.

26. See S.R.O 1987/33/1.

27. *Abiah*, p.243. S.R.O 1987/33/1.

28. *Abiah*, p.244.

29. Raistrick, p.210.

30. Raistrick, pp.210-11.

31. The property known as Rosehill today is not the same as the property, No 43, Darby Road, which originally bore that name. The property now known as Rosehill was formerly known as The Grange, built by Richard Ford I in 1738 (see S.R.O 1681/179/3). It was acquired by Abraham Darby II in 1760 after the bankruptcy of Richard Ford II. Previous to that bankruptcy it had been occupied by Abraham Ford and his wife Jane. After 1760 it was let to Benjamin Wright who was the surgeon for Coalbrookdale until his death in 1794. In 1791 he purchased land from the Earl of Craven and built Green Bank Farm House. It was then that Rosehill was leased to the Coalbrookdale Company for occupation by Richard Dearman.

32. Raistrick, pp.211-12.

33. Raistrick, p.215. The partnership between Joseph Rathbone, Abraham III, Samuel Darby, William Reynolds and Hannah Mary Rathbone was dissolved in September 1794. See S.R.O 1681/179/2.

34. Raistrick, p.216.

35. Formalised in Articles of Partnership dated 1 February 1798, S.R.O 1987/33/2.

36. For a detailed summary see Raistrick, p.312. Also see the trust deed relating to Samuel Darby's shares S.R.O 1987/33/1.

37. S.R.O 1987/33/1 – 37, 37A, S.R.O 1681/138/4 dated June 1794.

37a S.R.O 1681/138/4 dated June 1794.

38. S.R.O 1681/179/2.

39. For a more detailed summary see Raistrick, pp.216-218.

40. Raistrick, p.218.

41. Trinder, *Industrial Revolution in Shropshire*, p.72.

42. Abiah made her Will on 14 March 1782. See Abiah P.217/8.

43. For a full description of Deborah's memorable visit to America see *Deborah*, pp.127-216.

44. *Deborah*, pp.220-22.

45. Raistrick, p.221.

46. Raistrick, p.222. The visit of the Prince and Princess of Orange is graphically depicted in the model of the Ironbridge Gorge on display in the Museum of the Gorge at the Wharfage, Ironbridge, (Ironbridge Gorge Museum Trust).
47. Raistrick, p.203.
48. Raistrick, p.121-23.
49. Raistrick, p.164 and p.315.
50. Raistrick, pp.156-57. Adam Heslop left Ketley and set up his own foundry near Whitehaven, Cumberland, where he built at least fourteen of his engines.
51. Raistrick, pp.159-59.
52. *Historic Buildings in Telford* No 20, published by Telford Development Corporation (refer to IGMT).
53. Although Thomas Telford adapted the design of the Longden-on-Tern Aqueduct to Chirk and Pontcysllte, the work was undertaken by William Hazeldine & Company.
54. *Historic Buildings in Telford* No 21, published by Telford Development Corporation (refer to IGMT).
55. Trinder, *Industrial Revolution in Shropshire*, p.70.
56. The location of the school in Coalbrookdale is not at present known but see VCH Vol XI Telford, p.72 Note 74. Also S.R.O 2280/6/95.
57. S.R.O 1987/30/2. Also see author's report to IGMT relating to Chancery Proceedings in 1786/87 between Joseph Rathbone, Abraham Darby, Samuel Darby, Sarah Darby and William Reynolds (partners in the Company of Rathbone and Company, otherwise known as the Coalbrookdale Company) and John Powys Stanley – Public Record Office Ref C12/1693/17.
58. See *Abiah*, p.250 – 30 March 1793.
59. S.R.O 1681/138/1-2 and see also 1681/138/3.
60. Purchase by Richard Ford from Smitheman and Giffard of one acre of land part of Spring Coppice (later known as Dale Coppice) in 1763 (S.R.O 1681/139/5). Lease of two acres of land in 1779 to John Rose by Abraham Darby (S.R.O 1987/38/1). Sale of piece of land to Richard Dayus by Richard Reynolds in 1783 (S.R.O 1681/131/15). Surrender of land forming part of Spring Coppice by Richard Ford to Richard Reynolds in 1791 (S.R.O 1681/131/19 see S.R.O 1681/139/5).
60a *Deborah*, p.250.
61. *Deborah*, p.289.
62. Raistrick, p.227.
63. *Deborah*, p.297.
64. Will of Richard Reynolds dated 9 May 1816. S.R.O 1987/30/1.
65. Abstract of Title S.R.O 1987/30/2.
66. S.R.O 1681/138/10. The partners in 1845 were Francis, Abraham and Alfred Darby.

CHAPTER VIII

The Napoleonic Years
Edmund Darby, Barnard Dickinson
and Francis Darby

THE TURN OF the century saw the Coalbrookdale Company in a prosperous state. Britain had been at war with France since 1793, and although the Company took no part in the armaments trade, they nevertheless shared in the prosperity which resulted from the mobilisation of the iron industry. When peace was signed at Amiens in 1802, Quaker families were overjoyed. In common with everybody else they believed that the great war was ended. Their joy was short lived however, because just over a year later the bitter conflict was resumed and was to last for another eleven years until Waterloo in 1815. These were to be eventful years for the family and the Company.

Family affairs were still dominated by the household at Sunniside. The situation was described in a letter written many years later in 1879 by Matilda Darby.[1] Referring to Sunniside she said "*three old ladies lived there together. Deborah Darby, Mary Rathbone, both widows and Aunt Sarah Darby, who seems to have been the Mistress of the House with Susannah to guide them all.*"[2] These were the old guard of the family, and with Rebecca Darby, widow of Abraham III who lived close by at the White House, they were the partners in the Company.

However, although the older generation still had a role to play, the future lay with the rising members of the next generation. These comprised the children of Abraham III and his brother Samuel. When Abraham III died in 1789 he was succeeded by six children, Ann, Mary, Francis, Joseph, Hannah and Richard. Of these, Mary died aged twenty-one in 1801 and Joseph died aged thirteen years in 1798. There were, therefore, four children who survived to take an active role in the Company during the next half century or so.[3]

107

Abraham III's brother Samuel died in 1796, leaving Deborah as his widow with two surviving children, Samuel and Edmund.[4] In the 1790s Samuel and Edmund were at Thomas Huntley's school, Hillside Academy in Burford, Oxfordshire, where they were joined by Francis and Joseph (Abraham III's sons) who were slightly younger.[5] Abraham III's daughters Ann and Hannah were at school in York.

Samuel and Edmund were totally different characters. Samuel II seemingly rebelled against his strict Quaker upbringing whilst Edmund followed the family traditions and conformed to the Darby pattern.

In 1798 after Samuel I's death, an agreement was entered into between Rebecca Darby, Mary Rathbone and Sarah Darby, under which the partnership continued as before with four shares, but with Mary Rathbone and Sarah also acting as trustees for Samuel I's share.[6] This was in anticipation that Samuel's share would be inherited by his two sons Samuel II and Edmund when they came of age in 1800 and 1803 respectively.

As far as Samuel II was concerned things started to go wrong almost immediately. In 1799 Deborah his mother expressed herself worried "*by the kind of companionship he was keeping and increasing desertion of Friends*".[7] This reached a climax in 1801 when a testimony against him was presented at the New Dale Meeting. He was excluded from the Society, a decision which his mother had to accept with immense anguish.[8] He was then twenty-two years old and entered into trade as a common carrier and started to borrow considerable sums against his inheritance from Mary Rathbone, leading to a writ being issued against him.[9] In 1803 he married Frances Williams of Welshpool and joined the Army.[10] It is difficult to comprehend how devastating this must have been for Deborah.

By way of compensation, the career of Edmund her younger son was following a much more amenable course. He had entered the Works after leaving school to the extent that by 1803 he was taking on an articled clerk '*to manage forges, mills, furnaces and foundries, and to keep accounts, yield books and day books*".[11] He had himself been trained by Richard Dearman and was clearly the rising star in the Darby firmament. He had inherited the family's tradition of energy and flair.

He had been present in 1801 when flood water caused an explosion of the Old (Upper) Furnace at Coalbrookdale.[12] This had to be rebuilt and it is probable that the adjacent "snapper" furnace was built while the main furnace was out of action.[13] This was probably part of the process of reconstruction at Coalbrookdale and at Horsehay which Richard Dearman as Agent Manager was planning at this period and in which Edmund participated .

South west prospect of Coalbrookdale (Vivares, 1758).

Lucy Darby (née Burlingham). Married Edmund Darby in 1803, widowed in 1810. Died at Ebbw Vale in 1870 and buried at Melksham, Wiltshire, next to her husband.

He came of age in 1803 and he then married Lucy Burlingham of Worcester.[14] She was the daughter of John Burlingham who was one of the leading master glovers of Worcester. He was a major employer of labour in the city.[15] He was also a customer of the Coalbrookdale Company[16] but Edmund seems to have become acquainted with the family mainly through Quaker Meetings.[17] Lucy was a very suitable and attractive spouse. She had beautiful deep blue eyes with long dark eye lashes, which were inherited through subsequent generations of the family.[18] Edmund and Lucy took up residence in Sunniside,[19] but this was intended to be a temporary arrangement, because in July 1803 Edmund was granted a ninety-nine year lease of five acres of the upper land behind Dale House, known as the Whales Back. He covenanted to build "one or more good and substantial dwellinghouses" at a cost of £2,000, within two years.[20]

This was clearly to be a prestige dwelling comparable to Sunniside and was possibly to be sited on the crown of the hill in the vicinity of or on the site of the tower shown in the 1758 engraving of South West Prospect of Coalbrookdale by Vivares (see Illustration). Foundations were laid but before further progress could be made, Edmund's plans were changed by the death of Richard Dearman in 1804. This meant that Edmund took over from Richard Dearman as Manager of the Works and he and Lucy moved into Dale House, recently vacated by Richard Reynolds. Edmund was released from his covenant to build the new house.[21]

The Company was in good shape when Edmund took over. Richard Dearman had managed the enterprise very well. He had guided the partnership through the complicated reconstruction of the 1790s which resulted in the splitting of its extensive operations into two manageable companies; he had steered the Company through a difficult financial period and had supervised its recovery to full order books; he had survived the setback caused by the explosion and loss of the Old Furnace in Coalbrookdale, and had set in train a programme of reconstruction; above all, he had throughout safeguarded the Company's reputation for innovation and excellence.

Edmund continued Richard Dearman's programme of reconstruction, and a third furnace was built at Horsehay in 1805.[22] The railway which had been built down Jiggers Bank in the late 1770s was abandoned in 1802, the rails removed for scrap and it was replaced by a new railway alongside the line of the canal to Brierly Hill above Coalbrookdale.[23]

The production of the Works during this period was astonishingly diverse. The Company had become one of the country's leading suppliers of steam engines including some designed by Richard Trevithick who had maintained his contact with Coalbrookdale.

An important innovation in the architectural use of cast-iron was the glass and iron roof installed in the picture gallery at Attingham Park near Shrewsbury during the enlargement of the Hall by John Nash in 1805-7. [24] This type of large-scale work was in addition to the production of a wide range of household goods.

While all this activity was going on it became necessary to deal with the lease of the Works which had been renegotiated with Richard Reynolds in 1794 and was due to expire in 1807. A new lease was, therefore, granted by Richard Reynolds in 1805 for a further period of twenty-one years. [25] The rent which had been dramatically reduced in 1794 was modestly increased.

With the Company once again in a sound condition, the thoughts of the family turned to the enlargement of their land holdings. Since Abraham II, little had been done to consolidate the Sunniside estate. After the abortive attempts by Abraham III to acquire the Manor of Madeley, it was Richard Reynolds who took over the acquisition of land, notably the purchase of the adjoining Stanley's Farm in 1788. The next big purchase to come on the market was the sale by auction at the Talbot Inn in Coalbrookdale of the Meadow and Strethill farms in May 1803. These two farms, comprising one hundred and sixty-seven acres of land lay to the west of Sunniside and stretched all the way down to the River Severn. They were outside the Manor of Madeley, although within the Parish. The bulk of the property, north of the Leighton turnpike road, consisting of some one hundred and fifty-one acres was purchased by Mary Rathbone, [26] while an eight acre field known as Upper Leesow near to Sunniside was purchased by Rebecca Darby, she being already the tenant of that field. [27]

These major acquisitions were accompanied by a series of smaller acquisitions by Sarah Darby of various properties in the Dale, which seemed to be part of a strategy to upgrade the properties in the upper part of the Dale. They were disposed of subsequently by her Will in 1821 and combined with a further series of acquisitions later by Frances Darby, led to a substantial expansion and consolidation of the family's property holdings, by the middle of the century.

In the meantime, Edmund was proceeding with his plans to improve the Works. He designed a new mill for Horsehay in 1806 [28] and embarked on the rebuilding of the forge furnaces. [29]

A considerable cloud appeared on the horizon that year when the government threatened to impose a tax on pig iron. Edmund became active with ironmasters in various parts of the country in opposition to this tax. [29] Competition within the iron industry was becoming intense. The Shropshire Coalfield was losing its leadership of the industry to the larger and increasingly more competitive concentrations of the industry in the Black Country and South Wales. Even within the Shropshire Coalfield, the pattern had changed. Coalbrookdale was no longer the largest iron-works. That title had been taken by the Old Park ironworks which had been established by Thomas Botfield, a local Dawley man who had established three furnaces at Old Park, Dawley in 1790.[30] Also in the northern part of the Coalfield, the old partnership of the Marquess of Stafford & Company had become the Lilleshall Company which soon started to expand and develop its operations.

Closer to home, however, the health of Mary Rathbone had deteriorated and she died at Sunniside on 17 March 1807, aged fifty-nine years. There were no children of her marriage to Joseph Rathbone. She left a Will dated 22 February 1805 and a codicil dated 7 November 1806. Under that Will and codicil she left Strethill Farm to Edmund for life and then to his son Abraham (IV)[31] and she divided her quarter share of the partnership between (a) Sarah Darby, (b) the children of her brother Abraham III and (c) Edmund Darby with provision for an annuity to be paid to Edmund's brother Samuel for life and thereafter to his children. She also released Samuel from his outstanding debts to her.[32]

This meant that the former quarter shares in the partnership became effectively third shares, but spread between a great number of individual holdings. A new partnership agreement was entered into on 10 August 1807. This created a co-partnership of seven hundred and twenty shares, with two hundred and forty allocated to Sarah Darby, two hundred and forty allocated to Edmund and Samuel, and the other two hundred and forty split between Rebecca and her children.[33] Sarah became the largest single shareholder and this reinforced her position as matriarch and guiding light of the family's affairs.

Sarah was now the last surviving child of Abraham II and Abiah who had built Sunniside in 1750/51. She had been born there. She was still living there accompanied by Deborah, widow of Samuel Darby[34] and by Susannah Appleby. Some three years previously in 1804, Francis Darby, eldest son of Abraham III had come of age and under the terms of his grandfather's Will he had inherited Sunniside and the Sunniside estate.

He could, therefore, have claimed possession of the property. There is no evidence that he made any attempt to do so, or even wished to do so. He was comfortably installed in the nearby White House and he was probably content to allow the formidable Sarah to continue living at Sunniside. He had now entered the Works and was learning the business in partnership with his cousin Edmund.

Other family affairs were, however, pressing. Samuel II had a violent nose bleed in November 1807 and his mother Deborah, who had been visiting Hay-on-Wye as part of her never-ending programme of travels, hastened to his side. Samuel was living at Berwick, Shrewsbury with his wife Frances, having settled down to family life after his tempestuous youth. Although he recovered temporarily, Deborah described him in her journal as *"My Beloved child who appears in a declining state of health"*. He died in the following February and was brought back to Dale House for burial. *(35)* At the end, despite having been excluded from the Society of Friends, there was a measure of reconciliation. He left a widow with one child Frances Anna (b.1806) and another child Mary born in 1807 after his death. The first child died in 1811 and it was Mary who grew to adulthood and inherited Samuel's property. *(36)*

On a much happier note, the other Darby cousins, the children of Abraham III were beginning to get married. First was the eldest child, Ann who married Barnard Dickinson on 9 April 1805. *(37)* Barnard Dickinson's family were Quakers who came from Beverley in Yorkshire. He was related to Deborah Darby. After attending school in York he took up a career in farming. He came to The Haye in 1804 as a farmer and married Ann Darby the following year. The property had been inherited by Francis Darby in 1804 and it seems likely that he had some rooms there while his sister and her husband were in occupation.

Francis Darby himself was the next to be married. *(38)* He had met Hannah Grant of Leighton Buzzard, Bedfordshire. Hannah came from an important Quaker family and was the daughter of John and Hannah Grant whose family was known to Abiah in the previous century. *(39)* They were married at Leighton Buzzard on 16 June 1808 and then they set up home at the White House and it seems likely that this was when Francis built a large wing on the eastern side of the White House. In the same month that he married Hannah, Francis gave some land close to the Burial Ground for the building of a new Meeting House. *(40)* The money for the building was donated by Richard Reynolds, and it replaced the old Meeting House originally built by Richard Ford at the southern end of Tea Kettle Row and expanded by Abiah in 1764 with funds provided in the Will of Abraham II.

Nearby at Sunniside, Sarah had built a grotto in the garden. This seemed consistent with the policy she was pursuing of up-grading the locality, and seemed to reflect echoes of the Goldney days when Thomas Goldney built a famous grotto at Clifton. *(41)*

While this was going on, Deborah's health started to deteriorate. During one of her frequent itineraries, this time in Bath, she was taken ill in April 1809. Although she seemed to recover by the summer, she

Francis Darby.

Hannah Darby (née Grant).

The Meeting House, Coalbrookdale. Built in 1808, demolished in the 1960s.

Barnard Dickinson.

weakened during the autumn. She became increasingly ill and in the New Year of 1810 she was confined to bed. Towards the end she was attended continuously by her son Edmund and his wife Lucy. She died in February 1810. She had lived a memorable life and was much mourned. She was described as being of a *"naturally sweet and amiable temper"* with a *"fine presence that never failed to keep hold of her audience."* She was said to be *"comly (sic) in person and active in ministry."* She had overcome the tragedy of her early marriage when her husband Samuel I had been afflicted by mental trouble and had devoted the rest of her life to her commitment to the ministry. Later she had suffered the immense indignity of her eldest son's behaviour and exclusion from the Society of Friends, but this was compensated by the exemplary behaviour of her younger son Edmund. She was fifty-six years of age.

Meanwhile Edmund had been following a policy of expansion and improvement in the Works. In 1809 he had installed a new rolling mill at Horsehay and had built two new furnaces at Dawley Castle which were blown in, in 1810. *(42)* He was, however, beginning to become concerned about the falling prices of iron. The price war initiated by Richard Crawshay of the Cyfarthfa Works in South Wales was showing itself in the Company's markets in Bristol and elsewhere.

A devastating act of fate intervened, however, in the summer of 1810, a matter of six months or so after the death of Deborah, when Edmund himself died suddenly of food poisoning while staying with his aunt at Melksham in Wiltshire. He was only twenty-eight years old. His widow Lucy, also twenty-eight was left with three children, Abraham IV, Alfred and Mary (named after Mary Rathbone). A fourth child, Deborah, was born after Edmund's death. *(43)*

Edmund's death was a truly savage blow not only to the family but also to the Company. It compared in its consequences with the early death of William Reynolds, just seven years earlier in 1803. He was virtually irreplaceable. He had proved himself to be the rising star of his generation and his loss at such a young age was incalculable.

What happened next is difficult to comprehend. Francis Darby was already involved in the Works and would by Darby traditions have taken over the management of the Works. In fact it was Barnard Dickinson who was chosen to undertake the superintendence of the operations.

Although married to Ann Darby, the oldest of the children of Abraham III, he nevertheless had no experience of the iron industry . He was a farmer and had been trained as such. The Dickinsons held forty-three shares, the same as Francis. It may, therefore, have been a decision of Sarah Darby who held two hundred and forty shares, or it may have been that Francis was disinclined to take on the management as he was in the

117

process of taking on the management of the Sunniside estate. Another possibility lies in the temperament of Francis. In the years to come he was to demonstrate a certain volatility of character and it is possible that this was already evident in 1810.

Whatever the reason, it was Barnard Dickinson who took over the responsibility for the Works, assisted by Francis Darby, and occupied Dale House. He took over at a difficult time. The war time economy was slowing down and the price war with the South Wales ironworks was intensifying year by year. It became increasingly difficult to maintain profitability and to sustain the level of investment needed to secure the future. Even so Barnard Dickinson seems to have done well in the circumstances and maintained a reasonably high level of output.

Within the family the next important event was the marriage of Richard Darby, youngest son of Abraham III and Rebecca. He had come of age in 1809. He was described at the time as being of "*the City of Bristol, wholesale ironmonger*".[44] Possibly he was in Bristol maintaining the Company's commercial connections, bearing in mind that Richard Reynolds, who had moved to Bristol in 1804, was by then quite elderly. In 1811 he married Maria Sorton of a Quaker family of Cheshire and presumably then returned to Coalbrookdale.[45] He was a shareholder in the Company and held the same number of shares as Francis and his sisters. Although he became involved in the affairs of the Company from time to time, he was not so active in management as Francis. He entered public life and took an active role in local politics. He followed the Whig persuasion unlike his brother Francis who was a Tory.[46] Above all, he had a life-long interest in the abolition of slavery and spent a great deal of time and effort on this cause as well as the Anti Corn Law league.[47]

Soon after the wedding of Richard and Maria, a question arose about the future of the land in Dawley on which the Horsehay Works and farm and some of the coal mines were situate. The land was owned by Mr Robert Slaney, Lord of the Manor, and was subject to two leases to the Company. Mr Slaney offered to sell the land, and after some protracted negotiations the Horsehay estate was purchased by Sarah Darby and leased back to the Company.[48]

At this time, the long Napoleonic Wars came to an end with the Battle of Waterloo in 1815, and the relative prosperity in the iron industry came to a sudden halt. There followed a period of extreme depression which lasted from 1815 until at least 1822. In 1816 there were twenty-four furnaces out of blast in Shropshire and only ten still making iron. That year Joseph Reynolds closed down and dismantled the Ketley furnaces.[49]

In 1818 the two furnaces in Coalbrookdale itself, the Old Furnace dating back to the seventeenth century and the 'New' Furnace built by

Abraham I in 1715, were blown out and thereafter no iron was ever again smelted in the Dale – a sad end, although it has to be acknowledged that the furnaces were small and the installations in Coalbrookdale had become old-fashioned and neglected. From 1818 onwards Coalbrookdale developed solely as a foundry using pig iron smelted elsewhere. The Company's furnaces at Horsehay and Dawley Castle continued in production throughout this difficult time.

Remarkably, in 1816 the parts for a footbridge over the River Liffey in Dublin were cast in the Dale and the following year a one hundred and twenty foot bridge over the Irwell in Salford was constructed. In 1820 the massive iron columns of the Macclesfield bridge over the Regent's Canal at Regents Park in London were cast in the Dale. Even so, the effects of recession had a devastating effect on the locality and social unrest was marked, leading eventually to the calling out of the Yeomanry. [50]

In this trying and difficult context, matters were made worse by an incident involving Francis Darby which occurred in the autumn of 1817. He had visited Park Gate[51] where he bathed in the sea and returned home very ill. It was thought his brain was affected, for which he was blooded. He was removed by his parents-in-law to Leighton Buzzard where he was installed in Linslade House[52] a nearby country house where he stayed for a year. He was diagnosed as having suffered a brain haemorrhage, and although he made a full recovery, the episode may have affected his position in the Company. During his absence the management was left entirely in the hands of Barnard Dickinson.

In the story of the Darby family, misfortune and joy often seemed to go hand in hand, and Francis' discomfiture was followed by much better news when the wedding took place of Hannah, his sister. In October 1818 she married William Tothill, the younger, merchant of Bristol and took up residence in that City. William Tothill was to become a distinguished business man in Bristol. He was one of the founders of the Great Western Railway and was one of the committee of four men who appointed Isambard Kingdom Brunel as Engineer of the Railway. He became the first Secretary of the Bristol Committee of the Railway. [53] And so finally, all the surviving children of Abraham III and Rebecca were married and settled down.

Ann   -   married Barnard Dickinson in 1805
Francis -   married Hannah Grant in 1808
Richard -   married Maria Sorton in 1811
Hannah   -   married William Tothill in 1818

To a greater or lesser degree, these four couples, together with the children of Edmund Darby, were to control the fortunes of the Coalbrookdale Company during the next thirty to forty years.

NOTES – CHAPTER VIII

1. Matilda Darby was the elder daughter of Francis Darby, eldest son of Abraham III. Matilda Darby married her cousin Abraham IV, the elder son of Edmund Darby, the younger son of Samuel Darby, brother of Abraham III.

2. Deborah Darby was the widow of Samuel Darby I. Mary Rathbone was the daughter of Abraham II, left a widow by the death in 1790 of Joseph Rathbone. Sarah Darby was the youngest (unmarried) daughter of Abraham II. All three were partners in the Coalbrookdale Company together with Rebecca Darby, widow of Abraham III who probably lived close by at The White House. Susannah Appleby was the companion of Sarah Darby, and she had come to live at Sunniside after the collapse of the Southwark foundry in 1779.

3. There were seven children of Abraham III and Rebecca:
   Abraham (1778-88) died of Scarlet Fever aged 10
   Ann (1779-1840) married Barnard Dickinson in 1805
   Mary (1780-1801) died 1801 aged 21
   Francis (1783-1850) married Hannah Grant in 1808
   Joseph (1785-c1798) died in c1798 (see S.R.O 1987/58/55)
   Hannah (1786-1859) married William Tothill in 1818
   Richard (1788-1860) married Maria Sorton in 1811.

4. There were 4 children born to Samuel and Deborah Darby
   Abraham (1777-1778)
   Samuel (1779-1808) married Frances Williams 1803
   Hannah (1780 lived 12 hours)
   Edmund (1782-1810) married Lucy Burlingham 1803
   Only Samuel and Edmund survived to adult years.

5. Thomas Huntley's wife was well-known for her excellent baking. It is said that she sold biscuits to travellers on the coaches passing the school at the top end of Burford, where they had to stop to put on the drag before descending the long steep hill. The next generation of Huntleys became involved in the making of biscuits commercially, and with the Palmers founded the famous firm of Huntley & Palmer.

6. S.R.O 1987/33/2.

7. *Deborah*, p.254.

8. *Deborah*, p.276.

9. See S.R.O 1987/33/2.

10. *Deborah*, p.297.

11. Raistrick, p.228.

12. Raistrick, p.227. According to Randall, the historian of Madeley, the members of the Darby family were much more concerned about death or injury to the workmen than about the loss of the furnace (see Raistrick's account above).

13. Trinder: *Darbys of Coalbrookdale*, p.45.

14. *Deborah*, p.290.

15. See *Deborah*, p.362. When George III came to Worcester, John Burlingham was deputed on behalf of the glovers to present the king with some gloves. There were numerous subsequent occasions when he was received by George III.
16. Trinder, *Industrial Revolution in Shropshire*, pp166-167.
17. *Deborah*, p.264, 270 and 285.
18. There is a portrait of Lucy Darby as an elderly lady on display in Rosehill, Coalbrookdale.
19. See *Deborah*, p.296.
20. S.R.O 1987/6/1.
21. The 99 year lease of the Whales Back was assigned to Sarah Darby in 1810 (S.R.O 1987/6/2). It seems that she turfed over the foundations. (See letter 1879 from Matilda Darby to Adelaide Whitmore, Bwlch RSO, Breconshire.)
22. Raistrick pp 121-125.
23. The railway alongside the canal continued in existence until the 1820s when it was replaced by a new railway along the Lightmoor Valley. See Trinder, *Industrial Revolution in Shropshire*, p.136.
24. Trinder: *Darbys of Coalbrookdale*, p.44.
25. S.R.O 1681/138/6.
26. S.R.O 1987/15/3-4.
27. S.R.O 1987/3/23-24.
28. Raistrick p.239.
29. Raistrick p.233.
30. Trinder: *Industrial Revolution in Shropshire*, p.73.
31. S.R.O 1987/15/8 and 9.
32. Copy Will and codicil in possession of IGMT.
33. S.R.O 1681/181/35. The parties to the co-partnership were: 1. Sarah Darby. 2. Rebecca Darby. 3. Edmund Darby. 4. Samuel Darby. 5. Francis Darby. 6. Edmund and Francis as trustees of marriage settlement of Barnard Dickinson and Ann Darby. 7. Edmund and Francis as executors of Mary Rathbone. 8. Barnard Dickinson.

The allocation of shares was as follows:

(1)	Sarah Darby	240 shares	
(2) (a)	Edmund Darby	150	} 240 shares
(3) (b)	Samuel Darby	90	
(3) (a)	Rebecca Darby	68	
(b)	Rebecca Darby p.p. Hannah and Richard Darby	56	
(c)	Francis Darby	43	
(d)	Edmund and Francis as trustees of settlement of Barnard Dickinson and Ann Darby	28	240 shares
(e)	Barnard Dickinson	15	
(f)	Edmund and Francis as trustees for Hannah and Richard	30	
		720 shares	

34. It is possible that Deborah lived for a time in the summerhouse behind Dale House which was left to her in Samuel I's Will, (see S.R.O 1987/17/7-8) but it was subsequently occupied by her brother Robert Barnard and his wife Hannah who came to live in Coalbrookdale in 1806. See *Deborah*, p.316. Samuel, Deborah's eldest son was living with his wife and family at Berwick, Shrewsbury, while Edmund and his wife and family lived at Dale House.
35. *Deborah*, pp.324-327.
36. See S.R.O 1987/17/7-8.
37. Extract from Barnard Dickinson's journal. IGMT. *Deborah*, p.45.
38. S.R.O 1681/179/12.
39. *Deborah*, p.327.
40. S.R.O 1987/31/6.
41. The grotto at Sunniside was embowered in honeysuckle and had written over the entrance the following sentences:- "*Enter in Stranger, undismayed, as no bat or toad here lurks, and if thy breast of blameless thoughts approve thee, not unwelcome shalt thou tread my mansion. Here quietly meditate upon the past, the present and the future; what thou owes the Supreme Creator, and what is due to thy companions through this Vale of Tears! Oh Vale whose gloom is brightened by the Transcendent Crown of Glory held up to view, which those whose life is spent in virtuous deeds clearly behold through Faith, the Christian mirror.*"
42. See Raistrick, pp.235 and 245; also Trinder: *Industrial Revolution in Shropshire*, p.237.
43. There were 6 children of the marriage of Edmund and Lucy Darby:-
    Abraham IV born 30 March 1804
    Corbyn born 21 March 1805, died in infancy
    Samuel Maude born 13 May 1806 died 1807
    Alfred born 21 December 1807
    Mary born 21 December 1808
    Deborah born 12 October 1810.
44. S.R.O 1987/31/6.
45. It is not clear where Richard and Maria Sorton lived on their return to Coalbrookdale. It is assumed that they moved into Rosehill, which had been occupied by Richard Dearman until his death in 1804. Sarah Darby had taken a lease of the house for 21 years from October 1807 and may have made it available to Richard and Maria. This is certainly where they lived later. The balance of the lease was given to Richard by Sarah in her Will dated 1821. The freehold was purchased by Richard in the late 1820s, when the properties inherited by Samuel Darby II were sold under the marriage settlement of his only surviving daughter Mary to the Reverend Edward Pryce Owen of Wellington on 6 December 1825. Maria's mother, Ann Sorton made a Will in 1824 leaving £2,000 to her daughter for a home,

although she herself did not die until 1835. (S.R.O 1681/181/31). Rosehill was the home of the family for the rest of the century.

46. S.R.O 1987/56/6. See letter from Edward Edwards (surgeon) to Benjamin Edwards dated 17 January 1836, in which there is a reference to the Wenlock Council – "The Radicals have been beaten at Wenlock – Mr Anstice is the new Mayor". Richard Darby is named as one of the chosen councillors.

47. See Raistrick, p.294.

48. The property was disposed of by Sarah Darby's Will (1821) in three ways:
    (a) As to 69 acres, one individual moiety to Francis, Richard, Ann and Hannah, children of Abraham III.
    (b) As to the same 69 acres, the other individual moiety, to Abraham IV, Alfred, Mary and Deborah, the children of Edmund and Lucy Darby.
    (c) As to 52 acres to Barnard and Ann Dickinson for life with remainder to their children.

49. Raistrick, pp.238-239.

50. Trinder: *Industrial Revolution in Shropshire*, p.382.

51. It is not known where Park Gate was. There are two places named Parkgate at the coast. One is in Hampshire near to Hamble River, Southampton. The other is on the Wirral near Gayton Sands, and it seems probable that the latter was the Park Gate visited by Francis Darby.

52. See *Journal of Matilda Darby* Part VI, dated 16 June 1872 and headed "The Story of the Leighton Bank as well as I remember it". Francis' stay at Linslade House and the reason for it, were remembered later when John Grant his father-in-law, proposed to leave his share in the Leighton Bank to Francis. The partners in the Bank made clear that Francis was not acceptable on account of the Linslade incident.

53. *History of the Great Western Railway* by E J MacDermot. Vol I, Part I.

CHAPTER IX

Years of Decline and Subsequent Recovery

THE DECADE STARTING in 1820 marked a low period in the history of the Coalbrookdale Company. The severe depression which followed the end of the Napoleonic Wars continued unabated until at least 1822. The atmosphere was revolutionary. Reductions in wage levels resulted in widespread strikes. A strike in 1820 amongst colliers and ironworkers led to the calling out of several troops of Yeomanry. Arbitration resulted in restoration of the old wage levels and further disturbance was avoided. But not for long. In January 1821 wage reductions were again announced. Action was taken by colliers and ironworkers to close down the ironworks. The Company's works at Dawley Castle and Horsehay were shut down. Once again the Yeomanry were summoned and a confrontation took place at Old Park, Dawley, where some three thousand were gathered on the cinderhills. After the reading of the Riot Act, the Yeomanry opened fire leading to the death of two men and the wounding of several others. Two suspected ringleaders were arrested and were convicted at the Assizes in March 1821. One of them was executed, but the other was reprieved. [1]

Fortunately the iron trade recovered during 1822 and there was a period of relative prosperity until 1830. The overall picture was, however, depressing. A visit to Coalbrookdale in 1821 by an engineer, Joshua Field, appears to suggest little activity. [2] Even so the Company was able to keep going during these difficult years although its profitability was reduced. [3] But perhaps the most depressing feature of this period is that the Company lost the inspiration and flair which had distinguished its existence from its early beginnings through to the Napoleonic period. The loss of William Reynolds and Edmund Darby in 1803 and 1810 was finally having its effect. Their successors were not able to continue the Company's unparalleled record of innovation and imagination. For the time being they no longer led the technological development of the industry.

Within the family, the fourth generation had finally taken over and the influence of the previous generation was coming to an end. Richard Reynolds had died in Bristol in 1816 and his son, Joseph Reynolds, was now Lord of the Manor of Madeley and was the Company's Landlord.[4] From the family's point of view an even more significant event was the death in 1821 of Sarah Darby, the last surviving child of Abraham II.

She had been born at Sunniside in 1752 when it was newly built and lived there all her life. After the death of Abiah in 1794, she was the undisputed head of the family. She was a highly competent business-woman with a proven ability as a Director of the Company during the period of 'petticoat government'. She directed affairs from her room, where her desk was littered with papers and was described as "*not unlike a lawyer's office*".[5] In making her Will, her first concern was to safeguard the interests of Susannah Appleby, who had come to Coalbrookdale in 1782 and had lived at Sunniside, virtually as a member of the family since then. Sarah had this in mind when she bought back from the Cranage family, the piece of land and houses next to the Meeting House which Abraham II had sold to the Cranages in 1748.[6] She converted the houses into the fine house which she named The Chesnuts (sic). The property was left to Susannah Appleby for life but there was an understanding that it would also be occupied by Lucy Darby and her family. On Susannah's death in 1827 it passed to Abraham IV, Lucy's son. Susannah was also given £4200 and certain other properties. Next to The Chesnuts was another property which Sarah had purchased from the Rose family during the same period. She named the property Rose Hill (now number 43 Darby Road and not the property now known as Rosehill) and possibly she intended to reconstruct the property in the same way as she had done with the Chesnuts.[7] This was also left to Susannah Appleby for life and then passed to the Dickinson family, who eventually sold it to Edward Edwards, the surgeon in the 1850s.[7]

Three other properties were given names by Sarah. One was called The Grove, consisting of two dwellinghouses and formed part of the little settlement near the Meeting House and at the southern end of the Rope Walk. Under the Will this passed to Hannah Tothill who sold it to Francis Darby in 1839.[8] Another pair of properties was called The Poplars and was situate on the land owned by the Thomas family near the Works. One of these passed to the Dickinsons and the other to Richard Darby.

The most important of the properties was situate at the bottom of the Dale, close to the River Severn. She called it Severn House (now the Valley Hotel). This comprised the land and property adjoining the River formerly part of Meadow Farm. She described the house as a mansion house and she left it to the Dickinson family.[9]

She had also acquired a leasehold interest in 1807 of the property now known as Rosehill and she bequeathed the leasehold interest to Richard Darby who purchased the freehold reversion in 1825. Rosehill which Richard may have already occupied under the lease on a tenancy from Sarah, became the family home of Richard and Maria and their children and was occupied until the death of the youngest of their seven children, Rebecca Sarah Darby in 1908.

Finally, Sarah had purchased an acre of land adjoining Sunniside in 1809 and this she bequeathed to Francis Darby who had become the owner of Sunniside under his grandfather's Will on his twenty-first birthday in 1804. [10] All these dispositions of individual properties to the various members of the family was in addition to the trusts established for the land in Dawley (Horsehay) which comprised the ownership of the Horsehay furnaces and collieries. Sarah also held two hundred and forty shares in the partnership of the Company and one hundred and forty of these she transferred to the children of her brother Abraham III (i.e. thirty-five each to Francis Darby, Richard Darby, Ann Dickinson and Hannah Tothill) and one hundred to the children of her nephew Edmund Darby and his wife Lucy Darby (i.e. twenty-five each to Abraham IV, Alfred Darby, Mary and Deborah).

Sarah's Will set the scene in the Dale for the next twenty to thirty years. It is, therefore, worth summarising the way in which the various branches of the family had settled. At the very top of the hill, living in the White House, was Francis Darby and his wife Hannah (née Grant) with their two daughters, Matilda and Adelaide born in 1809 and 1817 respectively. With the death of Sarah, the old house Sunniside was left empty until it was demolished in 1856. This represented something of an enigma, because although it was the family home, and a fine house, it is apparent that Francis would have liked to have knocked it down. [11] He had, of course, built a new wing on The White House and was very content to stay there. In 1816 he had expanded the land holding of the Sunniside Estate by acquiring Furnace Bank Farm, forty-one acres in extent, from which the original Darby land holdings had been derived. [12] This meant that he owned all the land at the top of the hill and both literally and figuratively he was the undisputed head of the family. [13]

Below The White House was the deer park containing a herd, reputedly bred from deer brought back by Deborah Darby from her voyage to America in 1793-96. At the lower end of the deer park, adjoining the Bridleway (now known as Darby Road) was the Meeting House built in 1808.

Opposite the Meeting House was the Rope Walk with its settlement of dwellings, which included The Grove, owned by Hannah Tothill.

The upper part of Coalbrookdale (William Westwood, 1835). The house to the left is Dale House, built by Abraham Darby I 1715-17, enlarged and improved by his grandson Abraham III in 1776. Next to Dale House is Rosehill, built by Richard Ford I c.1738 and renovated in 1791 for the occupation of Richard Dearman.

The Chesnuts (sic), Darby Road. Built by Sarah Darby c.1818 for occupation by Susannah Appleby. Subsequently the home of Abraham Darby IV.

Severn House (The Valley Hotel). Built by George Goodwin, master collier c.1757. Subsequently occupied by Henry Dickinson.

Immediately below the Meeting House was the recently constructed house named The Chesnuts. This provided a rather grand home for Susannah Appleby until her death in 1827. Also living with her however, was Lucy Darby (née Burlingham) with her four children, Abraham IV (born 1804), Alfred (born 1807), Mary (born 1808) and Deborah (born 1810).[14]

Lower down the hill was the residence of Richard and Maria Darby (née Sorton) now known as Rosehill. This was the property built by Richard Ford c1738 and subsequently occupied by Benjamin Wright the surgeon, and Richard Dearman. Richard and Maria had seven children of whom four lived to mature years.[15]

Next door at Dale House lived Barnard and Ann Dickinson with a large family of eleven children of whom most survived to adult years.[16] The one who was most important to the family story was Henry Dickinson (1812-86) who married Deborah Darby, daughter of Lucy Darby in 1841. Sarah Darby gave Severn House to the Dickinsons in 1821 and this eventually became the home of Henry Dickinson. When Barnard and Ann Dickinson left Dale House in 1838, they moved to Eastfield, next door to Severn House and Lucy Darby moved into Dale House.

Behind Dale House and Rosehill was a property called Mount Pleasant. This had started life as a summer house and was converted into a dwelling house by Richard Ford II. At the time of Sarah Darby's death it was occupied by Robert Barnard who was Deborah Darby's brother.[17] He died in 1830.

All these members of the family kept closely in touch with each other. They visited each other regularly and organised entertainments for each other. The only members of the family who lived away from the Dale were Hannah, who was married to William Tothill[18] and lived in Bristol (but who visited the Dale regularly) and Mary, surviving daughter of Samuel II, who in 1827 married the Reverend E Pryce Owen of Wellington.[19] The family also kept in touch with the Reynolds family and particularly the Anstices who lived in Madeley Wood and controlled the Madeley Wood Company. Altogether it was a very agreeable life. On the whole the family kept true to its traditions as 'plain Quakers'. Despite the reduced profitability of the Works, the family were regarded as wealthy, and behaved accordingly.

Richard Darby followed his Whig inclinations and took an active part in public life. He was much involved in the campaign for the abolition of the Slave Trade. This had long been a subject of commitment within the family. As early as 1792, Hannah Mary Rathbone, whose husband William, was the importer of the earliest bales of American cotton to reach the United Kingdom, recorded that "*it was decided in the House that the slave trades should be abolished.*[20] Richard was also involved in local politics and was active in the Anti-Corn Law league. Perhaps his earnestness showed in his social life because the parties held at his house were described by his niece Adelaide as '*dull*' and '*stiff*'.

A similar earnestness imbued the Dickinson household and this showed itself in an increasing commitment by Barnard Dickinson to his religious life. In 1824 Barnard first spoke as a minister and was acknowledged as one in 1827. Thereafter his work in the ministry took over his life. He was joined in the ministry in 1830 by his wife Ann by which time they had decided to sever their connection with the Company. In his account book for 15 December 1830, Francis Darby recorded:

> *My Brother and Sister Dickinson offered all their shares in the Coalbrookdale Company for sale to the Coalbrookdale Company which being declined by the Company purchasing. They then offered them to my Cousin Abraham Darby; who with his own family, consisting of his Mother and brother Alfred and two sisters have agreed to purchase them at the price stated in the Coalbrookdale Company's books at the 4th of 8th month last – deducting 10% from that amount.*"

Barnard and Ann Dickinson had forty-three shares in the Company but how they were split within the family of Lucy Darby is not known.

One of the matters which Barnard Dickinson dealt with before retiring was the renewal of the lease of the Works, which was due to lapse in 1827. The future of the Coalbrookdale Works had been in question, and it had been mooted whether the whole operation should be consolidated at Horsehay, but in the end, Coalbrookdale was reprieved and the lease was renewed by Joseph Reynolds, who had succeeded his father Richard Reynolds, as the owner of the freehold.[21] The renewal of the Lease coincided with the arrival in management of Abraham Darby IV in 1826 and his brother Alfred in 1828, both at the age of twenty-three. Abraham IV started in the Dawley Colliery office and familiarised himself with the coal and iron mines and with the furnaces. Alfred started in the Horsehay office and became involved with the forges and foundries.[22]

Also, at this time Barnard Dickinson's eldest son Joseph Dickinson, aged twenty-one, was appointed Assistant Manager at Horsehay. It followed, therefore, that when Barnard Dickinson retired there was already in place a young and energetic management team. By this time Francis Darby was forty-seven years of age and was content to assume the role of elder statesman while continuing his involvement in and responsibility for the Coalbrookdale foundry.

The take-over of the Works by the new management had an electrifying effect. A decade or more of poor performance had ended and a more vigorous management soon became evident, which was to take the Company to its greatest ever level of prosperity over the next twenty years.

Changes were initiated by Abraham IV and Alfred both in the technical processes (under Abraham) and in working conditions and the management of labour (under Alfred). A great deal of laxity and poor work practices had crept in during the 1820s and these had to be rectified. The new arrangements did not come without difficulty and it took much of the 1830s to bring the new regime into effect. All this took place against a background of social and industrial discord. These were turbulent times. Strikes amongst miners took place in 1831.[23] The great debate about the Reform Bill of 1832 split society and although Shropshire as a whole was against reform, there was considerable support for the Bill amongst the industrialists. Even so differences of opinion were evident even within families. Richard Darby followed the radical view whereas his brother Francis favoured the status quo. As well as these industrial and political divisions, Coalbrookdale began to be affected by health problems. In 1836 a typhus outbreak occurred which took many lives.

Within the Shropshire Coalfield adjustments were taking place in the balance of power. The Old Park Company, which earlier in the century had displaced the Coalbrookdale Company from its pre-eminence, and had subsequently expanded east of Dawley to Hinkshay and Stirchley,[24] had nevertheless itself conceded pride of place to the vast Lilleshall Company which, by 1819, had been described as *the greatest pig sellers in the world*.[25] The Ketley furnaces, which had been closed by Joseph Reynolds in 1816 were brought back into use in 1818 by a new company which then built new furnaces at Lawley. The Madeley Wood Company based at Bedlam Furnaces, established new furnaces at Blists Hill in 1834 and thereafter prospered well.

The new management of Abraham IV and Alfred enabled the Coalbrookdale Company to start the journey back to recovery and eventually to regain its pride of place. This was done not only through improvements in efficiency but also by importing into the Works new technological advances which originated elsewhere. In the previous century these might well have been the prerogative of the Company itself but the flair for innovation had been lost. Thus, Joseph Hall's method of producing wrought-iron by 'pig boiling' was introduced at Horsehay from Staffordshire in 1832 and the following year the guide rolling mill was imported from the Black Country some years after its first operation there.[26] After 1833 the profitability of the Company started to improve significantly enabling the Company to expand its operations.[27] This led to the acquisition in 1839 of the Lightmoor Company which had been a neighbour of the Company since the 1730s[28] and the purchase of the Pool Hill Estate in 1838 leading to the development of the exceptionally good clay resources which existed close to Horsehay.[29] The hot blast furnace system invented by Neilson in 1828 was applied at the Horsehay and

Dawley Castle furnaces. Evidence that the Company had returned to the path of greatness was shown in 1838, when two wrought-iron plates measuring 10ft 7in by 5ft 1in were displayed in Liverpool. It was claimed that they were the largest ever rolled. [30] As if to compound this feat, the next year, the Company produced 800 tons of iron plates for the hull of Brunel's SS Great Britain. The Company was once again back in the big time.

Equally exciting events were taking place in the foundry in Coalbrookdale, which was under the general surveillance of Francis Darby. The foundry which had been languishing during the 1820s was invigorated after 1830 when the work of reconstructing the Horsehay and Dawley Castle furnaces was taking place under the direction of Abraham IV. All the engines needed for that reconstruction were designed and made at the Coalbrookdale foundry. [31] A great leap forward was made when the foundry started to produce art castings in about 1834. There had for some time been a practice of producing decorative castings for architectural and ornamental purposes, but this did not compare with the superlative decorative works which had developed in the eighteenth and early nineteenth century in Bohemia, Saxony and Prussia. It is not yet clear how the technology was introduced to Coalbrookdale which became the first and pre-eminent foundry to develop art castings in Britain. There had been many visitors to Coalbrookdale from Central Europe as other countries sought to emulate the technological prowess of Britain in the iron industry. [32] One such visitor Count Burgstall was referred to in Adelaide Darby's diary for 8 July 1836. He had visited the works earlier in the century [33] and it was probably from visits like that, that a knowledge of Central European practice became available.

The credit for this new development is generally ascribed to Francis Darby, although this may be a simplistic view. It needs to be seen in the context of the renaissance which was taking place in the Company as a whole after Abraham IV and Alfred took over management. Francis had adopted a more worldly life-style and he had broadened his horizons by comparison with some of his contemporaries. Life at the White House had become relatively sophisticated and Francis' accounts show that he had developed a taste for books, silver, Coalport china and the purchase of pictures. He was a minor purchaser of furniture, silver and books at Lord Berwick's sale at Attingham Park in 1827. In the succeeding years he made a considerable collection of such items and he and his family lived in style as a man of property. Pride of place was accorded to his collections of paintings which occupied three rooms and were shown to visitors with great pleasure. [34] He obtained most of his pictures from London and Birmingham. By the mid-1830s, he had acquired a coat of arms, which appeared in his silver and porcelain. A cultivated man of taste, with a liking for artistic matters, he was clearly the man to be in charge of the foundry as it started to produce sculptures, busts, plaques and small ornamental objects like those made in the Czech and Prussian foundries. Soon the Company was producing fountains, gates, hall furniture, garden benches and a wide variety of decorative articles, many of which nowadays appear in salerooms all over the country.

It is difficult to form an accurate picture of Francis Darby. His portrait shows a man of genial disposition, but he was also a short-tempered man who was held in some awe by his daughters. His eldest daughter, Matilda, writing soon after his death, wrote *"My poor Father's life had not been happy. His marriage had not been congenial to him though I think he was very fond of Mama, but she became snappish with him as his health failed. He had been of violent temper in his days of health and he had an excitable temperament that was happiest in a very quiet life, and this quiet was disagreeable to Mama, who had been an only child and accustomed to see much variety in her Father's house, but I think her tastes were not refined like Papa's nor her mind as well cultivated so that she was not a companion to him...".*

Francis and Hannah had two daughters who were to play a conspicuous part in the affairs of Coalbrookdale. Living at the White House their closest neighbours were Abraham IV and Alfred. The eldest daughter, Matilda, when only fifteen became greatly attracted to Abraham IV then five years older and she formed a determination to marry him, which she did fifteen years later in 1839. Theirs was to be a happy and loving marriage. By the time of their wedding, the Company was restored to good fortune and there is little doubt that Abraham was the principal architect of that dramatic turnaround. A new building programme had been undertaken in Coalbrookdale and at the date of the wedding a new warehouse had been built (known now as the Great Warehouse). Great festivities accompanied the wedding which took place on 8 August 1839 at the Meeting House. Two hundred and fifty sheep were provided so that a present of meat could be given to the men in the Dale. A floral arch was constructed with the initials of the bride and groom underneath *"Prosperity to the House of Darby"*. Three cannons were available for a noisy send-off and an evening party took place in the new warehouse. The couple left by carriage for Birmingham – accompanied (unbelievably) by Matilda's sister Adelaide, who went with them on their honeymoon. They left Birmingham the next day, by train, for London and Southampton and then by steamer to Cowes for the regatta.[35]

Beneath the surface of this family unity, faint storm clouds were beginning to gather, which would lead in ten year's time to a crisis which would shake the family to its foundations. Adelaide, although eight years younger than Matilda, had fully expected to be married before her sister. A suitor had indeed been identified, a certain Mr Dawson, who had the advantage of being a Quaker, but, within the formalities expected by society at that time, he had been rejected by Adelaide's father, Francis Darby. Adelaide was perceived as the Darby heiress, and Mr Dawson, despite his Quaker credentials did not come up to expectations. There then followed a succession of suitors over the next ten years including William Tothill (rejected because the relationship of first cousin was too close)[36] and Archdeacon Beresford (too old with five children).[37] Perhaps the most appropriate match would have been Alfred Darby who sought Adelaide's hand with some persistence over a period of years. Each time he was rejected by Adelaide in increasingly vitriolic terms, and so, as the years passed she was perceived to be 'on the shelf', notwithstanding her wealth and eligibility. This situation festered within the family for the next decade.

While the situation was developing, Francis Darby was pursuing the policy, which he had already started, of expanding the Sunniside estate.

Under the marriage settlement of Mary Darby (daughter of Samuel II) with Reverend E Pryce Owen of Wellington in 1827,[38] it was decided to dispose of the lands which Samuel I had inherited under the Will of Abraham II in 1764 (i.e. the properties assembled by Richard Ford in 1738 and purchased by Abraham II under the bankruptcy of Richard Ford II). The property was split three ways. First, the principal house (i.e. the house now known as Rosehill) was purchased by Richard Darby.[39] Secondly, the property and ornamental gardens known as Mount Pleasant (formerly the summerhouse) with the orchard attached situate behind Rosehill and Dale House was sold to Lucy Darby.[40] Thirdly, the balance of the property, consisting of Tea Kettle Row, land and orchard at the rear and crown of the hill known as The Whales Back was sold to Francis Darby.[41] The latter piece of land was subject to a ninety-nine year lease then held by Lucy Darby and originally granted to her husband Edmund in 1803.[42] By far the most important piece of land acquired by Francis however was the purchase in 1837 of seventy acres, part of the former Stanley's (Cawbrook) Farm previously purchased by Richard Reynolds from John Powys Stanley in 1788.[43] This extended the Sunniside estate by including the land to the west of Sunniside House and the high land behind Dale House and the Works as far as Captain's Coppice. The ownership also included the field acquired by Rebecca Darby out of the sale of Strethill Farm in 1807 and transferred to Francis in 1827.[44]

Francis appeared to be intent on 'tidying up' the environs of The White House. Below The White House and close to the junction of the Rope Walk and Darby Road lay the settlement which had grown up in the mid-eighteenth century on either side of the Company's original railway from Cocks Wood. The settlement is most clearly shown in the view of 'Coalbrookdale from the north east' by William Westwood published in 1835.[45] Francis Darby already owned some of these properties but between 1838 and 1841 he had acquired the rest. Once he had

134

Coalbrookdale from the north east (extract) (William Westwood, 1835). This view shows properties (to the right of the picture) at the junction of Darby Road and the Rope Walk, which were demolished by Francis Darby in the 1840s.

The Severn Warehouse, built in 1834.

purchased them all, he demolished the lot and threw the rubble into the Rope Walk Coppice. *(46)*

One other development which took place at this time was the construction of Marnwood Hall on the extreme west of the parish adjoining the boundary with the parish of Buildwas. A piece of land between the parish boundary and the western edge of Strethill Farm (owned by Abraham IV) was acquired by Reverend John Bartlett who was appointed incumbent of the Buildwas Church in 1822.

Abraham IV agreed in 1828 to exchange land from Strethill Farm for an equivalent area of land to the north, thus facilitating the building of the Hall in the 1830s. *(47)* John Bartlett was married to a daughter of William Reynolds and was thus related by marriage to the Darby family. He became involved in public affairs in the parish of Madeley and constructed a small school adjoining Marnwood Hall entrance gates, which became a Dame School (the ruinous stone building still survives). After his death in 1861, Bartlett was commemorated by an obelisk in Market Square, Ironbridge, since relocated in a car park in Waterloo Street. *(48)*

By the 1830s, the Coalbrookdale operation was in need of rationalisation. A first step was taken with the construction in 1834 of the Severn Warehouse on the Wharfage (now the Museum of the Gorge). *(49)* The opportunity for further rehabilitation came when a new lease was negotiated with Joseph Reynolds in 1830. *(50)* This lease was for thirty-four years, compared with twenty-one years for the previous leases, but it had the unusual feature that after nine years the rent was to be dramatically reduced to a nominal level. This was probably in recognition of the fact that the site was in need of substantial investment.

This investment followed with the construction in 1838 of the Great Warehouse (now the Museum of Iron). The Severn Warehouse and the Great Warehouse were built on the strength of the Company's increasing prosperity and in the expectation of better times to come. Appropriately the wedding celebrations of Abraham IV and Matilda Darby the following year, 1839, with its message of "Prosperity to the House of Darby" was a fitting end to a decade which had seen Coalbrookdale recover from the decline which had afflicted it in the 1820s.

NOTES – CHAPTER IX

1. A full account of these events may be read in Trinder: *Industrial Revolution in Shropshire*, pp.382-385.
2. Raistrick, pp.242-243 quoting from Hall J.W, 'Joshua Fields' diary of a tour in 1821 through the Midlands, Trans' Newcomen Society, Vol. VI 1925-6, pp.1-41.
3. Raistrick, p.240 and Appendix 7, p.319.

4. By his Will, Richard Reynolds left his substantial estate to Hannah Mary Rathbone, his daughter by his first marriage to Hannah Darby and to Joseph Reynolds, his son by his second marriage to Rebecca Gulson. The two beneficiaries agreed to partition the estate, so that in 1824, Joseph Reynolds became the absolute owner of the Manor of Madeley S.R.O 1681/137/5-7 also S.R.O 1987/30/1-2.
5. *Deborah*, p.305.
6. S.R.O 1987/31/1-2 & 3. Abraham II sold a piece of land 30 yds x 27 yds at the southern end of his property adjoining the bridleway which became Darby Road, to George Cranage. Two houses were built on the land. The property was sold to Sarah Darby in 1809 (S.R.O 1987/17/5-6) by Edward Cranage (son of George Cranage) and she converted them within the next ten years to the fine property which she named The Chesnuts (sic). On her death it was occupied by Susannah Appleby (died 1827) and Lucy Darby. It was inherited on Susannah's death by Abraham IV, Lucy's elder son.
7. In 1821 Rose Hill (now No 43 Dale Road, adjoining The Chesnuts) was occupied by William Edwards the surgeon of the Dale and son-in-law of the previous surgeon, Benjamin Wright. He and his sons Edward and Benjamin Edwards continued to practice at Rose Hill and an adjoining cottage built in 1829 (S.R.O 1987/56/26). Between 1851 and 1855 Edward Edwards purchased Rose Hill from the Dickinson family and purchased the adjoining cottage in 1855 (S.R.O 1681/179/8). Edward Edwards lived there until his death in 1870 (S.R.O 1987/28/17)
8. S.R.O 1987/5/2-4.
9. Severn House became occupied by Henry Dickinson (1812-86) sixth child of Barnard and Ann Dickinson and married to Deborah Darby (Lucy Darby's daughter) in 1841 (see Adelaide Darby's diary 17 March 1841). Henry Dickinson emerged as the most influential of the eleven Dickinson children. Deborah died in 1855 and Henry then married Susannah Hadwen.
Barnard and Ann Dickinson lived in Dale House until 1838 and then built the fine property known as Eastfield (now known as Dale End House) literally on the field to the east of Severn House. Ann died in 1840 and Barnard in 1852.
10. S.R.O 1987/27/3-4. The land was bought by Sarah Darby in 1809 from Richard Reynolds. The purchase complemented a somewhat similar purchase of land adjoining the White House by Francis Darby in 1806. S.R.O 1987/27/1-2.
11. S.R.O 1987/56/12. In a letter written by Edward Edwards, surgeon, of Rose Hill, he states that *"Sunniside House stands uninhabited. Francis Darby does not intend to live there. He wishes it was down. He would like to see a pleasure ground there instead".*

12. S.R.O 1987/19/33-36. Furnace Bank Farm had remained in the same family through various marriages since 1705 when it was bought out of the Manor of Madeley by George Dukesell. The family had done well and had considerable properties elsewhere in Shropshire (see S.R.O 1987/19/29). One of their ventures was a bank in Bridgnorth which collapsed in 1814 causing their bankruptcy. Furnace Bank Farm was put up for auction at the Tontine Hotel, Ironbridge, in April 1815, where it was bought by Francis Darby.

13. The subconscious superiority of The White House was demonstrated later by Adelaide Darby when approached in marriage by Mr Alfred Darby. She confided to her diary *"I rather think Miss Darby of The White House is of more importance than ever Mrs Alfred Darby will be"*. (Adelaide's Diary 29 December 1841.)

14. In addition to the four children mentioned there had been two other children who died in infancy; Corbyn (born 1805) and Samuel Maude (born 1806).

15. The children of Richard and Maria Darby were:
    Richard Sorton born 1812 (married Anna Wilkinson)
    Maria Louise born 1814 (died unmarried ? 1854)
    Caroline Anne born 1815 (died unmarried 1838)
    Abraham Maude born 1817 (died 1818)
    William Henry born 1819 (married Sarah Littleboy 1854, died 1882)
    Charles Edward born 1822 (died unmarried 1884)
    Rebecca Sarah born 1832 (died at Rosehill 1908).

16. Information about the Dickinson family is incomplete.
    Ann and Barnard Dickinson had eleven children:-
    Joseph (born 1806, married Lucy Midgley, died 1860)
    Mary Darby (born 1807, married Charles Sturges)
    Sarah (born 1808, died 1835, see Adelaide's diary 13 December 1837 and S.R.O 1987/56/5)
    Barnard (born 1809, left Coalbrookdale in 1831 for Manchester, see Francis Darby's account book 28 February 1831)
    Rebecca (born 1810, died 1828 at Darlington)
    Henry (born 1812 married (1) Rebecca Darby (1810-55) in 1841 and (2) Susannah Hadwen (1831-1886) died 1886
    Samuel (born 1814, died 1840 – See Adelaide's diary 6 September 1840)
    Francis (born 1816, married Sarah Ann Stevens, died 1901)
    Hannah (born 1816 married Joseph Sturge, 14 October 1846, see Adelaide's journal, 20 September 1846)
    Christopher (born 1818 married Sophia Browne, died 1904)
    William (born 1822 married Miss Bradley 1858).

17. Robert Barnard died in 1830 aged sixty-eight after many years of indisposition. (Francis Darby's accounts 21 March 1830). Three years before his death, Lucy Darby purchased Mount Pleasant, the ornamental gardens and the adjoining Orchard. This remained in her ownership until her death in 1870 and was inherited by Abraham IV and subsequently his widow Matilda until her death in 1902. The house was demolished later in the nineteenth century. (S.R.O 1987/51/2/3)

18. William and Hannah Tothill had five children:
    William (born 1819)
    Joseph (born 1821)
    Francis (born 1823, married (1) Jane Digby and
        (2) Miss Galbraith 1858)
    Sarah Hannah (born 1824, married 1854 to Colonel Munro,
        39th Regiment)
    Rebecca (born 1826).

19. See S.R.O 1987/38/4-7. Reverend E Pryce Owen was Vicar of Wellington 1828-41. He was better known as a painter and etcher. See D.N.B.

20. *Abiah*, p.246.

21. Raistrick, p.248/9. The lease appears to be missing from the Shropshire Record Office. It may have been intended to be retained as 1681/138/7. The plan attached to the lease is shown in Raistrick p.p 250-251 and is analysed in detail there.

22. Raistrick, p.256.

23. Trinder: *Industrial Revolution in Shropshire*, pp.386-7.

24. Trinder: *Industrial Revolution in Shropshire*, p.241.

25. Trinder: *Industrial Revolution in Shropshire*, p.239 quoting Gilbert Gilpin.

26. Trinder: *Industrial Revolution in Shropshire*, pp.238-9.

27. Raistrick, p.319. Appendix 7.

28. See S.R.O 1681/183/1-12 and 18. The Lightmoor Works originated in a ninety-nine year lease dated 1733 by the Earl of Craven of works of coal and ironstone in Little Dawley. The following year 1734, Thomas Stanley gave a lease of land at Loadcroft adjoining the River Severn for ninety-nine years. Thus what became the Lightmoor Works had an access to the River not far from the Coalbrookdale Company's Wharf. The leases expired in 1832 and 1833 respectively. The Lightmoor Works reverted to the Earl of Craven who gave a new lease for forty years to the Coalbrookdale Company from 1839 (S.R.O 1987/35/12-13).

29. Trinder: *Industrial Revolution in Shropshire*, p.239.

30. Raistrick, p.259 quoting from the Mechanics Magazine 1838.

31. Raistrick, p.261.

32. Refer to "Gold I gave for Iron", an exhibition produced by Wrexham Library Arts Centre in 1989. Text in IGMT Library.

33. Count Burgstall had seemingly been much taken with Ann Dickinson in her young days, presumably before she married Barnard Dickinson in 1804.

34. For example, see Francis Darby's account book for 26 April 1847.

35. Adelaide's journal, 2 August, 8 August 1839 et seq.

36. Francis Darby's accounts, 3 July 1848.

37. Francis Darby's accounts 2 March 1849.

38. S.R.O 1987/38/4.

39. S.R.O 1987/38/7.

40. S.R.O 1987/17/7-8 and 1987/38/6.

41. S.R.O 1681/179/4-5, 6 and 7 and 1987/38/5 and 6.

42. S.R.O 1987/23/1.

43. S.R.O 1987/30/3-4, 5 and 6. Stanleys Farm was purchased by Richard Reynolds in 1788 (S.R.O 1987/30/2). It consisted of a total of 230 acres of land, meadow, pasture and woodland with five homes and five gardens. It comprised the land forming the western flank of Coalbrookdale together with land on the eastern side of the Dale from Paradise fields down to the River at Ludcroft Wharf (i.e Museum of the Gorge).

44. S.R.O 1987/3/26-27.

45. Collection of Ironbridge Gorge Museum Trust.

46. The settlement included two dwellings purchased by Sarah Darby in 1809 and 1810 (S.R.O 1987/5 and 12) named The Grove and bequeathed to her niece Mary Tothill. Nine dwellings were purchased by Francis Darby in 1813 (S.R.O 1987/13) and the remainder were acquired by him between 1838 and 1841 (S.R.O 1987/4, 5, 7, 9, 12, 16 and 26). These transfers are all listed in the schedule of Francis Darby's freehold properties dated 19 March 1851 (S.R.O 1681/178/16).

47. See map of Strethill Farm. S.R.O/1987/55/2. Field Nos. 25, 26 and part of 19 were exchanged by agreement dated 10 March 1828 for roughly equivalent areas of land to the north comprising Marn Hill Meadow and part of Far Marn Hill (S.R.O 1987/32/4).

48. V.C.H. Vol XI Telford, pp.40, 72 and 73.

49. The Severn Warehouse had been completed by 20 September 1834 because Adelaide Darby's diary for that date contains the following entry:-
"...*When we had progressed as far as the Iron Bridge, we beheld the Coalbrookdale Company's Warehouse rising in turretted and embattled rivalship of these convincing and cemented proofs of the March of Improvements...*"

50. S.R.O 1681/138/8.

CHAPTER X

Francis Darby, Abraham IV and Alfred I

THE FOURTH DECADE of the nineteenth century started with a period of industrial and social unrest, as had the previous two decades. The background to the unrest was the rise of the Chartist movement, which came from the failure of the Reform Act, 1832 to improve the lot of the vast majority of the population. The country as a whole was getting wealthier but the wealth did not reach down to the working class who were close to real starvation. Adelaide Darby in her journal for 18 August 1842 records:

"We hardly think it safe to stir beyond the gardens, for the country is in a dreadful state and daily nearer and worse. There was a Chartist Meeting yesterday and today the Colliers have struck work. At Preston the Military have fired on the mob and the loss of life has been considerable; and in the Potteries – dangerously close – they have burned and pillaged the houses of magistrates and clergymen in a frightful manner – Trentham was considered in danger. So formidable an insurrection has not been known for years and the sanguine and hopeful look at each other and say 'Where is it to end?' – Plentiful and cheap as provisions are thro' the Mercy of Providence, the poor creatures having neither work nor wages, cannot buy, and trade is in such a state that if they all returned to their labours tomorrow there would be employment for but an inconsiderable number – People vilify the Corn Laws and Sir Robert Peel and the Parliament just prorogued for grouse shooting but can Christian men exist who having given all their energies to understand these difficult questions, and knowing that certain changes are needed, who could possibly for small and selfish motives look on and see their fellow creatures reduced to misery in their power to alter.". [1]

The latter part of the entry is a bit confused but the sentiment is clear. The Darby family were fully committed to the Anti-Corn Law League and it was this rather than the reform of Parliament sought by the Chartists which in the end improved the lot of the working man. The Corn Laws were passed to protect the domestic agricultural industry and had the effect of keeping out cheaper imported food. The National Anti-Corn Law League Bazaar was held at Covent Garden in London in May 1845. The ladies of the family had been working hard to prepare work for a stall[2] but the Company made a special effort and displayed for the first time art castings, which included statues of Goethe, Napoleon and Wellington and Benjamin Franklin and decorative cast-iron fountains.[3] The Corn Laws were repealed in the following year.

The family accepted their wider social responsibilities in the spirit which they had inherited from their Quaker forebears. This might today be described as benevolent paternalism, but it was far more than that. Their Quaker beliefs imbued them with commitment towards education, religious instruction and the assistance of the poor. Richard Darby became involved as a Guardian under the Poor Law. Abraham IV carried on the family encouragement of education. A new boys school was built by Abraham at his expense in 1840 in Wellington Road adjoining the Upper Furnace site. This incorporated earlier family initiatives in the locality which in turn followed on the school built at Sunniside by Abraham II.[4]

Whilst all this was going on members of the family started to broaden their horizons beyond Coalbrookdale and Horsehay. In 1844, Abraham IV took the lead in acquiring the Ebbw Vale Ironworks in South Wales. In this initiative he was joined by his cousins Henry Dickinson and William Tothill.[5] The other partners were Joseph Robinson, who was involved with Abraham in Liverpool, and Thomas Brown, who was the local manager. The works comprised four blast furnaces at Ebbw Vale, and another furnace at Sirhowy, situate in the next valley, north-west of Ebbw Vale.[5]

They also extended their interests outside the iron industry in the Liverpool area. It is not clear why this happened, beyond the fact that the family had close connections with the City through the Rathbone family, and maintained a warehouse in Liverpool.[6] They also had interests in the maritime industry. On 18 July 1844 Matilda, accompanied by Abraham IV and her sister Adelaide, launched and named an iron vessel "Richard Cobden" in Liverpool. It was a considerable occasion at which Abraham made a speech on the subject of Free Trade. Another member of the family present was William Henry Darby, son of Richard Darby.[7] Two months later, Richard Darby with another son, Charles Edward, were in Liverpool in connection with the sailing of another iron vessel.[8]

Two years later in 1846, Abraham and Alfred agreed to make five purchases of land in the neighbourhood of Liverpool for building purposes and for resale. Four of the purchases were at Aigburth and Garston on the south side of the city and the fifth was at West Derby on the east of

143

the city.*(9)* The total area was two hundred and seventy-two acres at a cost of £138,921.

This was a somewhat uncharacteristic venture, but Liverpool was expanding outwards at the time and it was seen as a simple matter of trading in a commodity.*(10)* In the event, it was to prove more complicated than that, but at the time it was seen as a sound commercial undertaking.

Against this widening background of interests in South Wales and Liverpool, the affairs at Coalbrookdale may have seemed less central to the family's future. The other branch of the family at Rosehill also started to move away. Richard Darby and Maria his wife had three surviving sons, Richard Sorton (b.1812), William Henry (b.1819) and Charles Edward (b.1822). The eldest son married Anna Wilkinson and moved to Hawkswood House, Sidbury, near Bridgnorth. He had health problems with eczema and developed other interests. The other two sons were trained in the works and might well have been expected to succeed in the management, but in 1846 they left the Dale to become joint managers of the Brymbo Iron Works, near Wrexham in North Wales. Curiously this re-ignited a connection which had lapsed one hundred years previously. Brymbo was the successor of the Bersham Iron Works some two miles away. Bersham was involved with the Dale following the marriage of Abraham I's second daughter Ann to John Hawkins (see Chapters 3, 4 and 6). It was subsequently bought by the Wilkinsons and it was John Wilkinson who established the Brymbo Iron Works in 1793.*(11)* William Henry Darby and Charles Edward Darby pursued distinguished careers at Brymbo and eventually took controlling interests in the Brymbo Steel Works.

Back in the Dale, the time had come to review the lease of the Works. This had last been negotiated in 1838 and was for thirty-four years with a considerable drop in rent after seven years. The lease was, therefore, of little value to Joseph Reynolds after 1845 and the freehold was sold by him to Francis, Abraham and Alfred Darby on 1 August 1845.*(12)* For the first time the Company owned the freehold of the Works. For the entire existence of the Company since Abraham arrived in the Dale in 1708, the premises had always been held on lease, usually for successive periods of twenty-one years. Having at last acquired the full rights to the property it was rather surprising when three months later, the very future of the Works became an issue. Adelaide Darby recorded in her journal *"It has been rather a stormy time beforehand and talk of giving up the Dale".*

The issue did not go away because eighteen months later in April 1847, Francis Darby recorded in his account book:

Abraham Darby IV.

Alfred Darby I.

Temple in woodland walk.

"*On the 3rd, A.D sat with me in the evening and informed me of his opinion that it would be best to relinquish carrying on the Colebrookdale foundry, in which, I dare say it would be right to agree, for it has long been rather unprofitable than otherwise.*" The views of both Abraham and Francis seem difficult to comprehend. The accounts of the Company appear to suggest that the foundry was by no means unprofitable. Its output would soon enable it to be described as the biggest foundry in the world. As recently as 1843, the Company had placed a proud clock tower on the newly erected Great Warehouse of 1838.

On the other hand, with the partners' interests broadened to South Wales and Liverpool, the direct management of the Coalbrookdale Works may have seemed burdensome. Also although the Company had ready access to the River Severn and to the recently reconstructed Holyhead Road, and the new Lubstree wharf of the Birmingham and Liverpool canal for distribution, all these facilities must have seemed a poor alternative to the new railway system which was singularly absent from Shropshire. It was ironic that the Company which had built the world's first steam locomotive was deprived of the benefit of the new form of travel.[13] To the far-sighted Abraham IV it may have seemed that Coalbrookdale had become distant from its markets.

However, nothing further was heard of the proposal to close the Works. A new railway was built from Shrewsbury to Wellington and from Wellington to Stafford and Wolverhampton in 1849.[14] Also by that time a decision had been made to appoint a manager for the Coalbrookdale Works, and Mr Charles Crookes took up the position in 1850 and resided at Paradise House,[15] near to where the Coalbrookdale Institute would soon be built.

If there had been serious doubts about the future of the Dale, this had not deflected Francis Darby from his policy of acquiring land and extending the Sunniside estate. This coincided with a policy of divestment of land being followed by Joseph Reynolds who had taken over as Lord of the Manor from his father Richard Reynolds. Joseph Reynolds had already in 1838 given a lease to the Coalbrookdale Company of land at the lower end of the Dale[16] and he had also in 1840 given a lease of Captain's Coppice on the west side of the Dale and Paradise Fields, Lincoln Hill Coppice and Dale Coppice which included the woodland walks designed by his father on the east side of the Dale.[16] He had also been giving long leases of land along the road leading to the New Pool and Oilhouse Coppice in the north east of the Dale.[17]

In 1840 he completed the latter transaction by conveying to Francis Darby twenty-one acres of Oilhouse Coppice together with the freehold reversion of the long leases previously granted.[18] In 1848 he conveyed

147

to Francis Darby the land at Paradise leading from Charity Row (owned by the Coalbrookdale Company) down to the land at the south end of the Dale already leased to the Company. *(19)*

In addition to these transactions, Francis Darby was able to purchase from Sir Joseph Hawley in 1848 several coppices (sixteen acres in extent) adjoining Oilhouse Coppice and at Castle Green along the eastern edge of Dale Coppice, together with lands and buildings known as Lodge Farm (nineteen acres) to the south. *(20)* On 30 January 1849, Francis Darby was able to record in his accounts, one senses with some pleasure, that the manorial rights of these various transactions were now *"vested in myself"*. Although his ownership did not extend much beyond Coalbrookdale itself, he must have felt some satisfaction in having at last achieved what his father (Abraham III) set out to accomplish in the previous century *(20a)*. These various transactions made Francis Darby the second largest landowner in the parish with four hundred and thirty-seven acres. *(21)* An additional one hundred and sixty-one acres was owned by Abraham IV mainly at the neighbouring Strethill and Meadow Farms. *(22)* Francis' income from the Coalbrookdale Company in the late 1840s was considerable. His accounts reveal the following figures: *(23)*

	£.	s.	d.
1844	5,901	7	6
1845	7,323	15	0
1846	12,471	1	4
1847	12,668	14	3
1848	9,558	5	9
	£47,923	3	10

Some of this income was spent on acquiring land but some of the rest was spent on acquiring pictures and books for his gallery and library at The White House. His pictures included a number of Dutch flower pieces and still life, also some good modern landscapes of the day, among which were two of Hampstead Heath by John Constable, as Francis found *"Mr Constable a talented young man"*. *(24)*

The lead given by Francis Darby in artistic matters was soon being followed by Abraham IV at the Chesnuts. Extensive improvements to the property were made in 1846 to house a picture gallery and a new piano. *(25)* Francis and Abraham had both become men of property and both led cultured lives with their families. There was a noticeable change in their way of life by comparison with their Quaker forebears. Unlike their ancestors they were gradually assimilated into leading Shropshire Society, *(26)* and they were no longer so dominated by the routines of the Society of

Friends. The local historian, John Randall, writing about the Darbys in 1880 said:-

"Of the later members of the Darby family we may speak in part from personal knowledge. Whilst adhering to the grand cardinal doctrine of the Inner Light they indulged their own ideas of the extent to which the strict discipline of the body should control their tastes. They were birth members but lax in their opinions and did not live by their strict Quaker rule. Francis Darby of the White House, had great taste and loved high art. He filled his rooms with costly paintings. Others indulged in a love of music and luxury."

Abraham IV and his wife Matilda were the first to break with the Society of Friends and to join the Church of England. In April 1848, Abraham and Matilda resigned their "birth right membership" and were then accepted into the Anglican communion. They joined the congregation at Little Wenlock church. [27] Although the break was nominally over the question of tithes, the drift away from the Society had been in prospect for many years. As early as 1839, when on honeymoon they had attended church services, with Adelaide commenting *"how beautiful are the prayers of the English Church".* [28] Over the years they became accustomed to attending church services as well as Meetings of the Society. [29] In the end it was a matter of personal choice rather than a gesture of religious preference.

At the beginning of the decade, and after the marriage of Abraham IV to Matilda, there was a first indication of Alfred's intention to propose to Matilda's sister, Adelaide. [30] This became a formal proposal of marriage at the end of 1841. [31] The proposal was rejected but was kept alive during the next five years. His final proposal was made and rejected in October 1846. Things were different this time however, because the previous year during the Anti-Corn Law League bazaar, the family had met the Christy family, and had visited their home at the Woodbines, at Kingston-on-Thames. [32] There they had met Rebecca Christy, described by Adelaide as a *"fine girl, distinguished in manner and very elegant in dress".*

She also had the great advantage of being from a strong and distinguished Quaker family. Evidently she had impressed Alfred because he proposed marriage to her in July 1847. [33] He then took a house in Clapham Common in London and they were married in May 1848 (Adelaide who liked to have the last word commented *"It was a vulgar affair they say"*). Adelaide was by then over thirty years old, and apart from the proposals from Alfred she had been through a number of affairs of the heart, some of which she had declined and others had ended in disappointment.

A number of factors now started to come together which would, within a few years, bring about a crisis within the family. First, Francis' health

149

which had for some time been a problem, started to deteriorate. He appears to have been afflicted with bladder trouble. His wife Hannah, probably worried by the fact that Adelaide was not married and therefore not provided for, started to press Francis to make a Will. During 1848 a Will was prepared which gave all his Coalbrookdale estates to his widow and to his daughter Adelaide during their joint lives and then to Adelaide; Hay Farm was to be given to Adelaide outright and his shares in the ironworks were to be given to his two daughters Matilda and Adelaide in equal shares subject to an annuity of £800 per annum to his widow. *(34)* Francis Darby declined to execute this Will after it was engrossed, allegedly saying that "*the Law would make a better Will for him than he could do for himself*". *(35)* The existence of this unexecuted Will, which substantially disinherited one of the sisters was not known to either of the sisters at the time. Significantly, relations between Hannah Darby and her daughter Matilda had become more strained. *(36)* As between the two sisters relations remained on a blissful level. Adelaide was almost invariably included in visits and travels by Abraham and Matilda *(37)* and they continued to relate to each other in the most endearing terms.

Another factor which started to intrude into affairs at this time was the fact that Abraham's home at The Chesnuts was proving inadequate for his position as the leading industrialist in the Dale and could not accommodate his increasing collection of paintings. Abraham had set his sights on Stanley Hall, Bridgnorth, which would have suited him admirably. At the time it was rented to another family. When it became available in 1849 it was offered by the agent to Alfred Darby who thereupon left Clapham Common and moved to Stanley Hall, thus thwarting Abraham's ambitions.

The obvious solution to Abraham's problems was to move to the old Sunniside which belonged to Francis Darby and had stayed empty since 1821 when Sarah Darby died. *(38)* Sunniside had always represented some sort of psychological problem to Francis. When Sarah died Francis wanted to knock it down, but he never did so, and it remained vacant throughout Francis' lifetime. Asked just before he died, whether he wished to demolish Sunniside, he is reputed to have replied "*No, I shall never do it. Matilda must do it*". *(39)*

Abraham seems to have made an approach to Francis about Sunniside, but Francis demurred. It is evident that, although they worked well together, there was a measure of antipathy between the two men, perhaps something of a personality problem caused by Francis' volatile state of mind. *(40)* All these matters came to an abrupt conclusion with the sudden death of Francis Darby on 20 March 1850, not from the bladder problem which afflicted him for so long but probably from angina pectoris. He died without making a Will. *(40)*

It would be happier to draw a veil over family affairs during the next twelve months. They were described by Matilda in a letter to her uncle Richard Darby as "*a very painful family affair*" but they were more than that because the results were devastating not just for the family but for Coalbrookdale itself, and led to the departure from Coalbrookdale in 1851 of Abraham and Matilda, with a lasting sense of grievance.[41]

Letters of administration were granted to the widow, Hannah Darby, but elements of dissent showed up almost immediately in the attempts to divide the family silver (which was considerable) into three parts; ie between the widow and two daughters. The situation deteriorated when Hannah Darby told her daughter Matilda about the unexecuted Will. The solicitor, reluctantly, supplied a copy of his instruction in September 1850. Matilda was '*thunderstruck*'.[39] Various partitions of the freehold land, etc, were proposed. The final one proposed by Mr Potts the Solicitor, was that Matilda should receive the Sunniside property and Adelaide, the Haye, with Hannah Darby receiving all personal property. The shares in the Works were to be split three ways. This would have worked very well as it would have allowed Abraham IV to restore and to develop Sunniside as a family home.

Unfortunately, Hannah Darby continued to needle her daughter and Adelaide adopted an unhelpful attitude with the result that by the end of December 1850, after seeking the approval and support of her husband Abraham and his brother Alfred, Matilda agreed to forfeit her share of all the freehold property, taking only her one-third of Francis' shares in the Works (free of debt).

This was contrary to Francis Darby's wishes. He had clearly expected that Matilda would take Sunniside. It was also contrary to the provision of Abraham II's Will, under which Sunniside and the property immediately around it and possibly The Hay Farm would have been inherited by Matilda and Adelaide as co-parceners. It is difficult to avoid the conclusion that the situation was brought about by the way in which Hannah Grant behaved towards her elder daughter in favour of the interests of her younger daughter. Adelaide was able to confide in her diary "*Mr Potts came to the Chesnuts and they sent for me. He has arranged for me to take, with the Hay and the whole of the freehold property M's* (Matilda's) *share of the debt. This makes it somewhat less unfair, it is about £7000. We are much happier than we were, i.e, I am.*" Adelaide was the clear winner.[42]

Abraham and Matilda immediately made a decision to leave Coalbrookdale. Having previously been deprived of the opportunity of living at Stanley Hall, and now unable to live at Sunniside they had to look elsewhere, and after some searching they decided on Stoke Court, a considerable country property in Buckinghamshire, built by a grandson of William Penn. They left The Chesnuts and Coalbrookdale and moved to Stoke Court in April 1851.[43] Before they left, the deeds transferring the freehold properties to Adelaide and the personal property to Hannah Darby the widow were completed.[44] It was also a condition of the settlement that land for a new Anglican church in Coalbrookdale (to be provided and endowed by Abraham IV and Matilda) would be conveyed for a nominal consideration to the Commission for New Churches by Adelaide. The land at Paradise in Coalbrookdale, on which the new church was built between 1851 and 1854, was duly transferred by Adelaide in November 1851.[45] Adelaide also built a wall round the Quaker Burial Ground. When Abraham and Matilda left Coalbrookdale, The Chesnuts where the family had lived since the 1820s was no longer needed as a family home; it was, therefore, made available to the Church Commissioners with an endowment of £800 for use as a vicarage.[46] Abraham also let Strethill Farm to his cousin Henry Dickinson.[47]

While all this family drama was taking place, the Company was progressing well under the management of Mr Charles Crookes. He was a designer rather than a works manager, and he was deeply sympathetic to the work which the Company had pioneered in art castings. A great opportunity presented itself when the proposals for the Great Exhibition were published. Under his guidance the Company designed and cast for the new Crystal Palace a set of ornamental gates, 60ft wide; an ornamental fountain entitled "The Boy and the Swan"; a statue of Andromeda exposed to a sea monster; a cast-iron altar rail; a huge cast-iron dome, 30ft high, sheltering a figure of an Eagle-Slayer with his bow, whose arrow had pinned to the underside of the dome, a slain eagle. For this work Charles Crookes had commissioned John Bell, a distinguished designer to assist. John Bell was responsible for Andromeda and the Eagle-Slayer while Charles Crookes was responsible for the ornamental gates and the cast-iron dome.[48]

The exhibition was opened by Queen Victoria and Prince Albert on 1 May 1851. It was an outstanding success (Adelaide had a seat in the nave, while Abraham IV and Matilda had seats in the gallery).[49] Andromeda was purchased by Queen Victoria for re-erection at Osborne House on the Isle of Wight. The splendid gates were re-erected in Kensington Gardens where they remain to this day.[50] The Boy & Swan was purchased by Wolverhampton Corporation for display in the Market Hall. Later it was dismantled from a public park but was rescued from a Corporation depot and re-erected back in Coalbrookdale where it now occupies an honoured position in front of the Museum of Iron.

The Company was riding the crest of a wave. Following the reconstruction undertaken by Abraham IV and Alfred in the 1830s and 1840s, it could reasonably claim to be the largest Foundry in the world, turning

Coalbrookdale Company fountain and gates for the Great Exhibition, 1851. The gates are now located in Kensington Gardens.

Coalbrookdale Company 'Boy and Swan' fountain, designed by John Bell, exhibited at the Great Exhibition of 1851, as restored and on display in Coalbrookdale.

Coalbrookdale Company statue 'Andromeda' by John Bell, exhibited at the Great Exhibition of 1851, and now on display at Osborne House, Isle of Wight.

out some 2,000 tons of finished iron per week. *(51)* Although Abraham IV had left the Dale in 1851, his departure, which caused consternation in the locality, *(52)* was tempered by the arrival back in Shropshire of Alfred and the birth of a new heir, Alfred II *(53)* whose arrival was accompanied by great festivities and processions in the Dale. At a meeting of the partners of the Company held on 12 November 1851, attended for the first time by Adelaide and her mother, as new shareholders, Abraham IV gave up management of the Company to Alfred who was appointed on a salary of £500 per annum. The future of the Company was, therefore, left in good hands. Alfred was entrusted with the general direction and control of the enterprise, and Charles Crookes continued as Manager, assisted by Samuel Cookson as the Engineer.

The family, therefore, settled down to a new rhythm. At the head of the Dale lived Francis' widow Hannah and her daughter Adelaide, newly installed as partners in the Company. They were joined in the White House shortly after Francis' death by Hannah's mother, Hannah Grant who had been widowed in 1842 and had lived on at Leighton Buzzard until moving to Coalbrookdale in August 1850. Richard Darby continued to live at Rosehill with his wife Maria with their daughter Rebecca. *(54)* Next door, at Dale House lived Lucy Darby, mother of Abraham IV and Alfred, with her daughter Mary.

At the bottom of Coalbrookdale was the residence of Barnard Dickinson at Eastfield (built in 1838 when Barnard had moved from Dale House). Sadly his wife Ann (née Darby) had died on 5 May 1840 and he had spent the ten years since then travelling extensively on Quaker business. He died on 30 April 1852, aged seventy-one. *(55)* Next door to Eastfield was Severn House *(56)* the present day Valley Hotel, the residence of Henry Dickinson. Henry had married Deborah Darby in 1841. *(57)* Deborah was the daughter of Lucy and Edmund Darby and sister to Abraham IV and Alfred. Although the Dickinson's had sold their shares in the Company in 1831, Henry's marriage to Deborah had brought him back into the mainstream of the family. Henry had also become involved in the Shropshire Banking Company in Wellington. This was the successor of the bank set up in Wellington in 1805 by Thomas Eyton, a local landowner in conjunction with John Wilkinson and Joseph Reynolds. It became the Shropshire Banking Company in 1836 when it united with other banking facilities in Coalbrookdale, Newport and Shifnal. *(58)* It was used by the partners of the Coalbrookdale Company.

Henry Dickinson had become a wealthy man and in 1850 he purchased the Little Ness estate, north of Shrewsbury from the Earl of Powys, at a cost of £42,000. *(59)* This comprised 1012 acres of land in Little Ness, Adcote, Prescott and Ensdon. He was destined to become involved in the Company's affairs again in the next few years.

NOTES – CHAPTER X

1. Adelaide Darby's Journal, 18 August 1845. Trinder: *Industrial Revolution in Shropshire*, pp.387-393.
2. Adelaide Darby's Journal, 22 January 1845.
3. Trinder, *Darbys of Coalbrookdale*, pp.53-54.
   Adelaide Darby's Journal, 7-13 May 1845.
4. VCH Vol XI Telford, p.74 – See also S.R.O 1987/31/9 which is a blank receipt of July 1836: "*Received July 1836 of Abraham Darby ...for purchase of a small piece of land described in the sketch annexed (*missing*) which piece of land has been enclosed within and forms part of the playground surrounding the Infant School at Coalbrookdale, Madeley, and an undertaking at the expense of Abraham Darby to execute to him a conveyance of the piece in fee.*"
   It is assumed that the transaction was completed for it is possible to identify the piece of land in question from the counterpart lease of the Ironworks of 1838 (S.R.O 1681/138/8 – No 17 on map). Also see memorandum on Indenture, 31 March 1902, that the School House and School Yard was purchased by Abraham Darby from his relative Richard Darby, 18 December 1830.
5. S.R.O 1987/59/4. See also History of the Ebbw Vale Works and Collieries (First Article) 1894 by H Joshua Phillips, IGMT Library.
6. Adelaide Darby's Journal, 26 April 1842. J G Kohl writing at Liverpool in 1842 states: "*Liverpool 1842. To see how many things are now made of iron in England, one must visit one of the iron warehouses. as for instance that of Coalbrookdale, at this place. Tables, sofas, vases, inkstands and an endless variety of articles fashioned into the most graceful forms may there be seen.*" – IGMT Museum Guide No 2.01, published 1979.
7. Adelaide Darby's Journal, 17-20 July 1844.
8. Adelaide Darby's Journal, 15 September 1844.
9. See The Darby Estate Act 1854. (17 and 18 Vict., c.14)
   The five purchases of land were:-
   a) 154 acres at Aigburth and Garston (Hopes Estate) £75,000
   b) 71 acres at Garston (Seddon Farm Estate) £34,400
   c) 11 acres at Aigburth (Aigburth Hall Estate) £5,575
   d) 23 acres at Aigburth (Riversdale Estate) £18,921
   e) 13 acres at West Derby (Tue Brook Estate) £5,000
10. In a letter dated 29 November 1887 (S.R.O 1987/51/2/2) Matilda says, "*He* (Alfred Darby) *and my husband as A & A Darby had recently bought freehold land in Liverpool not for a permanent investment, but as so much cotton or corn to sell again*".
11. See Brymbo Steel Works by I D Jones published 1991 by Bridge Books, 61 Park Avenue, Wrexham (ISBN 1 872424 13 9). Once again the family brought with them the tradition of innovation and enterprise. Charles Edward, the younger brother, took out a patent

for the tapping of gases from the furnace top and conveying them by a gas 'downcomer' to the boilers to supplement the fuel burned there. This was a system which had been tried at Horsehay in 1850/51, where it failed.

12. S.R.O 1681/138/10.

13. As early as 1831, Francis Darby had been involved with his father-in-law, John Grant of Leighton Buzzard, *"respecting the newly projected Railway for steam-carriage from Birmingham to London"*. (Francis Darby's accounts 26th January 1831). The railway was constructed through the Grant's land (for a description see Adelaide Darby's Journal, 24 September 1836, also a description of Adelaide's first ride on a steam railway, 1 May 1839).

14. See Trinder: *Industrial Revolution in Shropshire*, pp.255-258.

15. See *History, Gazetteer and Directory of Shropshire 1851* by Samuel Bagshaw.

16. See S.R.O 1681/143/12 and S.R.O 1681/153/11 and 1681/138/9.

17. See S.R.O 1987/21/2, and see also SRO 1987/17/1, 9, 10,and 11. Note also SRO 1681/180/1.

18. S.R.O 1987/21/2 see also S.R.O 1681/180/1.

19. S.R.O 1987/11/2.

20. S.R.O 1987/19/37 and 1681/178/5, 6 and 7. See also Francis Darby's accounts for 21 February, 24 March and 4 August 1848.

20a Francis Darby's accounts, 30 January 1849. S.R.O 1681/180/2.

21. S.R.O 2280/2/45-8.

22. S.R.O 2280/2/48.

23. Francis Darby's account book, 6 January 1849.

24. *Deborah*, p.339. Some of Francis Darby's collection. An example of his purchases is shown by the following entry in his accounts for 14 May 1848:

Christie & Manson

Lot 22 Philip Wouwermans "Le Defile du Duc de Vendome" in Mons Casimir Perier's Catalogue. Casimir Perier's frd who attended the sale assured Messrs Christie & Manson that the late Minister of the late French King Louis Phillipe gave £1200 for it.	£640.10. 0
Van Huysum Flower Piece from the Redleaff Gallery, Lot 120. 4ft 5in by 3ft and No 20 Smiths catalogue	£420. 0. 0
Do Van Huysum – Lot 39 Do	£ 55.13. 0
Do Hondechoeter lot 23 spaniel with a dead partridge etc	£ 36.15. 0
Do Lot 47 Weenix a dead partridge with other birds	£ 42. 0. 0
Do lot 55 Rachel Ruich fruit piece	£178.10. 0
Do Lot 61 D Teniers landscape with boors talking. Smiths catalogue No 161. 8in by 10 in.	£ 42. 0. 0
	£1415. 8. 0

25. Adelaide Darby's Journal, 21 July 1846.
26. Francis Darby's accounts, 13 September 1847.
27. Adelaide Darby's Journal, 11 April 1848, 24 September 1848 and 24 August 1849.
28. Adelaide Darby's Journal, 25 August 1839.
29. Adelaide Darby's Journal, 11 August 1844.
30. Adelaide Darby's Journal, 20 January 1840.
31. Adelaide Darby's Journal, 3 and 29 December 1841.
32. Adelaide Darby's Journal, 10 May 1845. Some panels of hand-painted Chinese wallpapers, rescued from The Woodbines by Lady Labouchere, on display at Rosehill, Coalbrookdale (IGMT).
33. Adelaide Darby's Journal, 16 July 1847.
34. Copy, watermarked 1848 of instructions for the Will of Francis Darby of Coalbrookdale, Esquire, IGMT.
35. Copy of letter written in 1851 from Matilda Darby to her uncle Richard Darby explaining why she and Abraham Darby left the Dale after the death of Francis Darby (IGMT).
36. Adelaide Darby's Journal, 18 November 1845.
37. For example, Adelaide was included in an important visit to Ebbw Vale, 11-17 July 1846, and to the Lake District in April 1848. Adelaide also joined Abraham and Matilda on a holiday in Belgium, Germany and Switzerland, 11 July to 1 September 1848.
38. S.R.O 1987/56/18.
39. Journal of Matilda Darby, Stoke Court, 4 October 1852.
40. Francis Darby's last illness seems to have started at the beginning of the 1840s or the end of the 1830s. It seems to have coincided with a recurrence of his latent 'psychological' problems. At that time he suffered 'a strange delusion' concerning his wife's faithfulness to him. It seems inconceivable that this referred to infidelity in the modern sense, but rather perhaps to her loyalty to him. He was a demanding man and was prone to violence. The marriage was clearly going through a bad patch to the extent that the intervention of his parents-in-law was invoked. It was probably this incident that persuaded his father-in-law, John Grant, to alter his Will so that his interest in the Leighton Buzzard Bank would not pass to Francis on John Grant's death. See journal of Matilda Darby dated 16 June 1872 headed "*The Story of the Leighton Bank as well as I remember it*".
41. See copy letter written by Matilda Darby, probably dated April 1851 to an addressee presumed to be Richard Darby. IGMT.
42. Adelaide Darby's Journal, 27 December 1850.
43. Journal of Matilda Darby, Stoke Court, 4 October 1852.
44. Memoranda of agreement dated 19 March 1851 were completed setting out the settlement of the estate of Francis Darby as agreed between the widow, Hannah Darby and her two daughters, Matilda Frances and Adelaide Anna. One of the memoranda signed by

Adelaide Anna is in the possession of IGMT. The conveyance of the freehold estate to Adelaide Anna was also completed on 19 March 1851 (see S.R.O 1681/178/16 and also S.R.O 1681/180/4, 5 and 6). The deed also dated 19 March 1851 vesting the personal property in Hannah Darby and making provision for payment of debts is in the possession of IGMT.

45. S.R.O 1681/180/7.
46. S.R.O 1681/179/14-15. The Chesnuts was used as a vicarage until 1901.
47. Adelaide Darby's Journal, 21 February 1851.
48. Barrie Trinder: *The Darbys of Coalbrookdale*, p.54.
49. Adelaide Darby's Journal, 29 April to 15 May 1851.
50. See letter from Abraham Darby to Lord Seymour S.R.O 1987/58/3.
51. Raistrick, p.266.
52. Adelaide Darby's Journal, p.337.
53. Alfred Edmund William Darby was born on 7 September 1850 (Adelaide's Journal for that date) followed by two sisters Alice Mary (born 1851), and Alfreda Lucy (born 1852).
54. The eldest son, Richard Sorton Darby, had moved to Hawkswood House, Sidbury, Near Bridgnorth. The 1851 census lists the two other sons, William Henry Darby and Charles Edward Darby as resident in the Dale, but they were already managing the Brymbo Iron Works near Wrexham.
55. S.R.O 1681/127/8 Copy Will of Barnard Dickinson, died 30 April 1852, proved 26 June 1852.
56. Severn House, now the Valley Hotel, Ironbridge, was built in 1757 by George Goodwin, master collier and partner in the Madeley Wood Company (V.C.H Vol XI, Telford p.28)
    It was purchased by Sarah Darby from the trustees of George Goodwin and passed under her Will to Barnard and Ann Dickinson and then to such of their children as they should appoint. They chose their son Henry.
57. Adelaide Darby's Journal, 17 March 1841.
58. V.C.H Vol XI Telford, p.228. Barrie Trinder: *Industrial Revolution in Shropshire*, p.234. The Shropshire Banking Company was taken over by Lloyds Bank in 1874 with a branch in Church Street, Wellington.
59. S.R.O 1987/41/83.

CHAPTER XI

The Days of the Triumvirate

WHEN ABRAHAM IV handed over management of the Company to his brother Alfred in 1851, the Company was in good shape. The coalfield as a whole had become segmented into spheres of influence split between some six main companies (See Map, p.162). The Coalbrookdale Company dominated much of the western parts including the parishes of Little Dawley, Little Wenlock and Lawley, as well as Coalbrookdale in the west of the Parish of Madeley. Most of the rest of the Parish of Madeley was dominated by the Company's former partner, the Madeley Wood Company, now run by the Anstice family regarded as near relatives through their relationship with William Reynolds.

The Company had achieved national renown through its activities in the Great Exhibition of 1851 and even if it no longer led the iron industry as it once had, it was assured of a good future in the development of art castings and domestic artefacts designed to suit the prosperous tastes of the new Victorian period.

Adelaide, once she had overcome the shock caused by the departure of Abraham IV and her beloved sister Matilda, settled down to a new way of life. Friendships with Broseley families led her to new activities in Bridgnorth and its neighbourhood. In particular in July 1851 she was invited to Dudmaston, near Bridgnorth, the home of William Wolryche-Whitmore.[1] During the next few months she met Henry Whitmore, a cousin of William Wolryche-Whitmore, resident at nearby Apley Castle.[2] By the end of November, the stage had been reached at which the Whitmore family made enquiries about her financial standing. It transpired that she was worth more than he was.[3] Within the month Adelaide and Henry were betrothed.[4] On 15 April 1852 they were married. Adelaide was then thirty-five years of age.

Over the years fate had dealt some cruel blows to the Darby family. Death at a relatively early age was a recurring theme[5] and always caused unfortunate results. This time, fate struck at Alfred who was only forty-four, and had just taken over control of the Company.

Coalbrookdale (W. W. Law, c.1850).

MINING ROYALTIES AND IRONWORKS 1840

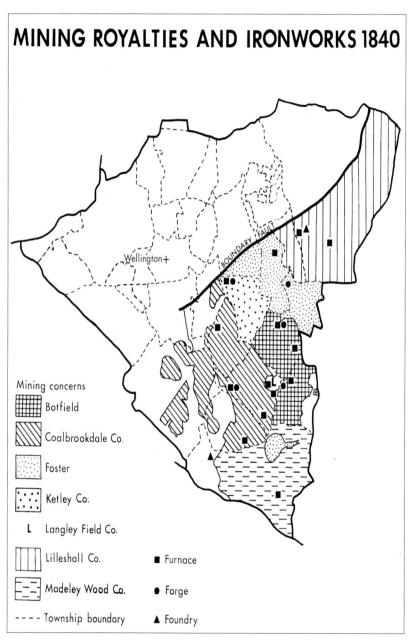

Mining concerns

Botfield

Coalbrookdale Co.

Foster

Ketley Co.

L Langley Field Co.

Lilleshall Co.

Madeley Wood Co.

---- Township boundary

■ Furnace

● Forge

▲ Foundry

Wellington +

BOUNDARY FAULT

MAP, COURTESY OF VICTORIA COUNTY HISTORY OF SHROPSHIRE (VOL. XI)

He died unexpectedly of erysipelas at his home Stanley Hall, Bridgnorth on 14 April 1852, just one day before Adelaide and Henry Whitmore were married.[6] The conjunction of the two events was dreadful.

Quite apart from the shock to the family, the problem was that for the first time, no member of the family trained in the Works was available to take over the management. Abraham IV had left the Dale and was now becoming increasingly involved in the expansion of the Ebbw Vale Works, although his return was briefly considered. The two sons of Richard Darby had moved to the Brymbo Ironworks at Wrexham and were fully committed there. In September 1852, a Company Meeting was held at which Mr Charles Crookes was appointed full manager having served with the Company since the 1830s. It was then decided that the partnership decisions should be left in the hands of a triumvirate, consisting of Henry Whitmore, Henry Dickinson and Francis Tothill (son of William Tothill)[7] and the situation was rationalised in January of 1854 when the three signed a declaration that all properties held by them were held in trust for the Coalbrookdale Company.[8] Their services were called upon very quickly when in 1853, the Company acquired the Manor of Lawley and property and mines in Lawley, Wellington and Dawley. This had the effect of consolidating the ownership of the Company on the northern reaches of its sphere of influence and shows that the Company was still expanding. Indeed, following the success of the Great Exhibition in 1851, the Company took part in the International Exhibition in Dublin in 1853 and the bigger International Exhibition in Paris in 1855.[9]

On the family front, however, the death of Alfred was causing unexpected difficulties. In July 1852 Alfred's widow Rebecca (Miller Christy) was granted Letters of Administration to her late husband's estate and then questions arose about the properties in Liverpool which Alfred and Abraham were developing for housing purposes. Five estates were involved, and at the time of Alfred's death, the conveyances for three of them had been completed. The two others in Aigburth and Garston had not been completed, even though development had taken place and money expended. This untidy situation required a decision as to whether the property passing on Alfred's death should be regarded as real estate, in which case it would pass to his infant son Alfred Edmund William Darby as heir-at-law or whether, being incomplete, the property should be regarded as an equitable estate, in which case it would pass as personal estate to Alfred's widow and children under the Statutes of Distribution. This difficult problem could only be resolved by an application to the Court of Chancery which promised to be a lengthy process. It was, therefore, agreed by the Court that an application should be made for a private Act of Parliament to enable the development to proceed. This was done and the Darby Estate Act 1854 was passed and given Royal Assent on 24 July 1854.[10]

The costs of the Act of Parliament and the Chancery proceedings, coupled with the delay to the development had a considerable effect on the profitability of the scheme. This was particularly unfortunate because Mary Darby, sister of Abraham and Alfred had been advised by Alfred to place her money in the project as an investment and her interests were therefore placed in jeopardy.[11] As a result Abraham IV and Matilda transferred to Mary their shares in the Coalbrookdale Works by way of compensation.[12] This was a blow to Abraham's finances and Matilda said that *"we were a good deal straitened after this transfer because at the same time Ebbw Vale Company had to provide Alfred's money there to the satisfaction of the Court of Chancery"*.[13]

Although they were happy in their married life at Stoke Court, the financial problems following Alfred's death came at a difficult time for Abraham. He was now fully committed to the development of the Ebbw Vale Works. This consisted of four blast furnaces at Ebbw Vale and another furnace nearby at Sirhowy which had been purchased in 1844 and three blast furnaces with puddling furnaces at the Victoria Ironworks and collieries purchased in 1848.[14] In 1852, the year of Alfred's death, the Ebbw Vale partnership purchased the Abersychan Ironworks and collieries, consisting of six blast furnaces and puddling furnaces and in 1855 they acquired extensive iron works, tin plate works and collieries in Pontypool consisting of four blast furnaces and associated works.[15] It was rapidly becoming a vast industrial empire with Abraham IV very much in the lead, and requiring considerable investment of capital, etc.

In the same year, 1855, Abraham IV and William Tothill became two of the five sponsors of the West Somerset Railway set up to bring iron ore from the Brendon Hills to Watchet harbour, east of Minehead.[16]

It was in the middle of all this activity that Abraham IV and Henry Dickinson suffered a truly cruel blow to their fortunes. It was early one morning in late November 1854 that Henry Dickinson arrived at Stoke Court with the devastating news that, two nights before, he had been sitting with his wife Deborah[17] in his study at Severn House, when Mr Allen, the Manager of the Shropshire Bank, Wellington, called to confess that he had speculated with the money placed in the Bank and had lost £200,000 and *"that the Bank was cleaned out and £30,000 was given notice to be wanted by Mr Foster which there was no means to pay"*.[18] £200,000 in 1854 was equivalent to over £11 million in 1997 terms, and prior to the Limited Liability Act 1879, proprietors of banks were absolutely liable to the last penny of their means to repay their creditors.[18a] This was, therefore, a shattering blow, the more so as there was need for the utmost

Adelaide Darby.

Henry Whitmore, MP.

Sunniside II (the White House). The original central portion was the home of Rebecca Darby, after the death of her husband Abraham III in 1789. The east wing (on the left of the picture) was built by her son, Francis Darby, c.1808. The west wing was built by Henry Whitmore (husband of Adelaide Darby) between 1862-65.

secrecy – only the two wives, Deborah and Matilda, were informed. We do not know how the crisis was resolved but sufficient resources were found to overcome the immediate problem as the Bank survived until it was taken over by Lloyds Bank in 1874.[19]

This major loss, combined with the disappointment of the Liverpool property was a severe setback to the family finances, and for some years Abraham and Matilda must have been worried about their future. In December 1857, Adelaide noted in her diary that *"Mama and I went to Stoke Court. We found Abraham and Matilda both ill from influenza and in trouble thinking they were coming to poverty!"*. [20] Thereafter Abraham had to devote his considerable energies and talents to the development of the Ebbw Vale Company, and this led to their departure from Stoke Court (and its eventual sale) and to the sale of the valuable collection of paintings, etc, which Abraham had been amassing since the 1840s. As Matilda put it, *"We did our best, my husband to earn, and I to learn details and to make the best of smaller means. We were very happy all the while"*. [21]

In complete contrast to the deteriorating fortunes of Abraham and Matilda, the prospects of Adelaide and her new husband Henry Whitmore were in the ascendant. Adelaide had married into one of Shropshire's most illustrious political families.

Henry was born at Apley Park in 1814, the third son of Thomas Whitmore who had represented Bridgnorth as Member of Parliament from 1806-1831. Before the Reform Act 1832, Shropshire returned twelve Members of Parliament and was unusual in that only one borough could be described as corrupt. Although the County was free of 'overtowering aristocratic territorial influence", its parliamentary representation was nevertheless practically hereditary in about a dozen families, of which the Whitmores in Bridgnorth was one.[22]

Although Shropshire was part of the Tory belt, the County nevertheless returned a solid cadre of at least eight Whigs, distinguished by the fact that they followed one leader (The Earl of Powys) in a way unknown at that time in any other English County. They were known as "The Shropshire Whigs" and were always treated as a group.[23]

Bridgnorth had been represented since the Reform Act 1832 by Thomas Charlton Whitmore, Henry's eldest brother. In June 1852, two months after his wedding to Adelaide, Henry was called upon to stand in a contested election at Bridgnorth, in succession to his brother. That election he won and thereafter he represented the constituency for some eighteen years until he accepted the Chiltern Hundreds in 1870.[24] Henry was a conservative and joined the efforts of Lord Derby and Benjamin Disraeli to unseat the Whig government of Lord John Russell and subsequently Lords Aberdeen and Palmerston. There was a brief success at the end of 1852 when Adelaide recorded in her Journal:- *"Very late division. Henry did not get away till 3 this morning. Too tired to say anything except "We have beaten them by 80". Ld Derby is safe now at present"*. In fact Lord Derby's government lasted less than a month. [25]

From 1852 onwards, Adelaide and Henry entered the upper reaches of London society. Life was a hectic round of receptions, balls, concerts, dinner parties and visits including a number of royal occasions. [26] Adelaide became a political hostess and appears to have undertaken her duties with considerable credit. Their acknowledged home was in Coalbrookdale where they were master and mistress of the White House which became known as Sunniside in 1856 when they demolished the old Sunniside. [27] But they spent much of their time in London whilst the House was in session and whilst the London season was in progress. The practice was to rent a London address each year, eg Chesham Place, Lowndes Street, Eaton Terrace and then to return to Sunniside, whence they would visit Apley, Bridgnorth, Willey and occasionally Stanley Hall (Mrs Alfred Darby) and more locally Uncle Richard Darby's house (ie Rosehill), Dale House (Lucy Darby and Mary) Severn House (Henry Dickinson) and Marnwood (Reverend Bartlett), as well as the Anstice family (Madeley Wood). Life was full to the brim.

The Sunniside estate remained much the same except that in 1853 the Hay Farm was sold to John Anstice. [28] They also started to improve Sunniside II by building a terrace in front of the house and undertaking alterations. [29] But inevitably the focus of their lives now centred on London where Henry was proving to be a diligent and committed politician. His prospects improved considerably in 1855 when he was given a parliamentary appointment by Disraeli. [30] Then, following the resignation of Lord Palmerston's government in March 1857 an election was held on 27 March. Henry was returned unopposed, at Bridgnorth. Adelaide recorded that *"The Bells rang there and at the Dale where we came home with 4 horses"*. [31]

The following February (1858) Henry went to the House to help present the Address to the Queen on the marriage of the Princess Royal to Prince Frederick William of Prussia, and then dined afterwards with Mr Disraeli. The political scene was hotting up and on 20 February the Government of Lord Palmerston was again beaten. On the 21st Adelaide said *"This has been a most exciting day...Lord Derby kissed hands as Premier today at 3 o'clock"*. During the next two days, she added, *"Everybody in a fever of expectation and the change astonishing to all"*. The following evening Adelaide had a dinner for fourteen at home, arranged long before the events of the past few days and was able to record with satisfaction *"curious it is that so many present had received appointments. Mr Seymour Fitzgerald to be Foreign Secretary, Mr Whiteside Att. General for Ireland, Col. Taylor and Henry, Lords of the Treasury"*. [32]

Disraeli was Chancellor of the Exchequer, and the following day they called on Lady Thesiger whose husband had been appointed Lord Chancellor and created Baron Chelmsford. [33] On 26 February 1858, Henry Whitmore was formally appointed Lord of the Treasury, and on the 6 March he was given the office of Keeper of the Privy Seal to the Duchy of Cornwall, the Queen's own gift, and in that capacity he went to Windsor to attend the confirmation of the Prince of Wales. [34] This was a most gratifying outcome to his political career. Within six years he had reached the higher levels of government and was associated not only with Lord Derby but also with Benjamin Disraeli, destined to become one of the great Prime Ministers of the nineteenth century.

Coalbrookdale shared in the glory when in October 1858 The Lord Chancellor and Lady Chelmsford stayed with Henry and Adelaide at the White House, by then renamed Sunniside. However, the Government of Lord Derby only lasted for just over a year and in the following June 1859, they were defeated and Lord Palmerston probably the most popular man in England, took over for his second Ministry which lasted until his death in 1865. Henry was, therefore, to spend the next few years in opposition until Lord Derby headed his third and last administration in 1866. [35]

During the decade of the 1850s other family events were taking place in Coalbrookdale. In 1853 Hannah Grant, mother of Hannah Darby, Francis' widow died at the White House. She had moved there in 1850 after the death of Francis Darby and lived there for the last three years of her life. [36] She had been a committed Quaker throughout her life and had been a great influence in the family, particularly on her grand-daughters Matilda and Adelaide.

Another sad occasion was the death of Henry Dickinson's wife Deborah (Darby) on 29 October 1855. She was the younger sister of Abraham IV and was aged only forty-five years. She had married Henry Dickinson in 1841. Her death came as a great shock. Anything affecting the Darby family was deeply felt in the Dale and the Works were closed on the day of her funeral. [37] Under the marriage settlement, Henry continued to receive £1000 per annum for life from Deborah's shares in the Coalbrookdale Company. [38] Three years after Deborah's death he married Susannah Hadwen. [39]

During this period of the 1850s, the landscape of the Lower Dale was being transformed by the building of the new parish church endowed and paid for by Abraham IV. The church was completed and consecrated in 1854. Shortly afterwards another new building started to appear below it. This was the Coalbrookdale Literary and Scientific Institution. This resulted from the efforts of a working party set up in 1853 under the chairmanship of Charles Crookes, Manager of the Works. [40] The building and the adjoining house for the librarian were designed by Mr Crookes and all the materials for construction were supplied by the Company from its own resources. In 1856 an associated School of art was founded which over the next seventy-five years or so was to make an enormous impact on the design capacity of the Works and also of neighbouring works such as the Coalport China Works and the Jackfield tile industry.

The Literary and Scientific Institution was completed in 1858 and virtually its first use was to celebrate the wedding of Mary Darby (sister of Abraham IV) and the Reverend William Jones of Baschurch. Mary was very popular in the Dale for manifold acts of kindness and generosity and her support for charities and every social and moral movement in the community. Her saintly behaviour led her to be known as the 'Queen of the Valley'. *(41)* She was a partner in the Works and in addition to her shareholding (enhanced by the transfer of Abraham and Matilda's shares in 1852) she owned property in Baschurch and Much Wenlock. *(42)* This presumably is how she came to know Reverend Jones, who was the Vicar of Baschurch. The wedding took place not in Coalbrookdale, but at Stoke Court, Buckinghamshire, home of Abraham and Matilda.

This did not in the least inhibit a week long programme of celebrations in Coalbrookdale, Horsehay, Dawley and Lawley. Mary Darby, at her own expense provided twenty-six oxen, forty-two sheep and calves, which were slaughtered, cut up and distributed, together with 1500 gallons of ale and 3200 loaves of bread, to upwards of three thousand employees at Horsehay, etc, and four hundred and seventy-seven at Coalbrookdale. The centre piece of the whole affair was a banquet in the new Literary and Scientific Institution, followed by an evening entertainment with a 15ft high bonfire with illuminations of the grounds of the Institution and of the Great Warehouse. *(43)*

The occasion was one of great euphoria and all concerned clearly felt that the Coalbrookdale Company and the Darby family were second to none in the Kingdom. The Company was doing well, and was approaching its optimum size. At this time it consisted of the ironworks in Coalbrookdale, Horsehay, Lawley, Lightmoor and Dawley Castle; limeworks in the Parish of Much Wenlock; Collieries, coalworks, ironstone works and brickworks in Madeley, Dawley, Little Wenlock, Much Wenlock and Wellington, and warehouses, yards and wharves in the City of Bristol and the Town of Liverpool. *(44)* In 1859 another warehouse in Bristol was acquired *(45)* and in 1868 the Company took an assignment of the Shutfield and Cherry Tree Hill Brickworks. *(46)* But by then, a process of contraction had begun.

The celebrations of Mary Darby's wedding effectively disguised the fact that Abraham IV and Matilda were still struggling with the consequences of the financial problems of the Shropshire Banking Company

Holy Trinity Church and Coalbrookdale Literary and Scientific Institution, 1859.

171

Dale House and Rosehill, pre-1864. The wooden bridge over the upper furnace pool replaced the cast iron bridge shown in the lithograph of the upper part of Coalbrookdale by William Westwood, dated 1835 (page 127).

and the difficulties arising from the Liverpool properties. The immediate family had pulled together extremely well to cope with the problems. After the death of Alfred and Deborah, they consisted of Lucy Darby and her eldest son and daughter, Abraham IV and Mary. Abraham was of course confronted with the need to expand the Ebbw Vale Company and an arrangement was made late in 1857 with the Bank of England for a loan or credit facility of £120,000. [47] This loan was guaranteed by the partners of the Company (Abraham IV, Henry Dickinson, William Tothill, Thomas Brown and Joseph Robinson, of Liverpool) and was secured by a transfer to trustees of the properties in Liverpool. It was also secured by a transfer to the same trustees of the property owned by Mary Darby in the parishes of Baschurch and Much Wenlock (Farley).

Lucy Darby, Abraham's mother, was also determined to play her part. She had already deposited all her available capital, some £41,000 with the Ebbw Vale Company on payment of interest. She also indicated her wish to transfer her shares in the Coalbrookdale Company to her son Abraham IV. Abraham's solicitor intervened to advise that because of possible claims that might still arise against Abraham, it would be better if the shares were transferred to trustees for the benefit of Abraham's wife Matilda. [48] This was done in February 1858. [49]

Two months later Lucy finally settled her affairs when she made a settlement of the £41,000 which was to remain with the Ebbw Vale Company during her lifetime and was then to be split predominantly between Abraham, Mary and Henry Dickinson with small bequests to her many nieces and nephews of the Burlingham and Southall families. [50]

After the wedding of Mary Darby and Reverend William Jones in 1858, Lucy Darby moved to Stoke Court to live with Abraham and Matilda. She left Dale House where she had lived since 1838 and stayed with Abraham and Matilda until she died in 1870. She left a good memory behind her in the Dale where she was remembered for her kindness and goodness which exemplified the relationship between the Darbys and their work people.

With the departure from Coalbrookdale of Lucy Darby, the curtain was falling on the fourth generation of the Darby family, the children of Abraham III. Hannah Darby, who had left the Dale to marry William Tothill of Stoke Bishop, Bristol, died in 1859. In less than a year, the death took place on 3 February 1860 of Maria Darby (Sorton) who was married to Richard Darby and lived at Rosehill. [51] Six months after she died, Richard accompanied by his daughter Rebecca, travelled to the continent and on 7 August 1860 he died in Brussels. [52] Before the year was out Hannah Darby, wife of Francis and mother of Matilda and Adelaide, died at Sunniside (The White House). Within a short space of time, the number of members of the family actually living in the Dale was reduced to

Adelaide at Sunniside (who spent much of her time in London), Rebecca (daughter of Richard and Maria) at Rosehill and Henry Dickinson at Severn House.

Hannah Darby had made a will in 1857 leaving most of her estate to Adelaide with a pecuniary legacy of £5,000 to her elder daughter Matilda. At least she was consistent, because this reflected the partiality to Adelaide which she had displayed at the time of her husband's (Francis') death in 1850. She must have been aware of the financial difficulties which had overtaken Matilda and Abraham IV since then, as she stayed quite frequently with Matilda and Abraham at Stoke Court during her latter years. Her only response to their difficulties was to increase the legacy of £5,000 to £8,000 by a codicil to the Will a few months before her death. *(53)*

At this time, fundamental technological advances were being made in the iron industry. In 1856 Henry (later Sir Henry) Bessemer invented a process for making what came to be known as mild steel. The year before J G Martien of New Jersey, United States of America, had experimented with a somewhat similar process of refining iron, the patent of which was purchased outright by the Ebbw Vale partnership under Abraham IV. Similar experiments were also being conducted under Mr George Parry the works chemist, at Ebbw Valve which pre-dated Bessemer's patent but were abandoned. In 1861, however, George Parry patented a process by which ordinary wrought-iron or scrap iron was converted into superior wrought-iron or cast steel. *(54)*

It was at this crucial time that Abraham IV decided to move to Ebbw Vale to take more direct personal control over events. He and Matilda, with his mother Lucy Darby left Stoke Court in 1861 intending to stay in Ebbw Vale for two years *(55)* although in the event, their removal from Stoke Court proved to be permanent and Stoke Court was eventually sold in 1869. *(56)* Abraham took over active management of the extensive Ebbw Vale enterprise in 1862. It then comprised nineteen blast furnaces, one hundred and forty-two puddling furnaces, ninety-nine heating furnaces and twelve hundred workmen's' houses. The colliery leases comprised some 75,000 acres of land, an altogether bigger operation than Coalbrookdale. The Company used their new patented process for several years until in 1866, Bessemer purchased the patent from the Ebbw Vale Company for £30,000 of which amount £10,000 went to Mr George Parry. Thereafter the Company inaugurated and operated Bessemer's process. Once again, a member of the Darby family was in the forefront of progress in the iron industry.

Another important milestone in progress was the passing of the Companies Act 1862, which introduced the concept of limited liability into company law. One of the first companies to convert into a limited liability company was the Lilleshall Company. *(57)* Two years later in 1864, Abraham IV took the lead in taking the Ebbw Vale Company along the same path. In that year a new limited liability company was formed with a capital of £4 million in shares of £50 each. *(58)* Abraham IV became Managing Director. The Company was further reconstructed in 1866 as The Ebbw Vale Steel Iron and Coal Company Limited.

The Company prospered and expanded under Abraham's inspired leadership until he retired in 1873. During this time he and Matilda lived at the Company's official residence Ebbw Vale Park near the blast furnaces. *(59)* Lucy Darby also lived there until her death in 1870. *(60)*

By way of contrast, the Coalbrookdale Company, still under the management of Charles Crookes, saw its future developing in a different way. Increasingly it was concentrating on the production of an astonishing variety of cast-iron products from its foundries. It was maintaining its high standards of excellence in decorative cast-iron, employing such artists as the Frenchmen P J Mene, and Carrier-Belleuse, and later Alfred Stevens and Christopher Dresser. The School of Art established in 1856 was also beginning to make its presence felt and increasingly the work of the Company's employees who had been students of the School of Art, was shown in the wide variety of patterns being created. The Company also contributed to the International Exhibition of 1862. The writer of the exhibition catalogue wrote of the Company:-

"While it furnishes millions of dwellings with stoves and other household necessaries of a cheap kind, it adorns also the mansions and palaces of the aristocracy...while they fabricate huge machines that move vast ships and weighty carriages over land and sea, they give due consideration to the requirements of a refined life."(61)

The Company was also developing its heavy engineering capacity and in 1863 they produced the Albert Edward Bridge carrying the new railway across the River Severn at Coalbrookdale, the longest single span bridge on the entire network of the Great Western Railway. *(62)*

The Company did not see a sustainable future in the production of iron and steel other than for its own purposes. The iron ore available in the Coalbrookdale Coalfield was not suitable for use in the Bessemer process as it then existed *(63)* and it was difficult to compete with iron works nearer the coast with more suitable supplies. The Company in the early 1860s had furnaces at Horsehay, Lawley, Lightmoor and Dawley Castle. There were too many for its own purposes and the first to go in 1861 were the Horsehay furnaces, started by Abraham II and Richard Reynolds over one hundred years before. *(64)*

Despite this setback, the local economy received a boost with the arrival of the railway in Coalbrookdale in 1864. The main line through

Shropshire from Shrewsbury to Wolverhampton had been opened in 1849 but it took another fifteen years before it reached Coalbrookdale. Branch lines had reached Lightmoor by 1858 and in 1862 the Severn Valley Railway was constructed along the southern bank of the River Severn. What was needed was the completion of the link between Lightmoor and the Severn Valley line, and this took place in 1864, using the Albert Edward Bridge fabricated in Coalbrookdale. *(64a)*

This provided a spectacular end to the career of Charles Crookes who retired in 1866. The fame of the Company was now world-wide. In 1866, the year that he retired, the Company despatched a cast-iron statue of the eminent colonial administrator, John Robert Godley for erection at Lyttleton near Canterbury, New Zealand. *(65)* The name of the Company could scarcely go any further.

Behind the scenes in the Company, however, all was not well. Charles Crookes for all his merit in the field of design, was not an ironmaster, and had no previous knowledge of iron making. *(66)* Abraham IV and Alfred had demonstrated in the 1830s and 1840s that running an ironworks needed strong leadership and management as well as a profound knowledge of the technology of iron making. Control of affairs under Charles Crookes were allowed to drift and the situation had become serious, particularly at Horsehay. *(66)* Radical change was called for and this came with the appointment of a new manager, William Gregory Norris in 1866. He took occupation of Dale House and was destined to steer the Company through a very turbulent period for the next thirty years and to ensure its survival through to the end of the century as a modernised and dynamic part of the iron industry.

W G Norris, like Charles Crookes before him, was not an ironmaster, and on the face of it, the partners were simply continuing the previous situation. His experience lay in the administrative side of the works. He had also been secretary of the committee set up to establish the Coalbrookdale Literary and Scientific Institution and the School of Art. But above all, there being no member of the Darby family available to take charge of the Company, he was the nearest thing to a member of the family that could be found. He was a Quaker and his mother was a member of the Luccock family, who had been with the Darby family in the Dale since the very beginning. Abraham I's stepmother was Joan Luccock and he took into apprenticeship a relative of hers, Thomas Luccock, in 1714. *(67)* The Luccocks had been involved in the Works from that date onwards. The appointment of their descendant, William Gregory Norris, was to prove to be a masterstroke.

His first task was to improve the quality of pig iron and in this he appears to have had the technical assistance of Abraham IV, for by introducing foreign ores and making other changes he was able to reduce the waste in the rolled iron from over twenty per cent to less than five per cent.*(68)* Within a few years the Company was once again able to compete with the demand for finished iron in any market in the land. There is other evidence that Abraham was linked to the Dale at that time because in September 1866, he and his wife Matilda appointed William Gregory Norris as trustee in the purchase of a house in Coalbrookdale. This was Woodside Cottage, backing on to Dale Coppice in the north east of the Dale.*(69)* Although the purchase was made at Abraham's request, the purchase money came from Matilda and the property was designated for her exclusive use. This seems to suggest that Abraham and Matilda may have been making provision for their possible return to Coalbrookdale. Indeed, they may have had good reason to make long-term provision because just before acquiring Woodside Cottage, the partners of the Ebbw Vale Company (including Abraham, Henry Dickinson and William Tothill) had made an accommodation with creditors for the appointment of Inspectors, presumably to control their assets.*(70)* It is not known whether this arose from the creation of the limited company at Ebbw Vale which was reconstructed in 1866 into the Ebbw Vale Steel, Iron and Coal Company Limited, but as they were introducing the Bessemer process at the time, they were undoubtedly involved in major capital investment.

Undoubtedly the partners at Ebbw Vale came under increasing financial pressure, because within two years the Inspectors directed Henry Dickinson to sell his Little Ness estate which he had acquired from the Earl of Powys in 1850.*(71)* The net proceeds of the sale were paid to the Inspectors. The property, however, remained within the family because Henry Dickinson sold the estate to Rebecca Darby of Stanley Hall, the widow of Alfred Darby.*(72)*

Meanwhile, the fortunes of Henry Whitmore and Adelaide were once again in the ascendant. Palmerston had died in 1865*(73)* and his successor as Prime Minister, Lord John Russell only lasted six months. Lord Derby and his conservative administration took office, with Disraeli as Chancellor of the Exchequer. Once again, Henry Whitmore was appointed Lord of the Treasury and Keeper of the Privy Seal to the Prince of Wales. He remained in office until 1868. Lord Derby resigned in 1868 and was succeeded as Prime Minister by Disraeli who held office for a further six months. Much of the time of the administration was taken up by the Reform Act of 1867 (known as the "Fancy Franchises" Bill) which enfranchised all male householders in the towns and men occupying houses worth £12 a year in the Counties.

His final two years as a government minister represented the high point of Henry Whitmore's political life. His career came to an end shortly afterwards when in 1870, he applied for the Chiltern Hundreds and retired from Parliament. In the same year, Lucy Darby's life came to a close at Ebbw Vale where she had been living with her son and daughter-in-law, Abraham IV and Matilda. She was eighty-eight years old and had lived the last sixty years of her life as a widow since the death of her husband Edmund Darby in 1810. She was buried next to him at Melksham in Wiltshire. She was the last of the fourth generation of the Darby family. Fortunately she died before she could be aware of the calamity which was about to befall the iron industry from 1870 onwards. There were few who could have foreseen the devastating events of the next ten to twenty years, and she was at least spared the turmoil which ensued.

NOTES – CHAPTER XI

1. Adelaide's diary, 15 July 1851 and 28 August 1851.
2. Adelaide's diary, 31 October, 1, 3, 7, 13, 24 and 28 November 1851.
3. Adelaide's diary, 28 November 1851 – "*I told her all of our family differences and at present I have not more than 500 a year – he has 400*".
4. Adelaide's diary, 26 December 1851.
5. Abraham I was 39, and his grandson Abraham III was 38. William Reynolds was 45 and Edmund Darby was only 28, Alfred Darby was 44.
6. Death certificate of Alfred Darby – IGMT Archive.
7. Henry Whitmore was married to Adelaide, who held one-third of the shares which devolved on the death of her father, Francis Darby in 1850; Henry Dickinson was married to Deborah Darby, daughter of Edmund and Lucy Darby, who held 88 shares; Francis Tothill, b1829 was the third son of William Tothill and Hannah Darby, who was entitled to shares under the partnership agreement of 1807 and under the will of Sarah Darby. See S.R.O 1681/178/10-15 and S.R.O 1681/179/9.
8. S.R.O 1681/181/55 and S.R.O 1681/178/10-15 and S.R.O 1681/179/9.
9. Trinder, *Darbys of Coalbrookdale*, p.55.
10. An Act for the better Division and Management of certain estates in the County of Lancaster, the Property of Abraham and (the late) Alfred Darby, Esquire 17 & 18 Vict, c.14. By a judgment of Vice-Chancellor Kindersley on 8 March 1856, it was decided that the Liverpool estates should be treated as personal property and would pass to the Widow and her three children and not to the Heir-at-law. (S.R.O 1987/59/2).
11. See letter dated 28 November 1887 from Matilda Darby to Mr Welton S.R.O 1987/51/2/3.

12. S.R.O. 1681/178/9 and 1681/181/51 and 52. These transactions comprised 88 shares from Abraham and 32 from Matilda. Mary already owned 88 shares and she, therefore, had a total of 208 shares (S.R.O 1987/51/2/3).
13. See note 11 above.
14. The Ebbw Vale Company which had been owned since the late eighteenth century by Messrs Harford Partridge & Company failed in 1842 and was kept going by trustees until 1844 when it was purchased by a partnership comprising Abraham Darby IV, Henry Dickinson, Joseph Robinson, William Tothill and Thomas Brown, who was appointed the managing partner of the concern. In 1848 they took over the lease of the Victoria Ironworks and Collieries from Sir Benjamin Hall (later Lord Llanover). See History of the Ebbw Vale Works and Collieries (first article) written in 1894 by H Joshua Phillips, F.I.C., F.C.S – copy in IGMT Library and Archive.
15. In 1852 the Ebbw Vale Company bought the Abersychan Ironworks & Collieries, situate about twelve miles away, from the New British Iron Company. In 1855 the company acquired four blast furnaces in Pontypool together with the Osborne Forge, Pontymoile Tinplate Works and the Lower Mills and Collieries. See History of the Ebbw Vale Works and Collieries (First and Second Articles) written in 1894 by H Joshua Phillips, F.I.C., F.C.S – copy in IGMT Library and Archive.
16. The mineral railway was established in 1855 by the West Somerset Mineral Railway Act 1855. Abraham Darby IV was Chairman until his death in 1878. He was also involved in the Brendon Hills Iron Ore Company of which he was managing director until 1873. See The West Brendon Hills Iron Mines by Roger Sellick, published by David and Charles 1962.
17. Deborah Darby younger sister of Abraham IV and Alfred who married Henry Dickinson in 1841. They lived at Severn House (now the Valley Hotel, Ironbridge).
18. Journal of Matilda Darby, 20 August 1855.
18a The present day equivalent of £11.8m pounds shows the staggering effect of inflation during the past fifty years. I am indebted to Mr Michael Lowe, J.P., F.C.A., Chairman of the Ironbridge Gorge Museum Trust for the calculation.
19. VCH Vol XI (Telford), p.229.
20. Adelaide's Journal, 4 December 1857.
21. Letter from Matilda Darby to Mr Welton of Quilter Ball & Company dated 29 November 1887 S.R.O 1987/51/2/3.
22. Sir Lewis Namier, Structure of Politics at the accession of George III. Volume 2. The following chart shows how the Whitmore family represented Parliament from 1621 to 1870:-

BRIDGNORTH
(The dates denote tenure of a seat at Bridgnorth)

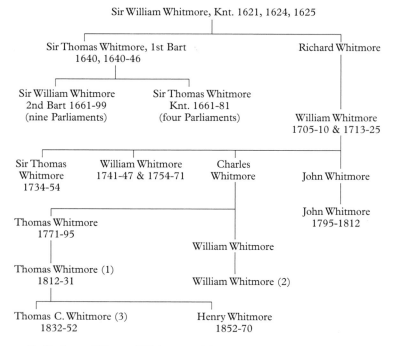

Sir William Whitmore, Knt. 1621, 1624, 1625

Sir Thomas Whitmore, 1st Bart
1640, 1640-46

Richard Whitmore

Sir William Whitmore
2nd Bart 1661-99
(nine Parliaments)

Sir Thomas Whitmore
Knt. 1661-81
(four Parliaments)

William Whitmore
1705-10 & 1713-25

Sir Thomas
Whitmore
1734-54

William Whitmore
1741-47 & 1754-71

Charles
Whitmore

John Whitmore

Thomas Whitmore
1771-95

John Whitmore
1795-1812

William Whitmore

Thomas Whitmore (1)
1812-31

William Whitmore (2)

Thomas C. Whitmore (3)
1832-52

Henry Whitmore
1852-70

1) Father of Henry Whitmore, J.P., D.L., High Sheriff 1805.
2) William Wolryche Whitmore of Dudmaston. Last seat in Bridgnorth at the Reform Act 1832, but was returned for the newly enfranchised borough of Wolverhampton.
3) Thomas Charlton Whitmore eldest brother of Henry Whitmore, married to Lady Douglas, eldest daughter of the 5th Marquess of Queensberry.
23. Vestiges of this Whig tendency could be discerned in County affairs until the end of the 1960s.
24. Adelaide's Journal, 21 June 1852, 7 and 8 July 1852.
25. Adelaide's Journal, 27 November and 17 December 1852.
26. Each year Adelaide seems to have attended what she described as *"The Drawing Room"*. A typical entry, 30 January 1858 – *"The Drawing Room. Our Princess Royal's last appearance. My Court dress was a green moire train – Henry's gift – and a white petticoat with Brussel's lace flowers, Feathers, Green leaves, White frosted flowers, Gold berries and red geraniums, Mrs W's* (Whitmore's) *diamonds. The Queen looked grave and the little princess took hardly any notice of anyone. I believe the Prince FW*

(Frederick Wilhelm) *of Prussia is all that can be wished and they really care for each other which is pleasant and rare in a Royal Marriage.*"

27. Adelaide's Journal, Appendix for 1856-1 November.
28. Adelaide's Journal, 31 December 1852. See S.R.O. 1681/143/28 and 29.
29. Adelaide's Journal, Appendix to 1857 (October) and 11 January 1858.
30. Adelaide's Journal, 12 October 1855 – "*H had yesterday a very gratifying letter from Disraeli offering him Lord Mandeville's appointment which he could not help accepting and I hope it will not be too much for him.*" The appointment is not specified, but Lord Mandeville who was MP for Huntingdon from 1852-1855 succeeded as the 7th Duke of Manchester in August 1855.
31. Adelaide's Journal, 27 March 1857.
32. Adelaide's Journal, 24 February 1858.
33. Adelaide's Journal, 25 February 1858. Lord Chelmsford's eldest son, the second Baron Chelmsford achieved fame (or notoriety) as Commander in Chief of the British Forces in the Zulu War 1879.
34. Adelaide's Journal, 26 February 1858 and 6 March 1858.
35. Henry Whitmore was again appointed Lord of the Treasury during the conservative administration of Lord Derby and Disraeli 1866-68.
36. Adelaide's Journal, 11 and 21 May 1853.
37. Adelaide's Journal, 29 October-5 November 1855.
38. See Duplicate Marriage Settlement dated 26 October 1858 (marriage of Mary Darby and Reverend William Jones) – Recital of Marriage settlement dated 16 March 1841 – Deborah Darby and Henry Dickinson. Deborah Darby was entitled to 88 shares in the Coalbrookdale Company.
39. Adelaide's Journal, 26 January 1858. Susannah Hadwen was the daughter of Isaac Hadwen, a Liverpool banker.
40. Raistrick, *Dynasty of Iron Founders*, pp.263-265.
41. Eddowes Shrewsbury Journal, November 3 1858 p.6. See also Adelaide's Journal, 30 March 1857.
42. Mary Darby owned the Hundred or Lordship of Pimhill, the Manor of Fennemore and property in the townships of Fennemore, Eyton and Middle in the Parishes of Baschurch and Middle. She also owned lands at Bradley and Wyke in the Parish of Much Wenlock.
43. Eddowes' Shrewsbury Journal, November 3 1858 – copy in IGMT archives.
44. See Deed of Indemnity dated 16 March 1858; The Ebbw Vale Company and Mary Darby. IGMT Archives.
45. See letter S.R.O 1987/58/50.
46. S.R.O 1681/178/21 and 22.

47. This loan or credit of £120,000 appears to have been made to the Ebbw Vale Company on 2 December 1857. See Deed of Indemnity dated 16 March 1858 between The Ebbw Vale Company and Mary Darby. IGMT Archives.

48. See letter from Matilda Darby to Mr Welton, dated November 1887. S.R.O 1987/51/2/3

49. S.R.O 1987/58/57-59.

50. For details of the distribution see the marriage settlement of Mary Darby and Reverend William Jones, dated 26 October 1858. IGMT Archives.

51. Adelaide's diary, 3 February 1860 (Appendix).

52. Adelaide's diary, 7 August 1860 (Appendix).

53. See copies of Will and Codicil of Mrs Hannah Darby dated 14 March 1857 and 14 May 1860 – IGMT Archives.

54. *History of the Ebbw Vale Works and Collieries, 1894*, by H Joshua Phillips (second article) IGMT Library. US Patent 16690, February 24, 1857.

55. Adelaide's Journal, Appendix 1861 – July 27.

56. Sale Catalogue of the Stoke Court and Mount Alexander Estates, British Museum. The property is now owned by Bayer Limited (1996).

57. *The Lilleshall Company Limited, a history 1764-1964* by W K V Gale and C R Nicholls, p.42.

58. *History of the Ebbw Vale Works and Collieries 1894*, by H Joshua Phillips (second article) IGMT Library. There also exists in the Shropshire Record Office (1987/59/4) an agreement for the purchase and sale of the various Ebbw Vale enterprises to new partners in 1864. It is not clear whether this was part of the process of converting into a limited liability company or whether it was a related transaction. The properties incorporated into the new company were the following:-
    1. Ebbw Vale Ironworks, Collieries and Mines
    2. Sirhowy Ironworks, Collieries and Mines
    3. Victoria Ironworks, Collieries and Mines
    4. Abersychan Ironworks, Collieries and Mines
    5. Pontypool Ironworks, Collieries and Tinplate Works
    6. Abercarn Collieries
    7. Six wharves at Newport
    8. The Hematite and Coal Gales (Royalties) in the Forest of Dean
    9. The Spathic Ore Mines, Brendon Hills, Somerset.

59. Adelaide's Journal, 1873.

60. S.R.O 1987/51/2/3.

61. Trinder, *The Darbys of Coalbrookdale*, pp.54-55.

62. The engineer of the Albert Edward Bridge was John Fowler.

63. It became usable at a later stage of development and was used by the Lilleshall Company from 1879 onwards at its Priorslee Furnaces, the only furnaces in the locality to be built for the production of steel by the Bessemer process – see *The Lilleshall Company Limited, a history 1764-1964* by W.K.V. Gale and C R Nicholls, p.56.

64. History of Horsehay Iron Works (1876) IGMT Library VCH Vol XI (Telford), p.121.

64a See *The Wenlock Branch*, by Ken Jones. ISBN 0 85361 500 4. Published by the Oakwood Press.

65. Trinder, *The Darbys of Coalbrookdale*, p.55.

66. History of Horsehay Iron Works (1876) IGMT Library.

67. Labouchere, *Abiah*, p.27.

68. History of Horsehay Iron Works (1876) IGMT Library.

69. Woodside Cottage is No 3113 on the Tithe Map 1847 although Abraham and Matilda never lived there, it remained in Matilda's ownership until her death in 1902. See letter from Matilda to Mr Welton dated 29 November 1887. (S.R.O 1987/51/2/3).

70 The indenture was made on 10 August 1866. It is not now available but is referred to in a Memorandum dated 25 March 1868 relating to the sale of the Little Ness Estate. IGMT Archives.

71. S.R.O 1987/41/83.

72. See S.R.O 1987/41/102-104. The conveyance to Rebecca Darby is not available, but was dated 25 March 1868 and is referred to in the Memorandum of that date relating to the sale of the Little Ness Estate. IGMT Archives.

73. *"With his death, the last candle of the eighteenth century went out"* (Guedella).

CHAPTER XII

The Fight for Survival

BY 1870 THE INDUSTRIAL Revolution which had started in Coalbrookdale more than one hundred and fifty years before was evolving into a new phase, based on steel, engineering, electricity and chemicals. The earliest phase based on coal and iron, which was pioneered in Shropshire in the eighteenth century was moving into relative decline. Although Britain was still the predominant world power, her position in world trade was being challenged by other countries notably the United States of America and continental Europe. Britain's share of world trade in manufacturing fell from 31 per cent in 1870 to 14 per cent in 1910.[1] The causes of decline were evident long before 1870 as other countries from the 1840s onwards were developing more efficient levels of industrial management and above all were establishing systems of state education which encouraged science-based and technical education.[1]

The decade started with the Franco-Prussian war of 1870, which brought to the attention of a startled Europe a newly unified and well-organised Germany. Europe, to repeat a quip of the day, *had lost a mistress and gained a master.*[2] It was not just the Prussian army which won the war so efficiently, it was also German industry and technology backed up by German science and education.

By way of contrast, Britain's progress in education was lamentable. It rested in the hands of the churches. Such schooling as existed was provided mainly by the Anglican National Society set up in 1811 and the British and Foreign School Society set up in 1814. Their efforts were supplemented from 1833 by a very small government grant. It was not until 1870 that the Elementary Education Act of that year[3] required the universal provision of primary education and set up school boards to provide education in areas where it did not exist or was not up to standard. Thanks to the efforts of the Darby family over the previous hundred years, Coalbrookdale was able to avoid the imposition of a school board.

State Secondary Education was not provided until 1902 leaving the way open for the public schools to fill the gap, based on the objectives laid down by Dr Arnold of Rugby School, which provided the Christian gentlemen who would be required for the new imperialism rather than the technocrats required to lead an industrial nation. The mould of British society was set for the next one hundred years. The situation was made worse from 1875 onwards by the collapse of British agriculture caused primarily by the development of the American prairies as grainlands which under the philosophy of free trade invaded the English Market.[4] By the end of the century the corn area of England and Wales had shrunk from eight million acres in 1871 to under six million.

It is doubtful whether considerations like this would have been perceived or carried much weight within the Shropshire Coalfields. More likely the trends would have been blamed on the activities of the trade unions which started to become evident in the Shropshire Coalfield during the early 1870s. Certainly this was the view taken by the historian of the Horsehay works writing in 1876 about *"the terrible pressure which was brought to bear on the coal and iron trades from 1871 to 1873"*. He commented – *"The reign of Unionism, and the age of strikers, which were quite unprecedented in the history of the iron trade, now bore heavily on these undertakings, causing immense losses, both of masters and men."* Whilst the activities of the trade unions were a prominent feature of the situation which had developed, and led to the passing of the Employees and Workmen's Act of 1875 (which legitimised the practice of "peaceful picketing")[5] the truth is that far more fundamental and widespread factors were at work, which resulted in the near devastation of large areas of the coalfield within the next ten to twenty years.

The decline within the area of the Coalbrookdale Company which had been first signalled by the closure of the Horsehay Furnaces in 1861 was followed by the closure of the Lawley Furnaces in 1870. Up until then Lawley had been expanding slowly as a community. In 1865 the Company and Lord Forester had given twelve acres of land for the construction of a Chapel of Ease, the building costs being largely borne by Henry Dickinson and Mrs Mary Jones (née Darby) the sister of Abraham IV. This was to become the Lawley Parish Church.[6] After the closure of the furnaces, mining in the locality also started to decline until by 1882 it had virtually ceased altogether.

Despite the closure of the Lawley Furnaces and the activities of the unions, the Works as a whole carried on and continued to make progress, In 1873 the Company won the Medal of Progress at the International Exhibition in Vienna[7] the highest award available and in the same year the Horsehay Works were said to produce all kinds of iron "from a rail bar to a wire rod".[8] It was clear that despite all the difficulties, the performance of the Company had been turned round since the days of Charles Crookes as manager. This was recognised by a loan to William Gregory

Norris of £50,000 in 1872 to enable him to purchase shares in the Company.[9] This was an unprecedented move because, except for the original shareholding of the Goldney family, no shares had ever been allowed to be held outside the Darby family. On the other hand, as already mentioned, Norris being descended from the Luccock family, was clearly regarded as one of the Darbys. His new status as a shareholder enhanced his position and authority within the Company and in effect he became Managing Partner and took charge of the Works.

At this time, mortality was beginning to catch up with the fifth generation of the family. In 1873, Mary Jones (née Darby) married to the Vicar of Baschurch died. Although living in Baschurch, she had continued to show her concern for her birthplace, demonstrated by her role in the building of the Lawley Church. In that same year, Abraham IV retired as the Managing Partner of the Ebbw Vale Company with all its various works in south-east Wales and its mineral resources in the Forest of Dean and in the Brendon Hills (he continued, however, as Chairman of the West Somerset Mineral Railway). He and Matilda had been living at Ebbw Vale House since 1861 but he had to vacate that property on his retirement. A return to Coalbrookdale must have been a possibility, particularly as he had maintained contact with William Gregory Norris since his appointment as Manager, and his wife Matilda, was also the owner of Woodside Cottage in Coalbrookdale.[10] In the event, however, he and Matilda moved to the beauty spot of Llangorse Lake near Brecon and settled there.[11]

Having decided not to return to Coalbrookdale, he appointed William Gregory Norris as the trustee of his interest in Strethill Farm which he had inherited on the death of his father Edmund Darby, in 1810.[12]

In 1876, three years after Abraham IV retired, his brother-in-law Henry Whitmore, husband of Adelaide Darby, died. He had retired from Parliament in 1870 having attained the height of his career as Lord of the Treasury in Lord Derby's second administration of 1866-68. As a parliamentarian he was most remembered for his opposition to the disestablishment of the Irish Church on the grounds that it would represent the beginning of a rift between Church and State. He had also transformed the family home at Sunniside (The White House) by the building of a new west wing between 1862-65.

At the time of Henry Whitmore's death the depression in the iron trade was really beginning to bite. In a report for 1876[13] William Gregory Norris stated that operations in that year had been affected with great difficulty and anxiety and although work had been reduced, stocks had been considerably increased. Although the foundry had sustained demand there had been a reduction of 11,000 tons in the production of the collieries, the forge had operated at only three-quarters of its capacity and the rolling mill produced only 10,429 tons against 14,516 the previous year. Sales of bar iron were down by £56,685. For the first time there was a hint of discontinuing colliery operations in Dawley, closing down the furnace at Dawley Castle and restricting the Works at Horsehay.

Writing at the end of 1876, the historian of the Horsehay Works reflected that *"unfortunately the present state of the Iron trade, together with the dark and gloomy appearance of the commercial atmosphere stamps with gloom the opening year, and to hope for a better state of things, seems very much like "hoping against hope"*. Little did he realise that a truly devastating blow was to occur in the following year 1877, when the total closure of the Botfield iron works at Old Park Dawley took place. *(14)* The dead hand of depression was finally entering the very heart of the coalfield. Great social distress resulted, aggravated by an outbreak of typhoid. The struggle for survival had started.

Matters were not helped by the death in November 1878 of Abraham Darby IV aged seventy-five years. Although he died in Breconshire, his body was brought by train to Coalbrookdale railway station and thence in procession through an *"immense concourse of people"* to the Coalbrookdale Church which he had built and endowed, where the interment took place. Every house in Coalbrookdale and Ironbridge had drawn blinds or closed shutters. *(15)* Although he left the Dale in 1851 after *"the very painful family affair" (16)* he had had an immense influence on the Dale. Without the work which he and his brother Alfred had done between 1830 and 1850, the Company might have failed. Even after he left the locality his advice and guidance was always available and his influence was ever-present.

In the year before Abraham IV died, his wife Matilda had had a serious illness. In the expectation that she might not recover she signed a deed appointing the Company shares which were held in trust for her under Lucy Darby's settlement dated 11 February 1858 to be transferred on her death to her nephew-in-law A E W Darby. In the event she unexpectedly recovered her health, but the appointment remained valid and was confirmed by her in a memorandum dated 22 August 1896. *(16a)* Matilda continued to have the benefit of the shares after Abraham's death.

Other shares which came into consideration at this time were ninety shares which had been held in the family of Revered E Pryce Owen formerly the Vicar of Wellington, who had married Mary Darby daughter of Samuel Darby II. Their son Hugh Darby Owen had inherited the shares and on his death they were offered for sale back to the Company in 1878. They were purchased by or on behalf of A E W Darby (Alfred II) in

1879.[17] In this way Alfred II started to acquire an interest in the Company and became active in the affairs of the Company.

With the death of Abraham IV in 1878, the emergence of his nephew the son of his brother Alfred and his wife Rebecca (née Christy) was a very welcome development, as an injection once again of young Darby blood into the family concern. In 1878 he was twenty-eight years old. He had been brought up at Stanley Hall, near Bridgnorth and had been schooled at Eton from 1864 to 1868[18] and subsequently at Merton College, Oxford. He had been brought up as a country gentleman and was much influenced by his two uncles, Alexander and Edmund Christy.[19] His mother Rebecca Darby had become interested in country pursuits and although of Quaker upbringing she, like some others of her generation joined the established church. It will be recalled that in 1868 she had purchased the Little Ness estate (north of Shrewsbury) from Henry Dickinson.[20] In 1875 Rebecca moved with Alfred and her daughter Alfreda Lucy from Stanley Hall to Little Ness House in the village of Little Ness. (Her other daughter Alice Mary had already married Alexander Wolryche-Whitmore in 1871 and was living at Dudmaston.)

The Little Ness estate consisted of a number of substantial farms and farmhouses. One of these, Adcott Hall became vacant at this time and Rebecca set about the ambitious project of converting it into a considerable mansion. She commissioned Richard Norman Shaw, the great Victorian architect to undertake the task. The result was that by 1881 he had completed the splendid mansion of Adcote, now known as Adcote School.[21]

Rebecca took up residence in 1881. In that year Alfred II married Frederica Louisa Julian Arthur and they established their home at Little Ness from where Alfred administered the joint estates. By then he was also deeply embroiled in the affairs of the Coalbrookdale Company. In 1880 he had become a trustee (with Francis Tothill) of the Company's land holdings in the manor of Lawley and the mines in Lawley, Wellington and Dawley.[22] He had also been involved in the renewal of the lease of the Dawley mines in 1877.[23] He had, therefore, started his induction into the affairs of the Company, although it has to be conceded that this was a long way short of the hands-on experience of the Works which his father Alfred and previous generations of the family had undergone. Times had changed however, and with the Company in crisis, William Gregory Norris was now firmly in charge.

Although over the years there had been little or no formal connection between the Coalbrookdale Company and the Ebbw Vale Company, the two companies had nevertheless become somewhat enmeshed, if only

Adcote House, Little Ness, home of Rebecca Darby (née Christy) and subsequently of her son Alfred Darby II. Since 1925 it has been the Adcote School.

Alfred Darby II.

because they were subject to the same control at partnership level. Also much of the Darby family money and assets had been invested in the Ebbw Vale concern. With the death of Abraham IV the connection was coming to an end and William Gregory Norris started to disentangle some of the mutual commitments. The process had started as far back as 1868[24] and by the time of the death of Abraham IV, the principal complication was the funding of a colliery known as Tyr Pentwys near Ebbw Vale leased separately by Abraham IV in which the Coalbrookdale Company had become involved. In these various negotiations Mr Norris had had dealings with financial consultants known as Messrs Quilter, Ball & Company of Moorgate, London, who were the advisers to the Ebbw Vale Company. As the overall situation of the Coalbrookdale Company deteriorated, Mr Norris commissioned Quilter Ball & Company for their advice.

It became evident that in order to survive there was a need for a massive retrenchment which would involve the closure or disposal of the Horsehay Works and the closure of the Company's warehouse in Bristol. It was proposed that the partnership should be converted into a limited liability joint stock company. A balance sheet was struck at August 1880 and consultation and negotiations with the various partners were undertaken.[25] The complication of the funding of the Tyr Pentwys was reduced to acceptable proportions by Matilda Darby who agreed to fund much of the liability from her resources as executor of Abraham IV. Others such as Henry Dickinson agreed to have their interests bought out. Resolutions were passed on 23 December 1880 to convert the partnership into a limited company and also to deal with the outstanding problem of the Tyr Pentwys colliery.[26] The Articles of Association of the Company were completed on 11 July 1881 and the next day the new company completed the agreement with the old partnership to purchase all the assets.[27]

For the purposes of the transfer the Company was valued at £305,000. The Company then issued the following shares:[28]

		£
349	ordinary shares of £250 each	87,250
480	preference shares of £100 each ($£50$ to be treated as paid which left £24,000 uncalled for)	24,000
650	preference shares of £100 each (fully paid up)	65,000
	Cash, payable over a period of years at 5% interest	128,750
		£305,000

190

Engineering shop, Coalbrookdale.

191

As a result of these various transactions the principal shareholders of the new company were Mr A E W Darby (Alfred II), Mrs Matilda Darby, William and Francis Tothill and on a lesser scale Mrs Adelaide Whitmore and William Gregory Norris.

The policy of the new company seems to have been to consolidate its core activities back to Coalbrookdale which throughout this exceptionally difficult period seems to have remained profitable. In fact expansion of the Coalbrookdale operation was taking place. The 1883 Ordnance Survey map shows that an Erecting Shop (now part of what later came to be known as the Engineering Shop) had been built alongside the Wellington Road on what had originally been the Lower Furnace site. Alongside the Erecting Shop was an Assembly Shop. Perhaps this is where the Company had built a massive pair of double blowing engines for the main Ebbw Vale Furnaces which were delivered and installed at Ebbw Vale in 1879. [29]

Between the Erecting Shop/Assembly Shop and the Great Warehouse new offices were built, presumably for the new company, incorporating or replacing earlier buildings shown on the 1849 Tithe map.

Outside Coalbrookdale the situation was grim. The Company closed down the Lightmoor and Dawley Castle furnaces in 1883 and for the first time since 1709, the Company ceased altogether to smelt iron ore. [30] Three years later in 1886, the forges at Horsehay were closed down. The effect on Dawley, Lawley and Little Dawley was devastating with unemployment and near starvation being the order of the day. The Horsehay Works was taken over in 1886 by the Horsehay Company, a partnership between H C Simpson formerly of Rotherham, Yorkshire and his brother. [31] Both were Quakers and they developed the heavy engineering side of the works concentrating on the manufacture of bridges, roofs and girders.

At the eastern end of the Madeley Parish, the situation was slightly less dire because the Madeley Wood Company managed to keep their furnaces operating, albeit on a lower level of output until the next century when the Blists Hill furnaces were finally blown out in 1912. The Coalport China Company was an important employer as also was the newly developing tile industry at Jackfield on the other side of the River Severn.

In the northern sector of the coalfield, the situation was also somewhat more optimistic. The Lilleshall Company was the dominant employer. Under the chairmanship of Granville Leveson-Gower, Second Earl Granville and with John Horton and his son Thomas Ellwood Horton as principal managers, the company had been following a policy of investment, notably in engineering. In 1861 the New Yard Engineering Works in Oakengates was started under the management of John Lloyd who had been recruited from Boulton and Watt's Soho Foundry in Smethwick.[32] By the 1880s the New Yard Works had an established reputation as manufacturer of industrial railway locomotives as well as winding, pumping and colliery ventilating engines. Even more importantly the basic Bessemer process of making steel had advanced to the point at which the local Shropshire iron ores could be used for conversion into steel. The Lilleshall Company decided to invest in steel making and in 1882 it laid down new blast furnaces at Priors Lee, even though this signalled the end of its old and uneconomic Lodge furnaces which were blown out in 1888. By virtue of this high level of investment the Lilleshall Company went on to become a company of national significance.

Despite these brighter trends the effect of the long depression of the 1870s and 1880s was appalling. The population of the coalfield declined from 57,572 in 1881 to 49,877 ten years later. But it was the central areas of the coalfield round Dawley which were the worst hit. The population of Dawley, which had been over 11,000 in 1861 was reduced to 9,200 in 1881 and then to 6,996 in 1891, an overall loss of 40%. The area never really recovered and dereliction of the former workings and their spoil mounds set in to become a marked feature in the next century.

In Coalbrookdale, the Company, which had lacked the level of investment which had characterised the Lilleshall Company in the previous two decades started to expand in two directions. First it developed a great variety of stoves, with associated work on smoke abatement for which it won the Silver Medal at the Smoke Abatement Exhibition, South Kensington in 1882. Secondly it developed its engineering capacity and produced a great number of steam engines, and high pressure and heavy duty pumps for mines and docks and harbour work. Its art castings department continued to thrive. Slowly the Company weathered the storm and was restored to profitability. In order to pay for the new developments the Company issued debenture stock worth £60,000 on the freehold holdings of the Company.[33] In 1886 Alfred Edmund William Darby (Alfred II) became Chairman of the Company and William Gregory Norris continued as Manager until he retired in 1897.

During this period the three sons of Richard and Maria Darby who had been brought up in Rosehill and had been involved in the Works during their early years reached the end of their lives – William Henry Darby (d.1882), Richard Sorton Darby (d.1883) and Charles Edward Darby (d.1884). The eldest son Richard Sorton Darby had left Coalbrookdale to live at Hawkwood House, Sidbury, Near Bridgnorth. When his father Richard Darby died in 1860, he was left a farm at Common Wood, Holt in Denbighshire.[34]

The two younger sons William Henry Darby and Charles Edward Darby, after training at Coalbrookdale, moved to Brymbo near Wrexham where they successfully managed the Iron Works together with the Minera Lime works and collieries. After their deaths in 1882 and 1884 the Brymbo Steel Company was established and John Henry Darby, son of William Henry Darby became Managing Director. He possessed the Darby family flair and was involved in the commissioning at Brymbo of the first basic open hearth furnace in Great Britain. *(35)* John Henry Darby at Brymbo and his cousin Alfred II at Coalbrookdale carried the Darby family banner on into the seventh generation since Abraham I to be involved in the iron industry.

The deaths of the three Darby brothers in 1882-84 left their sister, Rebecca Sarah Darby surviving them at Rosehill the family home in Coalbrookdale. Under the Will of their father Richard Darby *(34)* the property had been left to Rebecca and two of her brothers, William Henry Darby and Charles Edward Darby, but there was a provision in the Will that she could continue to live there during her lifetime. She was over ten years younger than her brothers and she outlived them both. She lived at Rosehill until her death in 1908. She had remained true to the Quaker faith. Living next door to William Gregory Norris at Dale House and fortified by the arrival of the Quaker Simpson family at Horsehay, they formed the nucleus of the now diminished number of the Society of Friends attending the Meeting House in Darby Road.

The other principal member of the Darby family to remain in Coalbrookdale was Adelaide Whitmore, widow of Henry Whitmore who maintained her home at Sunniside (The White House). She had also retained her London home at 68 Eaton Place and it seems probable that towards the end of her life she spent an increasing amount of time at her London address. In 1883 she had expanded the Sunniside estate to its final ultimate size by the acquisition of Green Bank Farm to the east of the Sunniside estate in the Manor of Little Dawley. *(36)*

In 1886 Henry Dickinson died aged seventy-four years. He had been brought back into the mainstream of the Darby family by his marriage to Deborah Darby (sister of Abraham IV and Alfred) in 1841. After her death in 1855, he remained involved in the Company's affairs and was a trustee of its assets until it was converted to a joint stock company in 1881. He was best known, however, as a director of the Shropshire Banking Company in Wellington until it was taken over by Lloyds Bank Limited in 1874. He had of course also been involved with Abraham IV and William Tothill in the partnership of the Ebbw Vale Iron and Steel Works. The Dickinson family became a considerably extended family. Henry Dickinson had six brothers and three sisters and they spread out over many parts of the country beyond Coalbrookdale. *(37)*

At the time of Henry Dickinson's death, Alfred II had become Chairman of the new Coalbrookdale Company Limited. He was living in considerable style with his wife Frederica (née Arthur) at Little Ness. His mother Rebecca Darby was living in even greater style at Adcote, nearby. A daughter, Frances Muriel Darby was born in 1882 followed by a son Alfred Alexander Maurice Darby, born some twelve years later in 1894. They enjoyed a country life style bound up with the church of Little Ness and the village school with events such as the Hunt Ball and charity occasions at Adcote.

During the 1890s the economic situation began to improve. It was a slow process with many setbacks, but signs of the future were beginning to emerge. In 1871 the Castle Iron Works had been established at Hadley by Nettlefold & Chamberlain of Smethwick and after passing through several sets of hands, it was purchased in 1910, by Joseph Sankey & Sons Limited of Bilston, and was destined to become the greatest maker of motor car wheels in Europe. C & W Walker, established at Donnington in 1857 was becoming well-known as a maker of gas holders and gas equipment. John Maddock & Company, which had started by manufacturing nails at Stirchley, moved to Oakengates in 1878. The centre of gravity within the coalfield had clearly moved to the northern area around Oakengates, Donnington, Hadley and St Georges, where the leading player was the Lilleshall Company.

The Coalbrookdale Company was also returning to stability and was once again employing a considerable workforce. In 1893 there was a revaluation of the enterprise and a reduction of share value agreed in the Chancery Division of the High Court.[38] In 1897, William Gregory Norris retired as Manager of the Company. He had had a rough ride, but it was largely thanks to his efforts that the Company had survived the great depression of the 1870s and 1880s. In the process the Company had contracted back to its original site but it was once again a viable and dynamic part of the community.

Sadly, within the next four years the two sisters, Adelaide and Matilda, who had been at the heart of the *"very painful family affair"* in 1850, came to the end of their lives. It was Adelaide Whitmore, the younger of the two, who died first on 10 July 1899 aged eighty-two years. She had made a will the previous year leaving the Sunniside estate and Green Bank Farm to her sister Matilda.[39] Matilda moved back to her birthplace at Sunniside, and she too died there on 16 December 1902 aged ninety-three years. On her death the property passed to Alfred II. It was valued for estate duty at £151,000.[40] He had already inherited Strethill Farm on the death of Abraham IV and so all the family property was finally united into one ownership. It was this ownership which maintained the link between the family and Coalbrookdale, particularly after 1908, when Rebecca Darby, the daughter of Richard Darby, died at Rosehill. *(41)*

In the meantime, after the retirement of William Gregory Norris In 1897, he was succeeded by Duncan Sinclair, who was Manager from 1897 to 1904. During his tenure the Company embarked on its last major expansion. In 1901 new foundries and workshops were built at Dale End (now the factory of Merrythought Company Limited makers of teddy bears and other soft toys) and in 1903, the Lower Furnace Pool was finally built over. *(42)* Mr Sinclair was briefly succeeded by Mr B S Brooksbank from 1904 to 1906 to be followed by Mr W S Malcolm, who was Manager from 1906 to 1929. *(43)*

In 1911, William Gregory Norris died at Dale House. This marked the end of an era for Dale House which had been built by Abraham I in 1717. For nearly two hundred years it had been regarded as the Darby family home. Even when individual members of the family were living in much grander houses, Dale House retained its primary status. It had been seen as the home of the manager of the Works and above all it had always been occupied by Quaker families. When Mr Norris died, the contents of the House were auctioned and the House was advertised for letting. *(44)*

Life had also changed at Little Ness and Adcote. In 1909, Rebecca Darby, widow of Alfred I, died at Adcote, the splendid house she had built in 1881. After his mother's death, Alfred II and his wife Frederica with their two children, moved their home from Little Ness to Adcote and thereafter maintained the considerable style and standard of living which Rebecca had established. The daughter Frances Muriel (known as Muriel) enjoyed an outdoor life but was also an accomplished musician. She studied music for a short period at Dresden. Her brother Alfred Alexander Maurice (known as Maurice) was also popular and was a lively and high-spirited youth. Brother and sister were greatly devoted to each other. Maurice attended school at Eton from 1907-11.

With the advent of the Great War in 1914-18, Maurice joined the 1st Battalion Grenadier Guards. He died from wounds on 15 March 1915 at Neuve Chapelle. His body was recovered from the battlefield by his uncle, Sir George Arthur, who was Lord Kitchener's secretary and had sufficient influence to arrange for the body to be returned for burial at Little Ness, a most unusual occurrence. Muriel, much distraught at her brother's death in action went to London to undertake war work. There she married Captain Mordaunt Leckonby Cope in 1917. The marriage was not a success and the couple executed a deed of separation in 1919. Subsequently Muriel executed another deed in 1924 assuming the additional surname of Darby and then became known as Frances Muriel Cope-Darby.

Muriel Cope-Darby.

*Maurice Darby.
Died of wounds, Neuve
Chapelle, 1915.*

With the end of the Great War a period of change and depression affected the country. In 1922 an alliance of ironfounding companies was set up. This was known as Light Castings Limited. The companies included in the alliance were the Coalbrookdale Company Limited, The Planet Foundry Company Limited of Guide Bridge, Manchester, M Cockburn & Company Limited of Falkirk and McDowall Steven & Company Limited also of Falkirk. Each remained as a separate company and retained its individual identity. Alfred II remained as Chairman of the Coalbrookdale Company with W S Malcolm as Manager. *(45)*

On 23 July 1925 Alfred II died unexpectedly at Adcote aged seventy-five years. Because of the impact of death duties Adcote had to be sold and became a well-known girls school. *(46)* Alfred's widow Frederica Darby moved back to Little Ness. Muriel inherited the Sunniside estate and came to live there in 1927, having altered the house to contain some of the possessions which had formerly belonged to her father and to Francis Darby. Once again a member of the Darby family was living in the Dale. Muriel regarded her years in Coalbrookdale as the happiest of her life. She entered into local activities and became deeply committed to the welfare of those living in the Severn Gorge. Because of her musical talents, she taught the choir in Holy Trinity Church of whose living she was the Patron. The music there became exceptional. She held many of the choir practices round the piano at Sunniside. *(47)*

In memory of her brother Maurice, she arranged for H S Goodhart-Rendell, President of the Royal Institute of British Architects to design a memorial to him in the form of a Decorated Chancel at the church. *(48)*

The connection between the family and the Company had come to an end with the death of Alfred II, but shortly after his death, Light Castings Limited was in 1929 absorbed by a larger grouping known as Allied Ironfounders Limited, of which the Coalbrookdale Company became a wholly owned subsidiary. In 1962 the company was transferred absolutely to Allied Ironfounders Limited and in 1973, Allied Ironfounders Limited was taken over by Glynwed Foundries Limited, the present owners.

In 1935, Muriel Cope-Darby died at Sunniside, the last member of the family to live in the Dale. Her main heir was her niece Rachel Katharine Hamilton-Russell, who was her closest and dearest relative. Rachel was the daughter of Olive Mary Wolryche-Whitmore and Eustace Scott Hamilton Russell, younger son of the 8th Viscount Boyne. Muriel had been a bridesmaid at the wedding of Olive and Eustace at St Peter's, Eaton Square in 1906 and was overjoyed by the birth of their only child Rachel in 1908. Muriel and Olive were first cousins and had spent much time together in their youth. *(49)* As Rachel grew up she became a regular visitor to Muriel at Sunniside. She recalled with great affection and fondness that Muriel had taken her on her first visit overseas to Florence in Italy. The magic of that occasion remained with her to the end.

The Sunniside estate was largely kept together during the second World War but soon afterwards Rachel, who had in the meantime married George (later Sir George) Labouchere of the Foreign Office in 1943 and was fully committed to a career in the diplomatic service, came under pressure from the beneficiaries of Muriel's Will to wind up the estate. This was done in the 1950s, and the local authority, the Borough of Wenlock, purchased Sunniside and the area around it for the development of the Sunniside housing estate. Sunniside itself was demolished by the local authority in 1960.

In the meantime, the Coalbrookdale Company, then part of Allied Ironfounders Limited was approaching the 250th anniversary of the founding of the Company by Abraham I in 1709.[50] G F (Fred) Williams, Managing Director of the Coalbrookdale Works had carried out some excavations of the Old Furnace in 1947 and soon after the Board of Allied Ironfounders Limited agreed to save the Furnace and its surroundings. In 1957 the Board decided that the excavations should be completed to commemorate the 250th anniversary. This was done and a Museum of Ironfounding was established in some nearby buildings. The restoration of the Old Furnace and the Museum was opened on 15 October 1959.

Museum of Ironfounding, Coalbrookdale, 1959.

199

Postscript

A T THIS VERY TIME the City of Birmingham was campaigning for the creation of one or more new towns for the West Midlands. In April 1961, Mr A G Sheppard Fidler, City Architect of Birmingham was asked to advise the Ministry of Housing and Local Government (now the Department of the Environment) "*on the possibility of building a new town in Dawley...*" He came to the general conclusion that in spite of severe dereliction it was a splendid situation for a new town, with many advantages. He added the comment that "*undoubtedly the steep valleys leading down into the Severn and the Severn Gorge itself with the famous Iron Bridge, if tidied up, could become one of the show places of England and would attract tourists on a large scale*". Prophetic words indeed. Dawley New Town was designated on 16 January 1963, and a Development Corporation was set up to bring it about. The designated area of the New Town included eight hundred and forty acres of the Severn Gorge which was regarded as "*most valuable for amenity purposes*".

It has to be recalled that at that time, the preservation of the nation's industrial heritage was not regarded with the same enthusiasm as the preservation of country houses or other socially more acceptable features of our history. The work done by Dr Raistrick and Dr Williams to secure the preservation of the Old Furnace at Coalbrookdale was a pointer in a new direction. Mr Rex Wailes had already been appointed under the sponsorship of the Ministry of Housing and Local Government to carry out a survey of industrial monuments. The term Industrial Archaeology had been used for the first time in 1955 by Michael Rix of the University of Birmingham Extra-Mural Department who was a great enthusiast for the Severn Gorge. Also by 1960, another group of enthusiasts had come together under the leadership of Dr Ivor Brown to form the Shropshire Caving & Mining Club, and they were instrumental in salvaging material from the Rock Mine at Ketley, virtually the last of the shallow mines still surviving. Another influential voice was that of Geoffrey Godber, Clerk of the Salop County Council who set up an informal working party to survey buildings, etc. This included Mr J Horsley Denton, an expert on canals and railways, and Dr Barrie Trinder who subsequently became Senior Research Fellow of the Ironbridge Institute and Honorary Historian of the Ironbridge Gorge Museum Trust.

Quite independently, Mr G R Morton, Principal Lecturer in Metallurgy at the Wolverhampton and Staffordshire College of Technology prepared a report on the preservation of Shropshire Industries.

All this enthusiasm started to produce a climate of opinion in the early 1960s which was sympathetic to the preservation of the area's industrial history and the creation of a feeling that "*something needs to be done*". It has to be conceded, however, that little or nothing would or could have happened without the intervention of a major authority. The designation of Dawley New Town (subsequently to be enlarged to become Telford New Town) provided the opportunity for that to happen.

Even so, nothing was inevitable and it took three years between 1964 and 1967 for the ideas to evolve within the Development Corporation. [51] There is a tendency these days to argue that the Ironbridge Gorge Museum Trust evolved out of the Coalbrookdale Museum of Ironfounding. Although this is a happy thought, it is not accurate. The Development Corporation was following a different and very much wider agenda.

The agenda was set out in the Corporation's Policy Plan for the Severn Gorge. [52] Within the Development Corporation was a small group of officers whose enthusiasm was equal to those outside the Corporation. These included John Madin and Michael Holt, the consultant planners, Mr Ceri Griffiths the Corporation's Chief Architect, Mr Lewis Jones, Miss Bishop (later Mrs Kate Ansell) and the author who was then the Corporation's Chief Legal and Administrative Officer. Their efforts led to the preparation of a set of proposals which were well received by the members of the Corporation who included Isaiah Jones and Viscount Boyne (both subsequently Deputy Chairmen of the Board) and Christopher Cadbury whose father, George Cadbury had been involved in the restoration of the Old Furnace.

The author made an approach to Mr Bruce Ball who had recently retired as Managing Director of the Lilleshall Company and when a meeting was convened by the Development Corporation on 15 February 1967 to discuss the proposals, Mr Bruce Ball was appointed Chairman of a working party. This was an inspired choice. In July 1967, the working party's final report was approved by the Development Corporation and the author was empowered to bring about the establishment of the Ironbridge Gorge Museum Trust as a Company Limited by Guarantee. The Museum Trust was formally registered on 18 October 1967. The following were the Honorary Officers at the inception of the Trust:-

Chairman	Mr E Bruce Ball C.B.E
Honorary Secretary	Mr E Thomas C.B.E
Honorary Treasurer	Mr Selwyn Devey
Honorary Curator	Mr Reg Morton

Mr Mike Lowe became the Auditor of the Museum and after many years distinguished service with the Museum, is now the Chairman. The Lord Lieutenant of the County, Lord Bridgeman, became the first President and led a first appeal for funds which raised £40,000. Two other members present at the inaugural meeting in February 1967 were Mr Jack Crabtree who subsequently became a Vice-President, as also did Mr Michael Darby the great, great grandson of Mr Richard Darby who lived at Rosehill and a descendant of Abraham I.

The very considerable voluntary effort which the Museum needed was soon harnessed by the establishment of a Friends organisation and the first Chairman was Mr Denis Roberts, who has also served on the Trust from its early days as Deputy Chairman and subsequently Vice-President. Mention must also be made of Ken and Dorinda Jones who have served the Friends organisation from the beginning.

In 1971 it was decided to set up a sister Trust, the Development Trust to undertake the daunting task of raising money for the development of the Museum. The Development Trust has proved singularly effective in raising many millions of pounds over the intervening years. Its first President was the Earl of Plymouth, followed by Sir Monty Finniston, Kt., Chairman British Steel Corporation. Since 1980 the President has been Sir Peter Gadsden, G.B.E. who was Lord Mayor of London in that year.

The first Chairman of the Development Trust was W. G. A. Russell and then Robin Martin, Chairman of Tarmac Ltd. After 1977 the Chairman was Bill Sidaway, O.B.E. (Chairman of Delta Metals Ltd), until his death in 1986. Since then the chairmanship has been held by Sir Ian MacGregor, Kt., Chairman of the National Coal Board, Sir Robert Scholey, Kt., C.B.E., Chairman of British Steel and Gareth Davies, C.B.E., F.C.A., Chairman and Chief Executive of Glynwed International Ltd. These gentlemen were greatly supported by Philip Trevor-Jones, Tim Rissbrook and Jeremy Beasley. The work of the Trust was directed successively by Tony Daniell, O.B.E., M.C., T.D., Mark Harwood-Little and Jim Stirling.

When Bruce Ball, C.B.E., retired as Chairman of the Museum Trust in 1978, he was followed by Tom Honess, C.B.E., who had just retired as Chairman of GKN Sankey Ltd. When Tom Honess retired in 1981 the Museum was extremely fortunate in persuading Philip Trevor-Jones, D.L., M.A., Chairman of Lowe & Fletcher Ltd, who until then had been involved in the Development Trust, to become Chairman of the Museum Trust. In 1987, when Philip Trevor-Jones became President of the Museum Trust, he was succeeded by Michael Lowe, J.P., F.C.A., the present Chairman, who previously had been enthusiastically managing the Museum's finances as Honorary Treasurer.

Rosehill (formerly The Grange), before restoration.

Dale House, before restoration.

Dale House, after restoration.

During the setting up of the Museum Trust, informal discussions had taken place with Glynwed Limited, the owners of The Old Furnace and the Museum of Ironfounding. As a result the company agreed to lease the Furnace and the Museum to the newly established Trust and in 1970, during a visit to Dawley New Town by HRH Princess Margaret, the lease was formally handed over, and the Museum became responsible for the Furnace and the surrounding area which Abraham I had originally taken on lease in 1709.

In 1973 Lord Bridgeman, the first President stood down and his place was taken by Lady Rachel Labouchere, a direct descendant of Abraham I. She remained President of the Trust for the next fourteen years until 1987. Those were perhaps the most momentous years of the Museum's growth. When she took over, Blists Hill had just been opened. The following year the Quaker Burial Ground came under the care of the Museum and in 1975 the restoration of Abraham III's Iron Bridge was completed. The same year Rosehill was purchased for the Museum by her for restoration.

In 1976 the Severn Warehouse, originally built by the Coalbrookdale Company in 1834 (see Note 49, page 141) was opened and the Coalport China Works Museum was also opened. The following year 1977, the Museum of the Year Award was granted to Ironbridge and in 1978 the European Museum of the Year was won.

In 1979 the Bicentenary of the Iron Bridge was celebrated and HRH The Prince of Wales, who had become Patron of the Museum visited the Gorge. Telford Development Corporation had shortly beforehand acquired the Great Warehouse, the Long Warehouse and the Old Furnace site from Glynwed Limited, and for the occasion of the royal visit, the Great Warehouse was converted to the Museum of Iron which Prince Charles formally opened.

In 1980 the Coalbrookdale Literary and Scientific Institution which was owned by the County Council was adapted and opened as a Youth Hostel. This was a project in which Mr Michael Darby took a special interest. In 1982 the Cover Building for the Old Furnace was erected and Dale House was acquired for restoration. The following year the Long Warehouse was opened to accommodate the Museum's Library and the Elton and Telford Collections and later the newly established Institute of Industrial Archaeology, which in conjunction with the University of Birmingham was to become the Ironbridge Institute.

In 1985, as she was approaching the end of her presidency it gave Lady Labouchere immense pleasure to witness the opening of Rosehill as a Darby family home. Restoration had taken place over the previous ten years. She had inherited from her aunt Muriel Cope-Darby some of the family furniture dating back to the early years of the nineteenth century together with family silver, porcelain, pictures and other artefacts. She donated much of this collection of family history to be displayed in period and interpretation rooms in Rosehill.

Her presidency finished with the ultimate accolade, when the Ironbridge Gorge was designated by UNESCO as a World Heritage Site, based very much on the events which had taken place in Coalbrookdale during the eighteenth century. She was succeeded as President by Philip Trevor-Jones.

In 1987 the Museum Trust was able to acquire the former office buildings of the Coalbrookdale Company and the Engineering Shop and other buildings on the site of the former Lower Furnace site. This was made possible by a gift of half the value of the buildings by Glynwed Limited, with the other half being a contribution from the National Heritage Memorial Fund.

In 1989 Lady Labouchere endowed a small subsidiary trust of the Museum Trust called Rosehill Trust under the chairmanship of Mr Denis Roberts, Vice-President and Deputy Chairman of the Museum Trust to manage a system of voluntary support for Rosehill and Dale House and the adjoining lands formerly part of the Sunniside Estate, including the Quaker Burial Ground. This has been operating most effectively and enthusiastically since Rosehill was opened in 1985.

Lady Labouchere died in 1996 aged eighty-seven years. The year before, she had been most gratified that her final objective of seeing Dale House restored was at least partially achieved. The restoration of Dale House had proved to be an immensely expensive and complicated process. In 1996, the restoration of Abraham Darby III's study where the planning of the Iron Bridge took place, was completed and was opened to the public, together with the entrance hall.

In 1996 the Upper Forge, dating back to 1783/84 and formerly owned by Telford Development Corporation, was restored with funds provided by the Corporation and handed over to the Museum Trust for use as a Study Centre. In this way the Museum Trust now has charge of all the important sites and buildings of the Coalbrookdale Company and of the Darby Family from 1708 until the present century.

The role of the Ironbridge Gorge Museum Trust in securing the present situation is unique and of national importance. The Trust has been supremely well served by three outstanding Presidents, Lord Bridgeman, Lady Labouchere and Philip Trevor-Jones and by four exceptionally able Chairmen, Bruce Ball, Tom Honess, Philip Trevor-Jones and Mike Lowe, supported by the equally able Denis Roberts. There have been only three Honorary Secretaries, the author (Emyr Thomas) from 1967-1988 and Michael Osborn from 1988-97 and Richard Clarke since

1997. There have been three totally committed Honorary Treasurers, Selwyn Devey, Mike Lowe and Derek Spencer.

All these have been wonderfully well supported by two Directors, Dr (now Sir) Neil Cossons and Stuart Smith and in recent years, Glen Lawes and the Deputy Director David de Haan. There have, of course, been many, many others who should be named, but these are the hard core of those who have seen the Museum develop from a brilliant concept to its present undoubted position as the pre-eminent independent Museum in the country.

While the Museum Trust was pursuing its meteoric rise, Telford Development Corporation was dealing with other consequences of the industrialisation set in motion by the Darby family. This was the largest single area of dereliction in Britain affecting over 5,000 acres of derelict land and 3,000 disused mine shafts. Most of the shafts and workings were in the area west of the Lightmoor fault where shallow mine working had taken place. Much of this was in Dawley and Lawley where the mining operations of the Coalbrookdale Company and of the Old Park Company took place. In a great many cases individual mine shafts had to be bored down to base rock and filled with cement slurry. In other areas where substantial coal reserves still existed, the problem was dealt with by open cast mining, the first scheme being at Princes End, Dawley, an area mined by the Coalbrookdale Company. This process continued until the Development Corporation went out of existence in 1991 and included the excavation of Newdale in 1987, the iron working community established by the Company in 1759. After 1991, British Coal continued open cast mining to the west from Horsehay to New Works and Coalmoor. And so finally, much of the evidence of the past workings of the Company was cleared away and re-landscaped. The shadow of the great collapse of the 1870s and 1880s was consigned to the past where it belonged.

One of the last outposts of the Darby empire to disappear was the original railhead for the works which Abraham II established in about 1750. This was called Cocks Wood to the east of Lydebrook Dingle, south of Coalmoor.(53) Part of Cocks Wood was affected by the construction of the Ironbridge bypass in 1989. The site is immediately to the eastern edge of the Lydbrook Dingle Bridge. The remainder of the site to the north of the bridge became a landfill site, thus bringing to an end the great endeavours of the Darby family which so famously flourished during the eighteenth and nineteenth centuries.

In this way the curtain was drawn on nearly three hundred years of industrial development of the highest importance. It is an incredible feature of that development that during the greater part of the period from 1709 to 1925 the Company was controlled and operated by no less than seven succeeding generations of one family, all descendants of Abraham I.

The divine spark which he brought to the enterprise was passed down to each generation in turn so that to the very end, each generation was able to make at least one significant and important contribution of national significance.

In Coalbrookdale, Abraham I changed the course of world history by showing how to smelt iron for casting by using coke instead of charcoal. His son showed how to build on that by extending the process to the uses of wrought-iron. The first iron wheel was produced in the Dale as was the first iron rail. This was followed by the world's first iron bridge and then the first steam powered railway locomotive. In the nineteenth century the Company turned to art castings and developed its foundries until it became the largest foundry in the world. Although operating outside the Dale, Abraham IV was in the forefront of the technology leading to the development of mild steel and John Henry Darby was responsible for the first open hearth furnace in Great Britain. This was a record, sustained over such a long period, which cannot be rivalled.

The three legged pot or 'kettle' which resulted from Abraham I's endeavours and which became so well known around the world is still at the heart of the operation to the present day. Glynwed p.l.c. which operates the Company in Coalbrookdale now produces the Aga cooker and the Rayburn cooker, both enjoying cult status. The Divine spark still glows.

NOTES – CHAPTER XII AND POSTCRIPT

1. *The Lost Victory* by Corelli Barnett (1995), pp.11-14.
2. *The Rise and Fall of the Great Powers* (1988) by Paul Kennedy, pp.241-248.
3. Elementary Education Act 1870. 33 & 34 Vict. c.75.
4. *English Social History* by G M Trevelyan (1942), pp.552-556.
5. Employers and Workmen's Act 1875, 38 & 39 Vict.c.90.
6. VCH Vol XI (Telford), p.281.
7. Trinder, *Darbys of Coalbrookdale*, p.55.
8. VCH Vol XI (Telford), p.121.
9. S.R.O 1987/58/60.
10. Woodside Cottage is No.3113 on the Tithe Map 1847. See Chapter XI. Deeds of property in IGMT archives.
11. Matilda and Abraham IV lived after 1873 at 'Treberfydd', Llangasty-Talyllin, Llangorse Lake, near Brecon. Abraham IV died there in 1878 and Matilda lived on there until late in the century when she returned to Coalbrookdale to live at Sunniside (The White House).
12. Edmund Darby inherited Strethill Farm under the Will of his Aunt Mary Rathbone. The property was devised in tail male. Abraham IV was entitled to the property during his lifetime and as he had no sons it passed to the son of Abraham's brother Alfred Darby, ie A E W Darby.

13. S.R.O 1987/58/9.
14. Trinder: *Industrial Revolution in Shropshire*, p.396.
15. Local press, 7 December 1878.
16. See Chapter X.
16a See letter from Mrs Matilda Darby dated 29 November 1887 (S.R.O 1987/51/2/3) and Memorandum dated 22 August 1896 (S.R.O 1987/58/69).
17. S.R.O 1987/58/61 and 62.
18. Eton College Register.
19. Alexander and Edmund Christy, known to Alfred Edmund William Darby as 'Uncle Mog' and 'Uncle Teddy'. They were connoisseurs of oriental porcelain and French furniture. It was their influence which inspired Alfred to build his valuable collection of Caughley porcelain, much of which is in the IGMT Coalport Museum and also at Rosehill House.
20. S.R.O 1987/41/104.
21. See *The History of Adcote School* by Rachel Lowe (1987) published by Adcote Old Girls Association.
22. S.R.O 1681/122/6 see also S.R.O 16181/122/1.
23. S.R.O 1681/119/6-7 and 1681/121/20.
24. S.R.O 1987/58/6.
25. A summary of the situation is contained in a letter to William Gregory Norris from Quilter Ball & Company, dated 6 December 1880. S.R.O 1987/58/29.
26. S.R.O 1987/58/10 and 11.
27. S.R.O 1987/58/69.
28. Copy of Articles of Agreement with 1st Schedule S.R.O 1987/58/64.
29. *History of the Ebbw Vale Works & Collieries* by Joshua Phillips (1894) (2nd article). Also Trinder, *Darbys of Coalbrookdale*, p56, picture.
30. Trinder: *Industrial Revolution in Shropshire*, p396.
31. VCH Vol XI (Telford), p122.
32. *The Lilleshall Company Limited – a history, 1764-1964* by W K V Gale and C R Nicholls, pp.46-49.
33. Indenture dated 19 April 1884. See deeds of Dale House in possession of IGMT.
34. Will of Richard Darby dated 1 March 1860. Copy in IGMT archives.
35. John Henry Darby was also instrumental in the introduction of the first by-product coke oven plant (Semet-Solvay) to be operated in conjunction with a steel plant. In 1908 he left Brymbo to design and erect the new steel plant at Normanby Park, Scunthorpe. He was awarded the Bessemer medal in 1912. He died aged 63 at Parkstone, Dorset.
36. Green Bank Farm formed part of the Earl of Craven's estate in Little Dawley. The Earl of Craven sold off his lands in Little Dawley in 1854. Green Bank Farm was purchased by Edward Edwards of Rose Hill, Coalbrookdale in 1855 (S.R.O 1987/28/3 and 1987/28/8).

Edward Edwards was the surgeon for Coalbrookdale, carrying on the medical practice started by Benjamin Wright in the previous century. By his Will dated 26 March 1870, Edward Edwards left the property, first to his sister and then to his brother Benjamin Edwards. If Benjamin Edwards died without issue, the property was to pass to William Henry Wright of Bolton, a descendant of the original Benjamin Wright. William Henry Wright mortgaged his expectancy to a bank in Bolton. They in turn sold their interest to Llewellyn William Mostyn who proved to be a nominee of Adelaide Whitmore. When Benjamin Edwards died childless in 1882, the property was duly conveyed to Adelaide Whitmore on 1 January 1883 (S.R.O 1987/28/22-24 Conveyance and endorsement).

37. For details of the family see 'Dickinson of Gildersome and Coalbrookdale' copy in IGMT Library.

38. S.R.O 1987/58/69.

39. S.R.O 1681/180/26 Probate of Adelaide's Will was granted to A E W Darby in September 1899. The property was transferred to Matilda Darby in March 1902.

40. Inland Revenue Affidavits – IGMT Archives.

41. After the death of Rebecca Darby Rosehill then known as The Grange was acquired by two sisters, the Misses Clemson. The surviving sister died in the early 1950s after which the property was made into a small hotel and restaurant. It was purchased for the Ironbridge Gorge Museum Trust with a major contribution from Lady Labouchere. It was restored and opened to the public in 1985.

42. VCH Vol XI (Telford), p.50.

43. Raistrick, *Dynasty of Ironfounders*, p.267.

44. *Wellington Journal*, 12 March 1912. Dale House was first let as a single house but soon after was divided into two flats, one entered from the back and one from the front. In the 1920s the upper flat was occupied by Mr and Mrs Prince. Mr Prince worked in the accounts office of the Company and was remembered for his ability to add up three columns of figures at once, in his head. The lower flat was occupied by Mr and Mrs Parker who remained in the flat until 1953 when the Company (unable to gain permission to knock Dale House down) obtained permission to convert it into a number of smaller flats. These remained as flats until 1981 when the building was acquired by Telford Development Corporation, who sold it the following year to the Ironbridge Gorge Museum Trust on condition that certain restoration works should be carried out. The Museum Trust subsequently undertook much more extensive restoration works and Dale House was opened to the public in 1994.

45. Raistrick, *Dynasty of Ironfounders*, p.269.

46. *History of Adcote School* by Rachel Lowe, published by Adcote Old Girls Association, 1987.

47. These are still remembered by Mr Onions of Tea Kettle Row.
48. The chancel at Holy Trinity Church needs to be restored every twenty-five years and this is undertaken by the Labouchere Trust set up by Lady Labouchere. The Trust also looks after the family graves at Coalbrookdale Church and Little Ness.
49. Frances Muriel Cope-Darby was the daughter of Alfred II. Olive Mary Wolryche-Whitmore was the daughter of Alfred II's sister Alice Mary who married Francis Alexander Wolryche-Whitmore in 1871. Muriel and Olive were, therefore, first cousins.
50. For a full description of the events leading to the preservation of the Old Furnace and the establishment of the Museum of Ironfounding in 1959, see Dr Raistrick's account in *Dynasty of Ironfounders*, pp.269-272.
51. For a fairly full description of this process see a report of the IGMT entitled 'Origins of the Ironbridge Gorge Museum Trust' published by the author, then Honorary Secretary of IGMT on 3 February 1982, the 15th anniversary of the inaugural meeting.
52. The Development Corporation's strategic objectives were described in the following terms in the Corporation's Policy Plan for the Severn Gorge published in the early 1970s.
"In taking the initiative in establishing the Trust, the Corporation had in mind a number of objectives.
First, it was recognised that the large-scale development involved in building the New Town might unwittingly destroy important surviving relics of the area's industrial past and that it was important to create an organisation to safeguard these.
Secondly, it was felt that in the Severn Gorge there was an unprecedented opportunity for creating an entirely new concept in museum work. This new concept was to designate the whole of the Severn Gorge and its adjoining localities as an authentic setting within which the development of the basic industries of the area could be demonstrated through the preservation insitu of the historic monuments of the Industrial Revolution. The conservation of the authentic setting is as much a part of the concept as the preservation of the monuments.
A third objective of the Corporation was that the preservation of the area's historic past would provide an increasingly valuable sense of tradition with which the New Town could be imbued..."
53. Cocks Wood was left in the Will of Abraham II to his widow Abiah Darby. It subsequently passed to Francis Darby who received an annual rent from the Coalbrookdale Company for the use of Cocks Wood and the Rope Walk, seemingly for timber extraction (See Francis Darby's accounts.)

Rachel Labouchere –
A Tribute

THIS BOOK HAS been produced as a tribute to Rachel Labouchere. She inherited from her aunt, Muriel Cope-Darby, large quantities of family papers, as well as furniture, furnishings, silver and porcelain, belonging to the Darby family. She took on the formidable task of marshalling all this material and ensuring that it would be preserved, mainly in Dudmaston, her family home, or in the Darby Houses, now restored in Coalbrookdale.

She was born Rachel Hamilton-Russell in 1908, a granddaughter of the eighth Viscount Boyne at 16 Grosvenor Gardens, London W1, her grandfather's London residence. Through her maternal line she was also descended from Alfred Darby and his wife Rebecca (née Miller Christy). She could, therefore, trace family descent from several distinguished Quaker families. As a Darby she represented the eighth generation from Abraham Darby I.

After a first marriage in the 1930s (dissolved in 1940) she married George Labouchere, whom she met during war service at the Admiralty in London. George, who was in the Diplomatic Service, had returned to the Foreign Office from Italy when Italy entered the war. He was then posted as First Secretary to the British Embassy in Stockholm where they were married. After the war, they served in Nanking, Buenos Aires, Vienna and Budapest until 1955, when George Labouchere became British Ambassador to Belgium. In 1960 Sir George, as he then was, was sent as British Ambassador to Madrid until his retirement in 1966.

After 1966, Rachel Labouchere was able to devote all her energies to the attainment of two long-term objectives. One was the transfer to the National Trust of Dudmaston, the historic home of the Wolryche Whitmore family. This she achieved in 1978. The other was to help in the rescue and furnishing of the Darby family homes at Dale House and 'Rosehill' in Coalbrookdale. Rosehill was the first of these and it was opened to the public in 1985 while she was still President of the Ironbridge Gorge Museum Trust. Dale House took longer but in 1995 it was partially opened to the public, a source of immense personal satisfaction to her.

Rachel Labouchere was deeply sympathetic to her Quaker background. By ensuring the survival of the Darby family records and the preservation in Coalbrookdale of representative memorabilia of the family she felt that she was helping to create a memorial to those members of the family who had gone before her, back through the generations to the first Abraham Darby who by his creativity and vision had heralded the start of the new industrial age and altered our lives forever.

Publication of this book has been sponsored jointly by the SESSIONS BOOK TRUST, a registered charity whose objectives are the encouragement of books of an educational, historical or religious nature; in close collaboration with the IRONBRIDGE GORGE MUSEUM TRUST whose principal objective is to secure the preservation, restoration, improvement, enhancement and maintenance of features and objects of historical and industrial interest in the area of Telford New Town and the surrounding districts of East Shropshire, including the provision of an industrial museum and the organisation of meetings, exhibitions, lectures, publications and other forms of instruction relevant to the historical and industrial development of East Shropshire.

The writing of the book is intended to be a tribute to Rachel Labouchere. It is, therefore, the wish of the sponsors and of the author that any eventual profit from the publication shall accrue to the Rosehill Trust (established by Rachel Labouchere) and used for the benefit of Dale House, Rosehill, the Quaker Burial Ground and the maintenance of the lands associated with those properties.

Bibliography and Abbreviations

Raistrick, Arthur, PhD., M.Sc. *Dynasty of Ironfounders: The Darbys and Coalbrookdale.* Published 1953 by Longman Green & Company. Revised 2nd edition published 1989 by Sessions Book Trust in association with Ironbridge Gorge Museum Trust. ISBN 1 85072 058 4.

Trinder, Barrie. *The Industrial Revolution in Shropshire.* Published 1973 by Phillimore & Co Ltd. ISBN 0 900592 70 2.

Trinder, Barrie. *The Darbys of Coalbrookdale.* First published 1974. New edition published 1991 by Phillimore & Co Ltd in association with Ironbridge Gorge Museum Trust.

Labouchere, Rachel. *Abiah Darby of Coalbookdale, 1716-1793 Wife of Abraham Darby II.* Published 1988 by William Sessions Limited. ISBN Hard 1 85072 018 5   Card 1 85072 017 7.

Labouchere, Rachel. *Deborah Darby of Coalbrookdale 1754-1810.* Published 1993 by William Sessions Limited. ISBN 1 85072 100 9.

Gale, WKV & Nicholls CR. *The Lilleshall Company Limited, a history, 1764-1964.* Published by Moorland Publishing Co. 1979 on behalf of The Lilleshall Company Limited. ISBN 0 86190 000 6.

Stembridge, PK. *Goldney, A house and a family.* Published 1969. Third edition 1979. Printed by Burleigh Limited, Bristol.

Smiles, S. *Industrial Biography: Iron Workers and Tool Makers 1863.*

Jones, ID. *Brymbo Steel Works – A Collection of Pictures.* Published 1991 by Bridge Books, 61, Park Avenue, Wrexham, Clwyd. ISBN 1 872424 13 9.

Jones, Ken. *The Wenlock Branch.* Published 1998 by the Oakwood Press. ISBN 0 85361 500 4.

Darby, Francis. Accounts – extracts in IGMT Library.

Darby, Adelaide. Journal 1833-73 copy in IGMT Library.

Darby, Matilda Journal – extracts in IGMT Library.

P.R.O. Public Record Office of Chancery Lane, London WC2A and Ruskin Avenue, Kew, Richmond, Surrey, TW9 LDU.

S.R.O. Shropshire Records and Research Centre, Castle Gates, Shrewsbury, Shropshire, SY1 2AQ.

S.P.L. Shrewsbury Public Library Records – now in SRO.

IGMT ARCHIVES. Library and Archive, Ironbridge Gorge Museum Trust Limited, The Long Warehouse, Coalbrookdale, Telford, Shropshire TF8 7DX.

V.C.H. The Victoria History of the Counties of England. A History of Shropshire, Volume XI (Telford). Published for the University of London, Institute of Historical Research by Oxford University Press, 1985. ISBN 0 19 722763 5

T.S.A.S. Transactions of the Shropshire Archaeological Society.

N.L.W. National Library of Wales.

D.N.B. Dictionary of National Biography.

Index

Re-structuring of Coalbrookdale Company, 80

Death from Scarlet Fever, 90, 91

Children of Abraham and Rebecca, 103 (note 1), 120 (note 3)

DARBY, Abraham IV, son of Edmund Darby and Lucy

Strethill Farm, contingent interest, 113

Shares under Sarah Darby's Will, 113, 126

Living at the Chesnuts, 129

Purchase of Dickinson shares, 130

Entered works 1826, 130

Married Matilda Darby 1839, 133

Partner in Ebbw Vale Works, 143, 179 (note 14)

Art Collection at The Chesnuts, 148

Assimilation into Shropshire Society, 148

Joined C of E with Matilda 1848, 149

The Chesnuts proving inadequate, 150

Aspired to Stanley Hall, but acquired by Alfred, 150

Acquisition of Sunniside rejected, 150

Death of Francis Darby 1850, 150

Matilda deprived of succession rights, 151

Left Coalbrookdale for Stoke Court, 152

The Chesnuts made available as vicarage, 152

At Crystal Palace Exhibition, 152

Transferred shares to sister, Mary, 164, 179 (note 12)

Living in straightened circumstances, 164

Expansion of Ebbw Vale Works, 164

West Somerset Railway, 164

Shropshire Bank, loss of £200,000, 164

Financial problems 1857, 167, 170, 173

Credit facility with Bank of England, 173

Left Stoke Court, moved to Ebbw Vale, 174

Retired as Managing Director, Ebbw Vale, 186

Moved to Llangorse, Brecon, 186, 208 (note 11)

Died 1878, buried at Holy Trinity, Coalbrookdale, 187

DARBY, Adelaide, daughter of Francis Darby and Hannah

Living at White House, 126

Succession of suitors, 133, 134

Marriage proposed by Alfred I, 134, 139 (note 13), 149

Alfred's proposal finally rejected, 149

Adelaide 'on the shelf', 134, 149

Mother proposed Will favourable to Adelaide, 150

Father declined and died intestate, 150

Partition of estate, 151

Settlement favourable to Adelaide, 151

Agreed to donate land for Church, 152

At Crystal Palace exhibition, 152

Married Henry Whitmore 1852, 160

Entered London society, 168, 180 (note 26)

Henry Whitmore appointed Lord of Treasury, 168, 177

Lord Chancellor visited Sunniside 1855, 168

Henry Whitmore died 1876, 186, 194

Lived at Sunniside and 68 Eaton Place, 168

Purchased Green Bank Farm 1883, 194, 209 (note 36)

Died 1899, 195, 210 (note 39)

DARBY, Alice Mary, daughter of Alfred I and Rebecca

Married Alexander Wolryche-Whitmore 1871, 188

DARBY, Alfred I, son of Edmund and Lucy Darby

Shares under Sarah Darby's Will, 126

Living at The Chesnuts, 129

Entered works 1828, 130

Proposed marriage to Adelaide Darby, 134, 139 (note 13)

Married Rebecca Miller Christy 1848, 149

Residence Clapham Common and then Stanley Hall, 149, 150

Appointed Manager 1851, 155

Death 1852, letters of administration, 163

Problems with Liverpool estates, Darby Estates Act, 1854, 164

DARBY, Alfred Edmund William (Alfred II), son of Alfred Darby I and Rebecca

Born 1852 at Stanley Hall, 155, 188

Matilda Darby appointed shares to be transferred, 187

Purchased shares of Hugh Darby Owen, 187

Brought up at Stanley Hall, educated Eton and Oxford, 188

Moved to Little Ness 1878, 188

Married Frederica Arthur 1881, 188

Trustees of company lands etc in Lawley, 188

Principal shareholder in limited company, 192

Appointed Chairman 1886, 193

Inherited Sunniside estate 1902, 195

Moved to Adcote 1909, 196

Died at Adcote 1925, 198

DARBY, Alfred Alexander Maurice, son of Alfred Darby II and Frederica

Born at Little Ness 1894, moved to Adcote 1909, 195, 196

Educated Eton, joined Grenadier Guards, 196

Died from wounds 1915, 196, 197

Body returned for burial at Little Ness, 196

Chancel, Holy Trinity, Coalbrookdale dedicated to his memory, 198, 211 (note 48)

DARBY, Alfreda Lucy, daughter of Alfred and Rebecca Darby

Moved from Stanley Hall to Little Ness 1875, 188